Elements of Literature®

Third Course

The Holt Reader

HOLT, RINEHART AND WINSTON

ISBN 978-0-03-099628-3

ISBN 0-03-099628-7

 8 9 1409 12 11

4500282716

Contents

To the Student

A Book for You

Teachers open the door, but you must enter by yourself.
—*Chinese Proverb*

The more you put into reading, the more you get out of it. This book is designed to do just that—help you interact with the selections you read by marking them up, asking your own questions, taking notes, recording your own ideas, and responding to the questions of others.

A Book Designed for Your Success

The Holt Reader goes hand in hand with *Elements of Literature*. It is designed to help you interact with the selections and master important language arts skills.

The Holt Reader has three types of selections: literature, informational texts, and documents that you may encounter in your various activities. All the selections include the same basic preparation, support, and review materials. Vocabulary previews, skill descriptions, graphic organizers, review questions, and other tools help you understand and enjoy the selections. Moreover, tips and questions in the side margins ensure that you can apply and practice the skills you are learning as you read.

A Book for Your Own Thoughts and Feelings

Reading is about *you*. It is about connecting your thoughts and feelings to the thoughts and feelings of the writer. Make this book your own. The more you give of yourself to your reading, the more you will get out of it. We encourage you to write in this book. Jot down how you feel about the selection. Write down questions you have about the text. Note details you think need to be cleared up or topics that you would like to investigate further.

A Walk Through the Book

The Holt Reader is arranged in collections, just like *Elements of Literature*, the book on which this one is based. Each collection has a theme or basic idea. The stories, poems, articles, or documents within the collection follow that theme. Let's look at how the arrangement of *The Holt Reader* helps you enjoy a collection as a whole and the individual selections within the collection.

Before Reading the Collection

Literary and Academic Vocabulary

Literary and academic vocabulary refers to the specialized language that is used to talk about books, tests, and formal writing. Each collection begins with the literary and academic terms that you need to know to master the skills for that collection.

Before Reading the Selection

Preparing to Read

From experience, you know that you understand something better if you have some idea of what's going to happen. So that you can get the most from the reading, this page previews the skills and vocabulary that you will see in the reading.

Literary Focus

For fiction selections—stories, poems, and plays—this feature introduces the literary skill that is the focus for the selection. Examples and graphic elements help explain the literary skill.

Reading Focus

Also in fiction selections, this feature highlights a reading skill you can apply to the story, poem, or play. The feature points out why this skill is important and how it can help you become a better reader.

Informational Text Focus

For informational, or nonfiction, selections, this feature introduces you to the format and characteristics of nonfiction texts. Those texts may be essays, newspaper articles, Web sites, employment regulations, application forms, or other similar documents.

Selection Vocabulary

This feature introduces you to selection vocabulary that may be unfamiliar. Each entry gives the pronunciation and definition of the word as well as a sentence in which the word is used correctly.

Word Study

Various activities reinforce what you have learned about the selection's vocabulary.

While Reading the Selection

Background gives you basic information on the selection, its author, or the time period in which the story, essay, poem, or article was written.

Side-Column Notes

Each selection has notes in the side column that guide your reading. Many notes ask you to underline or circle in the text itself. Others provide lines on which you can write your responses to questions.

A Walk Through the Book

Types of Notes

Several different types of notes throughout the selection provide practice for the skills introduced on the Preparing to Read pages. The notes help you with various strategies for understanding the text. The types of side-column notes are

- **Quick Check** notes ask you to pause at certain points so that you can think about basic ideas before proceeding further. Your teacher may use these notes for class discussions.
- **Literary Focus** notes practice the skill taught in the Literary Focus feature on the Preparing to Read page. Key words related to the specific skill are highlighted.
- **Reading Focus** notes practice the reading skill from the Preparing to Read page.
- **Literary Analysis** notes take basic comprehension one step further and ask you to think more deeply about what you have read.
- **Language Coach** notes reinforce the language skill found in the Preparing to Read pages of *Elements of Literature*.
- **Vocabulary** notes examine selection vocabulary, academic vocabulary, and topics related to how words are used.

After Reading the Collection

Skills Practice

For some selections, graphic organizers reinforce the skills you have practiced throughout the selection.

Applying Your Skills

This feature helps you review the selection. It provides additional practice with selection vocabulary and literary, reading, and informational text focus skills.

After Reading the Collection

Skills Review

On the first page of the Skills Review, you can practice using the collection's academic vocabulary and selection vocabulary.

Language Coach

The second Skills Review page draws on the Language Coach skills in the *Elements of Literature* Preparing to Read pages. This feature asks you to apply those skills to texts from throughout the collection.

Writing Activity

You may have found that you need more practice writing. These short writing activities challenge you to apply what you have learned to your own ideas and experiences.

Oral Language Activity

Writing Activities alternate with Oral Language Activities. These features are designed to help you express your thoughts clearly aloud. The features are particularly helpful if you are learning English or if you need practice with Standard English.

Collection

1

Plot and Setting

Literary and Academic Vocabulary for Collection 1

convey (KUHN VAY) *v.:* to suggest; communicate.
In this story, the author tries to convey an idea about war.

effect (UH FEHKT) *n.:* result.
Describe one effect of the narrator's actions.

excerpt (EHK SURPT) *n.:* passage; a part of a longer work.
Anna chose a short excerpt from the story that proves her point.

support (SUH PAWRT) *v.:* to back up; strengthen by giving evidence.
Support your ideas about the story by giving examples.

outcome (OWT KUHM) *n.:* result; ending.
The outcome of the story's conflict was revealed in the last paragraph.

plot (PLAHT) *n.:* the main story; a series of events.
The story's plot was full of tension and action.

conflict (KAHN FLIHKT) *n.:* the struggle or clash between opposing characters, forces or emotions.
The central conflict of the story is the struggle between the narrator and her mother.

foreshadowing (FAWR SHAD OH IHNG) *v.:* the use of clues to hint at what is going to happen later in the story.
By using the name Ship-Trap Island, the author is hinting at the dangers the narrator will face there; this is an example of foreshadowing.

setting (SEHT IHNG) *n.:* the time and place in which the action of a story takes place.
Part of what makes the story so exciting is its exotic island setting.

The Most Dangerous Game

by Richard Connell

LITERARY FOCUS: SUSPENSE AND FORESHADOWING

The **plot** of a story is a series of related events. These events take place as one or more characters take steps to resolve a **conflict,** or problem, of some kind. Some events are hinted at through the use of **foreshadowing.**

- Each event in this story will make you curious about what will happen next. That curiosity is called **suspense.**
- As you read, look for examples of **foreshadowing** that hint at what might happen later in the plot.

READING FOCUS: MAKING PREDICTIONS

Before you read "The Most Dangerous Game," take a few minutes to **make predictions** using a "plot impression." Plot impressions work like this: You are given some details from the story. Then, you weave the details together to create an impression of the plot as you **predict** it might be. Below are the details for a plot impression of "The Most Dangerous Game." What do you predict "the most dangerous game" is?

Key Details	
Rainsford, a big-game hunter	General Zaroff, another hunter
man overboard	fierce dogs
Ship-Trap Island	a trap
Plot Impression	

SKILLS FOCUS

Literary Skills
Understand foreshadowing.

Reading Skills
Make predictions.

Vocabulary Development

The Most Dangerous Game

SELECTION VOCABULARY

receding (RIH SEED IHNG) *v.* used as *adj.:* becoming more distant.

He could see the ship going away from him, receding in the distance.

disarming (DIHS ARM IHNG) *adj.:* removing suspicion or fears; charming.

"Don't be alarmed," said Rainsford, with a smile which he hoped was disarming.

imprudent (IHM PROOD EHNT) *adj.:* unwise.

Zaroff left the country after the revolution in Russia, for it was imprudent for an officer of the czar to stay there.

surmounted (SUHR MOWNT IHD) *v.:* overcame.

The general smiled the quiet smile of one who has faced an obstacle and surmounted it with success.

invariably (IHN VAR EE UH BLEE) *adv.:* always; without changing.

Zaroff said that his captives invariably choose the hunt.

WORD STUDY

DIRECTIONS: Match the vocabulary words on the left with the examples they best match on the right.

_____ 1. receding   **a.** a student who waits until the last minute to study for a test

_____ 2. disarming   **b.** a car as it drives away

_____ 3. imprudent   **c.** a message from the President that the aliens who have landed are very friendly

_____ 4. surmounted   **d.** a difficult item crossed off a to-do list

THE MOST DANGEROUS GAME

by Richard Connell

Mr. Kurtz, oil on canvas, 12 x 18 inches, Artist's collection © Paul Sierra.

A **READING FOCUS**

Underline the name of the island. What do you **predict** will happen in the story, based on this name?

_____

_____

_____

_____

_____

_____

"Off there to the right—somewhere—is a large island," said Whitney. "It's rather a mystery—"

"What island is it?" Rainsford asked.

"The old charts call it Ship-Trap Island," Whitney replied. **A** "A suggestive name, isn't it? Sailors have a curious dread of the place. I don't know why. Some superstition—"

"Can't see it," remarked Rainsford, trying to peer through the dank tropical night that was palpable as it pressed its thick warm blackness in upon the yacht.

10   "You've good eyes," said Whitney, with a laugh, "and I've seen you pick off a moose moving in the brown fall bush at four hundred yards, but even you can't see four miles or so through a moonless Caribbean night."

"Nor four yards," admitted Rainsford. "Ugh! It's like moist black velvet."

"It will be light in Rio," promised Whitney. "We should make it in a few days. I hope the jaguar guns have come from Purdey's.[1] We should have some good hunting up the Amazon. Great sport, hunting."

20 "The best sport in the world," agreed Rainsford.

"For the hunter," amended Whitney. "Not for the jaguar."

"Don't talk rot, Whitney," said Rainsford. "You're a big-game hunter, not a philosopher. Who cares how a jaguar feels?"

"Perhaps the jaguar does," observed Whitney.

"Bah! They've no understanding."

"Even so, I rather think they understand one thing—fear. The fear of pain and the fear of death." **B**

"Nonsense," laughed Rainsford. "This hot weather is making you soft, Whitney. Be a realist. The world is made up of two

30 classes—the hunters and the huntees. Luckily, you and I are the hunters. Do you think we've passed that island yet?"

"I can't tell in the dark. I hope so."

"Why?" asked Rainsford.

"The place has a reputation—a bad one."

"Cannibals?" suggested Rainsford.

"Hardly. Even cannibals wouldn't live in such a Godforsaken place. But it's gotten into sailor lore, somehow. Didn't you notice that the crew's nerves seemed a bit jumpy today?"

"They were a bit strange, now you mention it. Even Captain

40 Nielsen—"

"Yes, even that tough-minded old Swede, who'd go up to the devil himself and ask him for a light. Those fishy blue eyes held a look I never saw there before. All I could get out of him was: 'This place has an evil name among seafaring men, sir.' Then he said to me, very gravely: 'Don't you feel anything?'—as

B QUICK CHECK

Underline the sentences in lines 20–27 that tell how Rainsford feels about hunting animals. Circle the sentences that tell how Whitney feels about hunting animals.

---

1. **Purdey's** (PUR DEEZ): British manufacturer of hunting equipment.

Underline details in lines 41–59 that describe the setting and its effect on Whitney. What mood, or thoughts and feelings about the text, do these details help create?

_____
_____
_____
_____
_____
_____
_____
_____

B **READING FOCUS**

What do you **predict** will happen?

_____
_____
_____
_____
_____
_____
_____
_____

if the air about us was actually poisonous. Now, you mustn't laugh when I tell you this—I did feel something like a sudden chill.

"There was no breeze. The sea was as flat as a plate-glass window. We were drawing near the island then. What I felt was a—a mental chill, a sort of sudden dread."

"Pure imagination," said Rainsford. "One superstitious sailor can taint the whole ship's company with his fear."

"Maybe. But sometimes I think sailors have an extra sense that tells them when they are in danger. Sometimes I think evil is a tangible thing—with wavelengths, just as sound and light have. An evil place can, so to speak, broadcast vibrations of evil. Anyhow, I'm glad we're getting out of this zone. Well, I think I'll turn in now, Rainsford." A

"I'm not sleepy," said Rainsford. "I'm going to smoke another pipe on the afterdeck."

"Good night, then, Rainsford. See you at breakfast."

"Right. Good night, Whitney."

There was no sound in the night as Rainsford sat there but the muffled throb of the engine that drove the yacht swiftly through the darkness, and the swish and ripple of the wash of the propeller.

Rainsford, reclining in a steamer chair, indolently[2] puffed on his favorite brier.[3] The sensuous drowsiness of the night was on him. "It's so dark," he thought, "that I could sleep without closing my eyes; the night would be my eyelids—"

An abrupt sound startled him. Off to the right he heard it, and his ears, expert in such matters, could not be mistaken. Again he heard the sound, and again. Somewhere, off in the blackness, someone had fired a gun three times. B

Rainsford sprang up and moved quickly to the rail, mystified. He strained his eyes in the direction from which the reports had come, but it was like trying to see through a blanket.

---

2. **indolently** (YN DUHL EHNT LEE) *adv.*: lazily.
3. **brier** (BRAHY UHR) *n.*: tobacco pipe made from the root of a brier bush or tree.

He leapt upon the rail and balanced himself there, to get greater
elevation; his pipe, striking a rope, was knocked from his mouth.
He lunged for it; a short, hoarse cry came from his lips as he
realized he had reached too far and had lost his balance. The cry
was pinched off short as the blood-warm waters of the Caribbean
Sea closed over his head. **C**

He struggled up to the surface and tried to cry out, but the
wash from the speeding yacht slapped him in the face and the salt
water in his open mouth made him gag and strangle. Desperately
he struck out with strong strokes after the receding lights of the
yacht, but he stopped before he had swum fifty feet. **D** A certain
coolheadedness had come to him; it was not the first time he had
been in a tight place. There was a chance that his cries could be
heard by someone aboard the yacht, but that chance was slender
and grew more slender as the yacht raced on. He wrestled himself out of his clothes and shouted with all his power. The lights
of the yacht became faint and ever-vanishing fireflies; then they
were blotted out entirely by the night.

Rainsford remembered the shots. They had come from the
right, and doggedly he swam in that direction, swimming with
slow, deliberate strokes, conserving his strength. For a seemingly
endless time he fought the sea. He began to count his strokes;
he could do possibly a hundred more and then—

Rainsford heard a sound. It came out of the darkness, a
high screaming sound, the sound of an animal in an extremity of
anguish and terror.

He did not recognize the animal that made the sound; he did
not try to; with fresh vitality he swam toward the sound. He heard
it again; then it was cut short by another noise, crisp, staccato.

"Pistol shot," muttered Rainsford, swimming on.

Ten minutes of determined effort brought another sound to
his ears—the most welcome he had ever heard—the muttering
and growling of the sea breaking on a rocky shore. He was almost
on the rocks before he saw them; on a night less calm he would
have been shattered against them. With his remaining strength he

80

90

100

110

C READING FOCUS

What has happened to
Rainsford? What do you
predict will happen next?

_____

_____

_____

_____

_____

_____

_____

D VOCABULARY

Selection Vocabulary

The word _receding_ means
"becoming more distant."
What was pulling away from
Rainsford?

_____

_____

_____

_____

_____

_____

_____

_____

Rainsford's thoughts **fore-shadow** events to come. What kind of men do you think Rainsford will encounter?

_____

_____

_____

_____

This paragraph creates **suspense** by leaving questions in our minds. What questions would you like answered?

_____

_____

_____

_____

_____

_____

_____

dragged himself from the swirling waters. Jagged crags appeared to jut into the opaqueness.[4]

He forced himself upward, hand over hand. Gasping, his hands raw, he reached a flat place at the top. Dense jungle came down to the very edge of the cliffs. What perils that tangle of trees and underbrush might hold for him did not concern

120   Rainsford just then. All he knew was that he was safe from his enemy, the sea, and that utter weariness was on him. He flung himself down at the jungle edge and tumbled headlong into the deepest sleep of his life. **A**

When he opened his eyes, he knew from the position of the sun that it was late in the afternoon. Sleep had given him new vigor; a sharp hunger was picking at him. He looked about him, almost cheerfully.

"Where there are pistol shots, there are men. Where there are men, there is food," he thought. But what kind of men, he

130   wondered, in so forbidding a place? **B** An unbroken front of snarled and ragged jungle fringed the shore.

He saw no sign of a trail through the closely knit web of weeds and trees; it was easier to go along the shore, and Rainsford floundered along by the water. Not far from where he had landed, he stopped.

Some wounded thing, by the evidence a large animal, had thrashed about in the underbrush; the jungle weeds were crushed down and the moss was lacerated; one patch of weeds was stained crimson. A small, glittering object not far away caught

140   Rainsford's eye and he picked it up. It was an empty cartridge. **C**

"A twenty-two," he remarked. "That's odd. It must have been a fairly large animal too. The hunter had his nerve with him to tackle it with a light gun. It's clear that the brute put up a fight. I suppose the first three shots I heard was when the hunter flushed his quarry[5] and wounded it. The last shot was when he trailed it here and finished it."

---

4. **opaqueness** (OH PAYK NIHS) _n._: here, darkness. Something opaque does not let light pass through.

5. **flushed his quarry:** drove the animal he was hunting out of its hiding place.

He examined the ground closely and found what he had hoped to find—the print of hunting boots. They pointed along the cliff in the direction he had been going. Eagerly he hurried along, now slipping on a rotten log or a loose stone, but making headway; night was beginning to settle down on the island.

Bleak darkness was blacking out the sea and jungle when Rainsford sighted the lights. He came upon them as he turned a crook in the coastline, and his first thought was that he had come upon a village, for there were many lights. But as he forged along, he saw to his great astonishment that all the lights were in one enormous building—a lofty structure with pointed towers plunging upward into the gloom. His eyes made out the shadowy outlines of a palatial château;[6] it was set on a high bluff, and on three sides of it cliffs dived down to where the sea licked greedy lips in the shadows. **D**

"Mirage," thought Rainsford. But it was no mirage, he found, when he opened the tall spiked iron gate. The stone steps were real enough; the massive door with a leering gargoyle for a knocker was real enough; yet about it all hung an air of unreality.

He lifted the knocker, and it creaked up stiffly, as if it had never before been used. He let it fall, and it startled him with its booming loudness.

He thought he heard steps within; the door remained closed. Again Rainsford lifted the heavy knocker and let it fall. The door opened then, opened as suddenly as if it were on a spring, and Rainsford stood blinking in the river of glaring gold light that poured out. The first thing Rainsford's eyes discerned was the largest man Rainsford had ever seen—a gigantic creature, solidly made and black-bearded to the waist. In his hand the man held a long-barreled revolver, and he was pointing it straight at Rainsford's heart.

Out of the snarl of beard two small eyes regarded Rainsford.

"Don't be alarmed," said Rainsford, with a smile which he hoped was disarming. **E** "I'm no robber. I fell off a yacht. My name is Sanger Rainsford of New York City."

---

6. **château** (SHA TOH) *n.*: large country house.

D **VOCABULARY**

Word Study

Personification is a kind of figurative language in which a nonhuman thing or something inanimate (not alive) is talked about as if it were human or alive. Underline the detail in this sentence that gives the sea a human quality. What kind of "person" is this sea?

_____

_____

_____

E **LANGUAGE COACH**

Prefixes usually change the meaning of a word. *Dis-* is a prefix meaning "take away." *Arms* is another word for "weapons." *Disarm* means "take away weapons." What do you think *discomfort* means?

_____

_____

_____

A **LITERARY FOCUS**

How does the author build **suspense** here? How is this suspense resolved?

_____

_____

_____

_____

_____

_____

The menacing look in the eyes did not change. The revolver pointed as rigidly as if the giant were a statue. He gave no sign that he understood Rainsford's words or that he had even heard them. He was dressed in uniform, a black uniform trimmed with gray astrakhan.[7]

"I'm Sanger Rainsford of New York," Rainsford began again. "I fell off a yacht. I am hungry."

190 The man's only answer was to raise with his thumb the hammer of his revolver. Then Rainsford saw the man's free hand go to his forehead in a military salute, and he saw him click his heels together and stand at attention. **A** Another man was coming down the broad marble steps, an erect, slender man in evening clothes. He advanced to Rainsford and held out his hand.

In a cultivated voice marked by a slight accent that gave it added precision and deliberateness, he said: "It is a very great pleasure and honor to welcome Mr. Sanger Rainsford, the celebrated hunter, to my home."

Automatically Rainsford shook the man's hand.

200 "I've read your book about hunting snow leopards in Tibet, you see," explained the man. "I am General Zaroff."

Rainsford's first impression was that the man was singularly handsome; his second was that there was an original, almost bizarre quality about the general's face. He was a tall man past middle age, for his hair was a vivid white; but his thick eyebrows and pointed military moustache were as black as the night from which Rainsford had come. His eyes, too, were black and very bright. He had high cheekbones, a sharp-cut nose, a spare, dark face, the face of a man used to giving orders, the face of an aris-

210 tocrat. Turning to the giant in uniform, the general made a sign. The giant put away his pistol, saluted, withdrew.

"Ivan is an incredibly strong fellow," remarked the general, "but he has the misfortune to be deaf and dumb. A simple fellow, but, I'm afraid, like all his race, a bit of a savage."

"Is he Russian?"

---

7. **astrakhan** (AS TRUH KUN) _n._: curly fur of very young lambs.

"He is a Cossack,"[8] said the general, and his smile showed red lips and pointed teeth. "So am I."

"Come," he said, "we shouldn't be chatting here. We can talk later. Now you want clothes, food, rest. You shall have them. This is a most restful spot."

Ivan had reappeared, and the general spoke to him with lips that moved but gave forth no sound.

"Follow Ivan, if you please, Mr. Rainsford," said the general. "I was about to have my dinner when you came. I'll wait for you. You'll find that my clothes will fit you, I think."

It was to a huge, beam-ceilinged bedroom with a canopied bed big enough for six men that Rainsford followed the silent giant. Ivan laid out an evening suit, and Rainsford, as he put it on, noticed that it came from a London tailor who ordinarily cut and sewed for none below the rank of duke.

The dining room to which Ivan conducted him was in many ways remarkable. There was a medieval magnificence about it; it suggested a baronial hall of feudal times, with its oaken panels, its high ceiling, its vast refectory table where two-score men could sit down to eat. About the hall were the mounted heads of many animals—lions, tigers, elephants, moose, bears; larger or more perfect specimens Rainsford had never seen. At the great table the general was sitting, alone.

"You'll have a cocktail, Mr. Rainsford," he suggested. The cocktail was surpassingly good; and, Rainsford noted, the table appointments were of the finest—the linen, the crystal, the silver, the china.

They were eating borscht, the rich red soup with sour cream so dear to Russian palates. Half apologetically General Zaroff said: "We do our best to preserve the amenities[9] of civilization here. Please forgive any lapses. We are well off the beaten track, you know. Do you think the champagne has suffered from its long ocean trip?"

B **READING FOCUS**

Circle the words in line 214 that Zaroff uses to describe Cossacks. **Predict** what Zaroff's remarks suggest about how he will behave later in the story.

---

8. **Cossack** (KAHS ak): member of a group primarily from Ukraine, many of whom served as horsemen to the Russian czars and were famed for their fierceness in battle.

9. **amenities** (UH MEN IH TEES) *n.:* comforts and conveniences.

How does General Zaroff's peculiar behavior build **suspense**?

_____

_____

_____

_____

_____

_____

_____

What do you **predict** the most dangerous game will be?

_____

_____

_____

_____

_____

250 "Not in the least," declared Rainsford. He was finding the general a most thoughtful and affable host, a true cosmopolite.[10] But there was one small trait of the general's that made Rainsford uncomfortable. Whenever he looked up from his plate he found the general studying him, appraising him narrowly. **A**

"Perhaps," said General Zaroff, "you were surprised that I recognized your name. You see, I read all books on hunting published in English, French, and Russian. I have but one passion in my life, Mr. Rainsford, and it is the hunt."

"You have some wonderful heads here," said Rainsford as he ate a particularly well-cooked filet mignon. "That Cape

260 buffalo is the largest I ever saw."

"Oh, that fellow. Yes, he was a monster."

"Did he charge you?"

"Hurled me against a tree," said the general. "Fractured my skull. But I got the brute."

"I've always thought," said Rainsford, "that the Cape buffalo is the most dangerous of all big game."

For a moment the general did not reply; he was smiling his curious red-lipped smile. Then he said slowly: "No. You are wrong, sir. The Cape buffalo is not the most dangerous

270 big game." He sipped his wine. "Here in my preserve on this island," he said in the same slow tone, "I hunt more dangerous game." **B**

Rainsford expressed his surprise. "Is there big game on this island?"

The general nodded. "The biggest."

"Really?"

"Oh, it isn't here naturally, of course. I have to stock the island."

"What have you imported, general?" Rainsford asked.

280 "Tigers?"

The general smiled. "No," he said. "Hunting tigers ceased to interest me some years ago. I exhausted their possibilities,

---

10. **cosmopolite** (KAHZ MAHP UH LYT) _n._: knowledgeable citizen of the world.

you see. No thrill left in tigers, no real danger. I live for danger, Mr. Rainsford." **C**

The general took from his pocket a gold cigarette case and offered his guest a long black cigarette with a silver tip; it was perfumed and gave off a smell like incense.

"We will have some capital hunting, you and I," said the general. "I shall be most glad to have your society."

290   "But what game—" began Rainsford.

"I'll tell you," said the general. "You will be amused, I know. I think I may say, in all modesty, that I have done a rare thing. I have invented a new sensation. May I pour you another glass of port, Mr. Rainsford?"

"Thank you, general."

The general filled both glasses and said: "God makes some men poets. Some He makes kings, some beggars. Me He made a hunter. My hand was made for the trigger, my father said. He was a very rich man, with a quarter of a million acres in the

300   Crimea,[11] and he was an ardent sportsman. When I was only five years old, he gave me a little gun, specially made in Moscow for me, to shoot sparrows with. When I shot some of his prize turkeys with it, he did not punish me; he complimented me on my marksmanship. I killed my first bear in the Caucasus[12] when I was ten. My whole life has been one prolonged hunt. **D** I went into the army—it was expected of noblemen's sons—and for a time commanded a division of Cossack cavalry, but my real interest was always the hunt. I have hunted every kind of game in every land. It would be impossible for me to tell you how

310   many animals I have killed."

The general puffed at his cigarette.

"After the debacle[13] in Russia I left the country, for it was imprudent for an officer of the czar to stay there. **E** Many

---

11. **Crimea** (KRY MEE UH): peninsula in Ukraine jutting into the Black Sea.
12. **Caucasus** (KAW KUH SUHS): mountainous region between southeastern Europe and western Asia.
13. **debacle** (DIH BAH KUHL) *n.:* complete failure or collapse. Zaroff is referring to the Russian Revolution of 1917, in which the czar and his government were overthrown.

C (LITERARY FOCUS)

Zaroff builds **suspense** by avoiding the question Rainsford asks. Why do you think Rainsford is so curious?

_____

_____

_____

_____

D (QUICK CHECK)

Notice the sequence of events as Zaroff tells about his past. Underline the words in lines 300–301 that tell when he received his first gun. Underline the words in lines 304–305 that tell when he shot his first bear.

E (LANGUAGE COACH)

Im- is a **prefix** meaning "not." *Imprudent* means "not prudent" or "not wise." What do you think *immature* means?

_____

_____

_____

_____

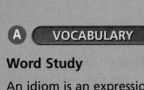

Word Study

An idiom is an expression that means something different from the literal definitions of its parts. Circle the idiom in this sentence. What does it mean?

_____

_____

_____

_____

_____

_____

noble Russians lost everything. I, luckily, had invested heavily in American securities, so I shall never have to open a tearoom in Monte Carlo[14] or drive a taxi in Paris. Naturally, I continued to hunt—grizzlies in your Rockies, crocodiles in the Ganges,[15] rhinoceroses in East Africa. It was in Africa that the Cape buffalo

320   hit me and laid me up for six months. As soon as I recovered I started for the Amazon to hunt jaguars, for I had heard they were unusually cunning. They weren't." The Cossack sighed. "They were no match at all for a hunter with his wits about him and a high-powered rifle. I was bitterly disappointed. I was lying in my tent with a splitting headache one night when a terrible thought pushed its way into my mind. Hunting was beginning to bore me! And hunting, remember, had been my life. I have heard that in America businessmen often go to pieces when they give up the business that has been their life." A

"Yes, that's so," said Rainsford.

330   The general smiled. "I had no wish to go to pieces," he said. "I must do something. Now, mine is an analytical mind, Mr. Rainsford. Doubtless that is why I enjoy the problems of the chase."

"No doubt, General Zaroff."

"So," continued the general, "I asked myself why the hunt no longer fascinated me. You are much younger than I am, Mr. Rainsford, and have not hunted as much, but you perhaps can guess the answer."

"What was it?"

340   "Simply this: Hunting had ceased to be what you call a sporting proposition. It had become too easy. I always got my quarry. Always. There is no greater bore than perfection."

The general lit a fresh cigarette.

"No animal had a chance with me anymore. That is no boast; it is a mathematical certainty. The animal had nothing but

---

14. **Monte Carlo** (MAHN TEE KAHR LOH): gambling resort in Monaco, a country on the Mediterranean Sea.
15. **Ganges** (GAN JEEZ): river in northern India and Bangladesh.

his legs and his instinct. Instinct is no match for reason. When I thought of this, it was a tragic moment for me, I can tell you."

Rainsford leaned across the table, absorbed in what his host was saying.

350 "It came to me as an inspiration what I must do," the general went on.

"And that was?"

The general smiled the quiet smile of one who has faced an obstacle and surmounted it with success. **B** "I had to invent a new animal to hunt," he said. **C**

"A new animal? You're joking."

"Not at all," said the general. "I never joke about hunting. I needed a new animal. I found one. So I bought this island, built this house, and here I do my hunting. The island is perfect for my

360 purposes—there are jungles with a maze of trails in them, hills, swamps—"

"But the animal, General Zaroff?"

"Oh," said the general, "it supplies me with the most exciting hunting in the world. No other hunting compares with it for an instant. Every day I hunt, and I never grow bored now, for I have a quarry with which I can match my wits."

Rainsford's bewilderment showed in his face.

"I wanted the ideal animal to hunt," explained the general. "So I said: 'What are the attributes of an ideal quarry?' And the

370 answer was, of course: 'It must have courage, cunning, and, above all, it must be able to reason.'"

"But no animal can reason," objected Rainsford.

"My dear fellow," said the general, "there is one that can."

"But you can't mean—" gasped Rainsford.

"And why not?"

"I can't believe you are serious, General Zaroff. This is a grisly joke."

"Why should I not be serious? I am speaking of hunting."

"Hunting? Good God, General Zaroff, what you speak of

380 is murder." **D**

B VOCABULARY

Selection Vocabulary
The word *surmounted* means "overcame." Underline words in this sentence that hint at this definition.

C READING FOCUS

Predict what this "new animal" could be.

_____

_____

_____

_____

_____

_____

_____

_____

_____

_____

D QUICK CHECK

Was your prediction correct? What is the game that Zaroff hunts?

_____

_____

_____

_____

The general laughed with entire good nature. He regarded Rainsford quizzically. "I refuse to believe that so modern and civilized a young man as you seem to be harbors romantic ideas about the value of human life. Surely your experiences in the war—"

"Did not make me condone[16] coldblooded murder," finished Rainsford stiffly.

Laughter shook the general. "How extraordinarily droll you are!" he said. "One does not expect nowadays to find a young
390 man of the educated class, even in America, with such a naive, and, if I may say so, mid-Victorian point of view. It's like finding a snuffbox in a limousine. Ah, well, doubtless you had Puritan ancestors. So many Americans appear to have had. I'll wager you'll forget your notions when you go hunting with me. You've a genuine new thrill in store for you, Mr. Rainsford."

"Thank you, I'm a hunter, not a murderer."

"Dear me," said the general, quite unruffled, "again that unpleasant word. But I think I can show you that your scruples[17] are quite ill-founded."

400 "Yes?"

"Life is for the strong, to be lived by the strong, and if need be, taken by the strong. The weak of the world were put here to give the strong pleasure. I am strong. Why should I not use my gift? If I wish to hunt, why should I not? I hunt the scum of the earth—sailors from tramp ships—lascars,[18] blacks, Chinese, whites, mongrels—a thoroughbred horse or hound is worth more than a score of them."

"But they are men," said Rainsford hotly. A

"Precisely," said the general. "That is why I use them.
410 It gives me pleasure. They can reason, after a fashion. So they are dangerous."

"But where do you get them?"

---

16. **condone** (KUHN DOHN) _v._: overlook an offense; excuse.
17. **scruples** (SKROO PUHLZ) _n._: feelings of doubt or guilt about a suggested action.
18. **lascars** (LAS KUHRZ) _n._: East Indian sailors employed on European ships.

The general's left eyelid fluttered down in a wink. "This island is called Ship-Trap," he answered. "Sometimes an angry god of the high seas sends them to me. Sometimes, when Providence is not so kind, I help Providence a bit. Come to the window with me."

Rainsford went to the window and looked out toward the sea.

420 "Watch! Out there!" exclaimed the general, pointing into the night. Rainsford's eyes saw only blackness, and then, as the general pressed a button, far out to sea Rainsford saw the flash of lights.

The general chuckled. "They indicate a channel," he said, "where there's none; giant rocks with razor edges crouch like a sea monster with wide-open jaws. They can crush a ship as easily as I crush this nut." He dropped a walnut on the hardwood floor and brought his heel grinding down on it. "Oh, yes," he said, casually, as if in answer to a question, "I have electricity.

430 We try to be civilized here." **B**

"Civilized? And you shoot down men?"

A trace of anger was in the general's black eyes, but it was there for but a second, and he said, in his most pleasant manner: "Dear me, what a righteous young man you are! I assure you I do not do the thing you suggest. That would be barbarous. I treat these visitors with every consideration. They get plenty of good food and exercise. They get into splendid physical condition. You shall see for yourself tomorrow."

"What do you mean?"

440 "We'll visit my training school," smiled the general. "It's in the cellar. I have about a dozen pupils down there now. They're from the Spanish bark *San Lucar* that had the bad luck to go on the rocks out there. A very inferior lot, I regret to say. Poor specimens and more accustomed to the deck than to the jungle."

He raised his hand, and Ivan, who served as waiter, brought thick Turkish coffee. Rainsford, with an effort, held his tongue in check.

B QUICK CHECK

How does Zaroff find men to hunt?

_____

_____

_____

_____

_____

_____

_____

A VOCABULARY

Word Study

Here, the word *game* means "competition for amusement." What associations come to mind when you hear the word *game*? What impression do you form of Zaroff when he uses this word to describe hunting men?

_____

_____

_____

_____

_____

_____

_____

"It's a game, you see," pursued the general blandly. **A** "I
suggest to one of them that we go hunting. I give him a supply

450   of food and an excellent hunting knife. I give him three hours'
start. I am to follow, armed only with a pistol of the smallest
caliber and range. If my quarry eludes me for three whole days,
he wins the game. If I find him"—the general smiled—"he loses."

"Suppose he refuses to be hunted?"

"Oh," said the general, "I give him his option, of course.
He need not play that game if he doesn't wish to. If he does not
wish to hunt, I turn him over to Ivan. Ivan once had the honor of
serving as official knouter[19] to the Great White Czar, and he has
his own ideas of sport. Invariably, Mr. Rainsford, invariably they

460   choose the hunt."

"And if they win?"

The smile on the general's face widened. "To date I have not
lost," he said.

Then he added, hastily: "I don't wish you to think me a
braggart, Mr. Rainsford. Many of them afford only the most
elementary sort of problem. Occasionally I strike a tartar.[20] One
almost did win. I eventually had to use the dogs."

"The dogs?"

"This way, please. I'll show you."

470   The general steered Rainsford to a window. The lights from
the windows sent a flickering illumination that made grotesque
patterns on the courtyard below, and Rainsford could see moving
about there a dozen or so huge black shapes; as they turned
toward him, their eyes glittered greenly.

"A rather good lot, I think," observed the general. "They
are let out at seven every night. If anyone should try to get
into my house—or out of it—something extremely regrettable
would occur to him." He hummed a snatch of song from the
Folies-Bergère.[21]

---

19. **knouter** (NOWT ER) *n.*: person who beats criminals with a knout, a
kind of leather whip.
20. **strike a tartar**: get more than one bargained for. A tartar is a violent,
unmanageable person.
21. **Folies-Bergère** (FAW LEE BER ZHER): famous nightclub in Paris.

480　　　"And now," said the general, "I want to show you my new collection of heads. Will you come with me to the library?"

"I hope," said Rainsford, "that you will excuse me tonight, General Zaroff. I'm really not feeling at all well." **B**

"Ah, indeed?" the general inquired solicitously.[22] "Well, I suppose that's only natural, after your long swim. You need a good, restful night's sleep. Tomorrow you'll feel like a new man, I'll wager. Then we'll hunt, eh? I've one rather promising prospect—"

Rainsford was hurrying from the room.

"Sorry you can't go with me tonight," called the general.
490　"I expect rather fair sport—a big, strong black. He looks resourceful— Well, good night, Mr. Rainsford; I hope you have a good night's rest."

The bed was good and the pajamas of the softest silk, and he was tired in every fiber of his being, but nevertheless Rainsford could not quiet his brain with the opiate[23] of sleep. He lay, eyes wide open. Once he thought he heard stealthy steps in the corridor outside his room. He sought to throw open the door; it would not open. He went to the window and looked out. His room was high up in one of the towers. The lights of the
500　château were out now, and it was dark and silent, but there was a fragment of sallow moon, and by its wan light he could see, dimly, the courtyard; there, weaving in and out in the pattern of shadow, were black, noiseless forms; the hounds heard him at the window and looked up, expectantly, with their green eyes. Rainsford went back to the bed and lay down. By many methods he tried to put himself to sleep. He had achieved a doze when, just as morning began to come, he heard, far off in the jungle, the faint report of a pistol. **C**

General Zaroff did not appear until luncheon. He was
510　dressed faultlessly in the tweeds of a country squire. He was solicitous about the state of Rainsford's health.

---

22. **solicitously** (SUH LIHS IH TUHS LEE) *adv.:* in a concerned manner.
23. **opiate** (OH PEE IHT) *n.:* anything that tends to soothe or calm someone. An opiate may also be a medicine containing opium or a related drug used to relieve pain.

B **READING FOCUS**

What do you **predict** Rainsford will do next?

_____

_____

_____

_____

_____

_____

_____

C **LITERARY ANALYSIS**

Describe the mood, or feelings, created by this setting.

_____

_____

_____

_____

_____

_____

_____

_____

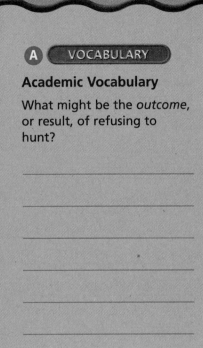

"As for me," sighed the general, "I do not feel so well. I am worried, Mr. Rainsford. Last night I detected traces of my old complaint."

To Rainsford's questioning glance the general said: "Ennui. Boredom."

Then, taking a second helping of crêpes suzette,[24] the general explained: "The hunting was not good last night. The fellow lost his head. He made a straight trail that offered no
520   problems at all. That's the trouble with these sailors; they have dull brains to begin with, and they do not know how to get about in the woods. They do excessively stupid and obvious things. It's most annoying. Will you have another glass of Chablis, Mr. Rainsford?"

"General," said Rainsford firmly, "I wish to leave this island at once."

The general raised his thickets of eyebrows; he seemed hurt. "But, my dear fellow," the general protested, "you've only just come. You've had no hunting—"
530   "I wish to go today," said Rainsford. He saw the dead black eyes of the general on him, studying him. General Zaroff's face suddenly brightened.

He filled Rainsford's glass with venerable Chablis from a dusty bottle.

"Tonight," said the general, "we will hunt—you and I."

Rainsford shook his head. "No, general," he said. "I will not hunt."

The general shrugged his shoulders and delicately ate a hothouse grape. "As you wish, my friend," he said. "The choice
540   rests entirely with you. But may I not venture to suggest that you will find my idea of sport more diverting than Ivan's?"

He nodded toward the corner where the giant stood, scowling, his thick arms crossed on his hogshead of chest. **A**

"You don't mean—" cried Rainsford.

---

24. **crêpes suzette** (KREYP SOO ZEHT) *n.*: thin pancakes folded in a hot orange-flavored sauce and served in flaming brandy.

© Julio Larraz, Casanova (1987), courtesy Marlborough Gallery, New York

"My dear fellow," said the general, "have I not told you I always mean what I say about hunting? This is really an inspiration. I drink to a foeman worthy of my steel—at last."

The general raised his glass, but Rainsford sat staring at him.

550 "You'll find this game worth playing," the general said enthusiastically. "Your brain against mine. Your woodcraft against mine. Your strength and stamina against mine. Outdoor chess! And the stake is not without value, eh?" **B**

"And if I win—" began Rainsford huskily.

"I'll cheerfully acknowledge myself defeated if I do not find you by midnight of the third day," said General Zaroff. "My sloop will place you on the mainland near a town." **C D**

The general read what Rainsford was thinking.

"Oh, you can trust me," said the Cossack. "I will give you my

560 word as a gentleman and a sportsman. Of course you, in turn, must agree to say nothing of your visit here."

"I'll agree to nothing of the kind," said Rainsford.

"Oh," said the general, "in that case— But why discuss that now? Three days hence we can discuss it over a bottle of Veuve Clicquot,25 unless—"

The general sipped his wine.

Then a businesslike air animated him. "Ivan," he said to Rainsford, "will supply you with hunting clothes, food, a knife. I suggest you wear moccasins; they leave a poorer trail. I suggest

570 too that you avoid the big swamp in the southeast corner of the

---

25. **Veuve Clicquot** (VOHV KLEE KOH): brand of fine champagne.

B QUICK CHECK

What "game" does the general plan to hunt?

_____

_____

_____

_____

C QUICK CHECK

What does Rainsford have to do to win the game?

_____

_____

_____

_____

_____

D VOCABULARY

Word Study

A *sloop* is a kind of boat or ship. Circle the clues in this paragraph that help you figure out this word's meaning.

island. We call it Death Swamp. There's quicksand there. **A** One foolish fellow tried it. The deplorable[26] part of it was that Lazarus followed him. You can imagine my feelings, Mr. Rainsford. I loved Lazarus; he was the finest hound in my pack. Well, I must beg you to excuse me now. I always take a siesta after lunch. You'll hardly have time for a nap, I fear. You'll want to start, no doubt. I shall not follow till dusk. Hunting at night is so much more exciting than by day, don't you think? Au revoir[27], Mr. Rainsford, au revoir."

580   General Zaroff, with a deep, courtly bow, strolled from the room.

    From another door came Ivan. Under one arm he carried khaki hunting clothes, a haversack of food, a leather sheath containing a long-bladed hunting knife; his right hand rested on a cocked revolver thrust in the crimson sash about his waist. . . .

    Rainsford had fought his way through the bush for two hours. "I must keep my nerve. I must keep my nerve," he said through tight teeth. **B**

    He had not been entirely clearheaded when the château

590 gates snapped shut behind him. His whole idea at first was to put distance between himself and General Zaroff, and, to this end, he had plunged along, spurred on by the sharp rowels[28] of something very like panic. Now he had got a grip on himself, had stopped, and was taking stock of himself and the situation.

    He saw that straight flight was futile; inevitably it would bring him face to face with the sea. He was in a picture with a frame of water, and his operations, clearly, must take place within that frame.

    "I'll give him a trail to follow," muttered Rainsford, and

600 he struck off from the rude paths he had been following into the trackless wilderness. He executed a series of intricate loops; he doubled on his trail again and again, recalling all the lore of the fox hunt and all the dodges of the fox. Night found him

---

26. **deplorable** (DIH PLAWR UH BUHL) _adj._: regrettable; very bad.
27. **au revoir** (AW RUH VWAR): French for "goodbye."
28. **rowels** (ROW UHLZ) _n._: small wheels with spurs that horseback riders wear on their heels.

leg-weary, with hands and face lashed by the branches, on a thickly wooded ridge. He knew it would be insane to blunder on through the dark, even if he had the strength. His need for rest was imperative and he thought: "I have played the fox; now I must play the cat of the fable." A big tree with a thick trunk and outspread branches was nearby, and taking care to leave not

610 the slightest mark, he climbed up into the crotch and stretching out on one of the broad limbs, after a fashion, rested. **C** Rest brought him new confidence and almost a feeling of security. Even so zealous a hunter as General Zaroff could not trace him there, he told himself; only the devil himself could follow that complicated trail through the jungle after dark. But, perhaps, the general was a devil—

An apprehensive night crawled slowly by like a wounded snake, and sleep did not visit Rainsford, although the silence of a dead world was on the jungle. Toward morning, when a dingy

620 gray was varnishing the sky, the cry of some startled bird focused Rainsford's attention in that direction. Something was coming through the bush, coming slowly, carefully, coming by the same winding way Rainsford had come. He flattened himself down on the limb, and through a screen of leaves almost as thick as tapestry, he watched. The thing that was approaching was a man.

It was General Zaroff. He made his way along with his eyes fixed in utmost concentration on the ground before him. He paused, almost beneath the tree, dropped to his knees and studied the ground. Rainsford's impulse was to hurl himself down

630 like a panther, but he saw the general's right hand held something metallic—a small automatic pistol.

The hunter shook his head several times, as if he were puzzled. Then he straightened up and took from his case one of his black cigarettes; its pungent incenselike smoke floated up to Rainsford's nostrils.

Rainsford held his breath. The general's eyes had left the ground and were traveling inch by inch up the tree. Rainsford froze there, every muscle tensed for a spring. But the sharp eyes of the hunter stopped before they reached the limb where

C QUICK CHECK

How does Rainsford avoid being captured and killed?

_____

_____

_____

_____

_____

_____

_____

_____

_____

_____

_____

_____

_____

_____

_____

_____

_____

_____

_____

_____

_____

_____

_____

_____

The first stage of the hunt is over. Who has won? What does Rainsford now know that he didn't know at the beginning of the story?

_____

_____

_____

_____

_____

_____

_____

_____

_____

_____

_____

640   Rainsford lay; a smile spread over his brown face. Very deliberately he blew a smoke ring into the air; then he turned his back on the tree and walked carelessly away, back along the trail he had come. The swish of the underbrush against his hunting boots grew fainter and fainter. **A**

Then pent-up air burst hotly from Rainsford's lungs. His first thought made him feel sick and numb. The general could follow a trail through the woods at night; he could follow an extremely difficult trail; he must have uncanny powers; only by the merest chance had the Cossack failed to see his quarry.

650   Rainsford's second thought was even more terrible. It sent a shudder of cold horror through his whole being. Why had the general smiled? Why had he turned back?

Rainsford did not want to believe what his reason told him was true, but the truth was as evident as the sun that had by now pushed through the morning mists. The general was playing with him! The general was saving him for another day's sport! The Cossack was the cat; he was the mouse. Then it was that Rainsford knew the full meaning of terror. **B**

"I will not lose my nerve. I will not."

660   He slid down from the tree and struck off again into the woods. His face was set and he forced the machinery of his mind to function. Three hundred yards from his hiding place he stopped where a huge dead tree leaned precariously[29] on a smaller living one. Throwing off his sack of food, Rainsford took his knife from its sheath and began to work with all his energy.

The job was finished at last, and he threw himself down behind a fallen log a hundred feet away. He did not have to wait long. The cat was coming again to play with the mouse.

Following the trail with the sureness of a bloodhound came

670   General Zaroff. Nothing escaped those searching black eyes, no crushed blade of grass, no bent twig, no mark, no matter how faint, in the moss. So intent was the Cossack on his stalking that he was upon the thing Rainsford had made before he saw it.

---

29. precariously (PRIY KAR EE UHS LEE) _adv.:_ unsteadily; in an unstable manner.

His foot touched the protruding bough that was the trigger. Even as he touched it, the general sensed his danger and leapt back with the agility of an ape. But he was not quite quick enough; the dead tree, delicately adjusted to rest on the cut living one, crashed down and struck the general a glancing blow on the shoulder as it fell; but for his alertness, he must have been smashed beneath it. He staggered, but he did not fall; nor did he drop his revolver. He stood there, rubbing his injured shoulder, and Rainsford, with fear again gripping his heart, heard the general's mocking laugh ring through the jungle.

"Rainsford," called the general, "if you are within the sound of my voice, as I suppose you are, let me congratulate you. Not many men know how to make a Malay man-catcher. Luckily for me, I too have hunted in Malacca.[30] You are proving interesting, Mr. Rainsford. I am going now to have my wound dressed; it's only a slight one. But I shall be back. I shall be back." **C**

When the general, nursing his bruised shoulder, had gone, Rainsford took up his flight again. It was flight now, a desperate, hopeless flight, that carried him on for some hours. Dusk came, then darkness, and still he pressed on. The ground grew softer under his moccasins; the vegetation grew ranker, denser; insects bit him savagely. Then, as he stepped forward, his foot sank into the ooze. He tried to wrench it back, but the muck sucked viciously at his foot as if it were a giant leech. With a violent effort, he tore loose. He knew where he was now. Death Swamp and its quicksand.

His hands were tight closed as if his nerve were something tangible that someone in the darkness was trying to tear from his grip. The softness of the earth had given him an idea. He stepped back from the quicksand a dozen feet or so, and, like some huge prehistoric beaver, he began to dig. **D**

Rainsford had dug himself in in France,[31] when a second's delay meant death. That had been a placid pastime compared

---

30. **Malacca** (MUH LAK UH): state in what is now the nation of Malaysia in southeastern Asia.
31. **dug himself in in France:** dug a hole for shelter from gunfire during World War I (1914–1918).

C **LITERARY FOCUS**

Who wins the second stage of this **conflict**?

_____

_____

D **READING FOCUS**

What do you **predict** Rainsford's idea will be?

_____

_____

_____

_____

_____

_____

_____

B LITERARY FOCUS

Who wins the third stage
of this conflict? According
to Zaroff, what will happen
the next day?

_____

_____

_____

_____

_____

_____

_____

_____

_____

to his digging now. The pit grew deeper; when it was above
his shoulders, he climbed out and from some hard saplings
cut stakes and sharpened them to a fine point. These stakes he
710 planted in the bottom of the pit with the points sticking up. With
flying fingers he wove a rough carpet of weeds and branches and
with it he covered the mouth of the pit. Then, wet with sweat and
aching with tiredness, he crouched behind the stump of a light-
ning-charred tree.

He knew his pursuer was coming; he heard the padding
sound of feet on the soft earth, and the night breeze brought him
the perfume of the general's cigarette. It seemed to Rainsford that
the general was coming with unusual swiftness; he was not feeling his way along, foot by foot. Rainsford, crouching there, could
720 not see the general, nor could he see the pit. He lived a year in
a minute. Then he felt an impulse to cry aloud with joy, for he
heard the sharp crackle of the breaking branches as the cover
of the pit gave way; he heard the sharp scream of pain as the
pointed stakes found their mark. **A** He leapt up from his place
of concealment. Then he cowered back. Three feet from the pit a
man was standing, with an electric torch in his hand.

"You've done well, Rainsford," the voice of the general called.
"Your Burmese tiger pit has claimed one of my best dogs. Again
you score. I think, Mr. Rainsford, I'll see what you can do against
730 my whole pack. I'm going home for a rest now. Thank you for a
most amusing evening." **B**

At daybreak Rainsford, lying near the swamp, was awakened
by the sound that made him know that he had new things to
learn about fear. It was a distant sound, faint and wavering, but
he knew it. It was the baying of a pack of hounds.

Rainsford knew he could do one of two things. He could
stay where he was and wait. That was suicide. He could flee. That
was postponing the inevitable. For a moment he stood there,
thinking. An idea that held a wild chance came to him, and,
740 tightening his belt, he headed away from the swamp.

The baying of the hounds drew nearer, then still nearer,
nearer, ever nearer. On a ridge Rainsford climbed a tree. Down

a watercourse, not a quarter of a mile away, he could see the bush moving. Straining his eyes, he saw the lean figure of General Zaroff; just ahead of him Rainsford made out another figure whose wide shoulders surged through the tall jungle weeds. It was the giant Ivan, and he seemed pulled forward by some unseen force. Rainsford knew that Ivan must be holding the pack in leash.

750   They would be on him any minute now. His mind worked frantically. He thought of a native trick he had learned in Uganda. He slid down the tree. He caught hold of a springy young sapling and to it he fastened his hunting knife, with the blade pointing down the trail; with a bit of wild grapevine he tied back the sapling. Then he ran for his life. The hounds raised their voices as they hit the fresh scent. Rainsford knew now how an animal at bay feels. **C**

He had to stop to get his breath. The baying of the hounds stopped abruptly, and Rainsford's heart stopped too. They must
760   have reached the knife.

He shinnied excitedly up a tree and looked back. His pursuers had stopped. But the hope that was in Rainsford's brain when he climbed died, for he saw in the shallow valley that General Zaroff was still on his feet. But Ivan was not. The knife, driven by the recoil of the springing tree, had not wholly failed. **D**

"Nerve, nerve, nerve!" he panted, as he dashed along. A blue gap showed between the trees dead ahead. Ever nearer drew the hounds. Rainsford forced himself on toward that gap. He reached it. It was the shore of the sea. Across a cove he could
770   see the gloomy gray stone of the château. Twenty feet below him the sea rumbled and hissed. Rainsford hesitated. He heard the hounds. Then he leapt far out into the sea. . . . **E**

When the general and his pack reached the place by the sea, the Cossack stopped. For some minutes he stood regarding the blue-green expanse of water. He shrugged his shoulders. Then he sat down, took a drink of brandy from a silver flask, lit a perfumed cigarette, and hummed a bit from *Madama Butterfly*.[32]

---

32. *Madama Butterfly:* famous Italian opera by Giacomo Puccini (1858–1924).

C READING FOCUS

Predict what Rainsford is trying to do with the sapling and the hunting knife.

_____

_____

_____

_____

_____

D QUICK CHECK

What does Rainsford hope to see when he climbs up the tree? What does he actually see?

_____

_____

_____

_____

E READING FOCUS

Trapped between his deadly pursuer and the sea, Rainsford jumps. Is the game over? What do you **predict** will happen next?

_____

_____

_____

_____

General Zaroff had an exceedingly good dinner in his great paneled dining hall that evening. With it he had a bottle of

780   Pol Roger and half a bottle of Chambertin. Two slight annoyances kept him from perfect enjoyment. One was the thought that it would be difficult to replace Ivan; the other was that his quarry had escaped him; of course the American hadn't played the game—so thought the general as he tasted his after-dinner liqueur. In his library he read, to soothe himself, from the works of Marcus Aurelius.[33] At ten he went up to his bedroom. He was deliciously tired, he said to himself as he locked himself in. There was a little moonlight, so before turning on his light, he went to the window and looked down at the courtyard. He

790   could see the great hounds, and he called: "Better luck another time," to them. Then he switched on the light.

A man, who had been hiding in the curtains of the bed, was standing there.

"Rainsford!" screamed the general. "How in God's name did you get here?"

"Swam," said Rainsford. "I found it quicker than walking through the jungle."

The general sucked in his breath and smiled. "I congratulate you," he said. "You have won the game."

800   Rainsford did not smile. "I am still a beast at bay," he said, in a low, hoarse voice. "Get ready, General Zaroff." **A**

The general made one of his deepest bows. "I see," he said. "Splendid! One of us is to furnish a repast[34] for the hounds. The other will sleep in this very excellent bed. On guard, Rainsford. . . ."

He had never slept in a better bed, Rainsford decided. **B**

---

33. **Marcus Aurelius** (MAR CUHS AW REH LEE UHS): emperor of Rome from A.D. 161 to 180 who wrote about the philosophy of Stoicism, which held that people should make themselves indifferent to both pain and pleasure.

34. **repast** (RIH PAST) *n*: meal.

Applying Your Skills

The Most Dangerous Game

VOCABULARY DEVELOPMENT

DIRECTIONS: Write vocabulary words from the Word Box on the correct blanks to complete the paragraph. Not all words will be used.

Word Box

receding
disarming
imprudent
surmounted
invariably

Rainsford climbed the tree and hid there. He wanted to jump on Zaroff when he saw him, but decided that doing so would be (1) _____ because he was unarmed. Zaroff had said that he (2) _____ finds his prey, so Rainsford was not surprised by his masterful tracking skills. As Zaroff walked away, Rainsford felt relieved that he had (3) _____ the odds and survived for at least one day.

LITERARY FOCUS: SUSPENSE AND FORESHADOWING

DIRECTIONS: Complete the chart below to illustrate how different elements of the story contributed to its **suspense**.

Detail	How does this create suspense?
While sailing past Ship-Trap Island, Rainsford hears gun shots.	I wondered why someone would be firing a gun so late at night.
Zaroff says that he invented a "new" animal.	

READING FOCUS: MAKING PREDICTIONS

While the author resolves the story's conflict in its final lines, he says nothing about the future for Rainsford. Will Rainsford remain on the island? Will he abandon hunting forever? What do you think will happen?

DIRECTIONS: On a separate piece of paper, write a paragraph in which you **make predictions** about Rainsford's future.

SKILLS FOCUS

Literary Skills
Understand how adding suspense can enrich a story and increase a reader's curiosity.

Reading Skills
Make predictions about a story's aftermath.

Liberty

by Julia Alvarez

LITERARY FOCUS: SETTING AND CONFLICT

The **setting** of a story is more than just the time and place where the action of the story happens. The setting also includes the events happening in the world around the character, and the general beliefs people hold at that time. For example, in a story that takes place before women had the right to vote, the characters might think very differently about women's abilities and rights than we do today. Their beliefs are an important part of the setting.

Using the same example, suppose a female character in such a story wants a job that was traditionally held by men. The beliefs of people may make it hard for the character to get the job. A struggle makes up another important part of a story—the **conflict**. The main action in a story often involves a character's attempt to resolve a conflict.

Record Settings   People sometimes take pictures, make videos, or write in a journal to help them remember special places and times. As you read "Liberty," think about how the narrator's life is changing, and make a list of the things she might want to record with pictures or in a journal.

READING FOCUS: ANALYZING DETAILS

The **details** a writer uses in a story can tell you many things. They can tell you about conflicts, settings, what might happen in the story's future, and what a character feels.

Use the Skill   As you read, create a chart like the one below to record the details in "Liberty," and decide what they tell about the action of the story.

Detail	What It Tells Me
Papi and Mami look scared when talking about leaving the country.	The situation is dangerous; they are worried about what might happen.
Mami would rather have visas than a puppy.	

SKILLS FOCUS

Literary Skills
Understand the relationship between setting and conflict.

Reading Skills
Analyze details.

Vocabulary Development

Liberty

SELECTION VOCABULARY

elect (IH LEHKT) *v:* choose as a course of action.

I elect to play with my dog Liberty instead of with my sisters.

distracted (DIHS TRAK TIHD) *adj:* not able to concentrate; unfocused.

She was so distracted, I had to shout to get her attention.

admonitions (AD MUH NISH UHNZ) *n:* scoldings; warnings.

When Mami forgot her admonitions to me about doing my homework, I knew something was wrong.

impression (IHM PREHSH UHN) *n:* idea; notion.

I had a strong impression that my father was keeping something secret.

inconsolable (IHN KUHN SOH LUH BUHL) *adj:* unable to be comforted; brokenhearted.

I was inconsolable and could not stop crying when they told me we had to leave.

resort (RIH ZAWRT) *v:* turn to something when in need.

When it started to rain, I had to resort to playing checkers indoors.

WORD STUDY

DIRECTIONS: The words *elect*, *impression*, and *resort* all have more than one meaning. Use a dictionary to look up the other meanings of each word. Then, fill in the blanks with the correct word. You will use each word twice.

1. I do not _____ to spend the afternoon watching television.

2. We spent our vacation at a beautiful _____.

3. I had the _____ that he was making fun of me.

4. If it does not stop snowing soon, we will have to _____ to our backup plan.

5. My foot left a deep _____ in the sand.

6. Every four years it is time to _____ a president.

LIBERTY

By Julia Alvarez

> **BACKGROUND**
> The Dominican Republic is an island located southeast of the United States in the Caribbean Sea. Julia Alvarez, the author of this story, lived in the Dominican Republic in the 1950s. At that time, a brutal dictator named Rafael Trujillo ruled the country. Under his rule, people had few rights. In addition, the secret police dealt harshly with those who opposed Trujillo. Julia's father opposed Trujillo. As a result, Julia and her family were forced to flee the Dominican Republic when she was ten years old.

A **READING FOCUS**

Circle the **details** the author provides about the dog's appearance. Underline the details that show Mami's feelings about the dog.

Papi came home with a dog whose kind we had never seen before. A black-and-white speckled electric current of energy. It was a special breed with papers, like a person with a birth certificate. Mami just kept staring at the puppy with a cross look on her face. "It looks like a mess!" she said. "Take it back." **A**

"Mami, it is a gift!" Papi shook his head. It would be an insult to Mister Victor, who had given us the dog. The American consul[1] wanted to thank us for all we'd done for him since he'd been assigned to our country.

---

1. **American consul** (KAHN SUHL): person appointed by the United States government to represent American interests and provide assistance to Americans living in a foreign country.

© Jerry Shulman/SuperStock

10   "If he wanted to thank us, he'd give us our visas,"[2] Mami grumbled. For a while now, my parents had been talking about going to the United States so Papi could return to school. I couldn't understand why a grown-up who could do whatever he wanted would elect to go back to a place I so much wanted to get out of. **B**

On their faces when they talked of leaving there was a scared look I also couldn't understand.

"Those visas will come soon," Papi promised. **C** But Mami just kept shaking her head about the dog. She had enough with

20   four girls to take on puppies, too. Papi explained that the dog would stay at the end of the yard in a pen. He would not be allowed in the house. He would not be pooping in Mami's orchid garden. He would not be barking until late at night. "A well-behaved dog," Papi concluded. "An American dog."

The little black-and-white puppy yanked at Papi's trouser cuff with his mouth. "What shall we call you?" Papi asked him.

"Trouble," Mami suggested, kicking the puppy away. He had left Papi's trousers to come slobber on her leg.

"We will call him Liberty. Life, liberty, and the pursuit of

30   happiness." Papi quoted the U.S.A. Constitution. "Eh, Liberty, you are a lucky sign!"

Liberty barked his little toy barks and all us kids laughed. "Trouble." Mami kept shaking her head as she walked away. Liberty trotted behind her as if he agreed that that was the better name for him.

Mami was right, too—Liberty turned out to be trouble. He ate all of Mami's orchids, and that little hyperactive baton of a tail knocked things off the low coffee table whenever Liberty climbed on the couch to leave his footprints in among the flower

40   prints. He tore up Mami's garden looking for buried treasure. Mami screamed at Liberty and stamped her foot. "Perro sin vergüenza!"[3] But Liberty just barked back at her. **D**

---

2. **visas** (VEE SUHZ): certificates granting official access to enter a country.
3. **"Perro sin vergüenza!"** Spanish for "Shameless dog!"

B LITERARY FOCUS

The author never directly names the **setting** of the story. Reread this paragraph and underline any words that show that the story might take place in another country.

C READING FOCUS

It is important to **analyze details** to help you learn about characters. Reread lines 16 through 18. What do they tell you about this family's situation?

_____

_____

_____

_____

_____

D LITERARY FOCUS

Based on the details given, what is your impression of one of the main **settings** of the story, the narrator's home?

_____

_____

_____

_____

_____

_____

_____

_____

_____

_____

_____

Selection Vocabulary
The word *distracted means* "not able to concentrate; unfocused." Underline the words in this sentence that might help a reader guess the meaning of this word.

"He doesn't understand Spanish," Papi said lamely. "Maybe if you correct him in English, he'll behave better!"

Mami turned on him, her slipper still in midair. Her face looked as if she'd light into him after she was done with Liberty. "Let him go be a pet in his own country if he wants instructions in English!" In recent weeks, Mami had changed her tune about going to the United States. She wanted to stay in her own

50 country. She didn't want Mister Victor coming around our house and going off into the study with Papi to talk over important things in low, worried voices.

"All liberty involves sacrifice," Papi said in a careful voice. Liberty gave a few perky barks as if he agreed with that.

Mami glared at Papi. "I told you I don't want trouble—" She was going to say more, but her eye fell on me and she stopped herself. "Why aren't you with the others?" she scolded. It was as if I had been the one who had dug up her lily bulbs. **A**

The truth was that after Liberty arrived, I never played with

60 the others. It was as if I had found my double in another species. I had always been the tomboy, the live wire, the troublemaker, the one who was going to drive Mami to drink, the one she was going to give away to the Haitians. While the sisters dressed pretty and stayed clean in the playroom, I was out roaming the world looking for trouble. And now I had found someone to share my adventures.

"I'll take Liberty back to his pen," I offered. There was something I had figured out that Liberty had yet to learn: when to get out of Mami's way.

70 She didn't say yes and she didn't say no. She seemed distracted, as if something else was on her mind. **B** As I led Liberty away by his collar, I could see her talking to Papi. Suddenly she started to cry, and Papi held her.

"It's okay," I consoled Liberty. "Mami doesn't mean it. She really does love you. She's just nervous." It was what my father always said when Mami scolded me harshly.

At the back of the property stood Liberty's pen—a chain-link fence around a dirt square at the center of which stood a doghouse. Papi had built it when Liberty first came, a cute little

80　house, but then he painted it a putrid green that reminded me of all the vegetables I didn't like. **C** It was always a job to get Liberty to go into that pen.

Sure enough, as soon as he saw where we were headed, he took off, barking, toward the house, then swerved to the front yard to our favorite spot. It was a grassy knoll[4] surrounded by a tall hibiscus hedge. At the center stood a tall, shady samán tree. From there, no one could see you up at the house. Whenever I did something wrong, this was where I hid out until the punishment winds blew over. That was where Liberty headed, and I was

90　fast behind on his trail.

Inside the clearing I stopped short. Two strange men in dark glasses were crouched behind the hedge. The fat one had seized Liberty by the collar and was pulling so hard on it that poor Liberty was almost standing on his hind legs. When he saw me, Liberty began to bark, and the man holding him gave him a yank on the collar that made me sick to my stomach. I began to back away, but the other man grabbed my arm. "Not so fast," he said. Two little scared faces—my own—looked down at me from his glasses.

100　"I came for my dog," I said, on the verge of tears.

"Good thing you found him," the man said. "Give the young lady her dog," he ordered his friend, and then he turned to me. "You haven't seen us, you understand?" **D**

I didn't understand. It was usually I who was the one lying and grown-ups telling me to tell the truth. But I nodded, relieved when the man released my arm and Liberty was back in my hands.

"It's okay, Liberty." I embraced him when I put him back in his pen. He was as sad as I was. We had both had a hard time with Mami, but this was the first time we'd come across mean

110　and scary people. The fat man had almost broken Liberty's neck,

---

4.　**knoll:** mound; small hill.

Word Study

The word *putrid* can mean "foul-smelling; rotten" and "very unpleasant." Use a thesaurus to find a synonym for *putrid*. Then write a new sentence using the synonym.

_____

_____

_____

_____

_____

D LITERARY FOCUS

Think back to what you read about Mami and Papi in lines 48 to 58. Predict how the two strangers might cause **conflict** in this story.

_____

_____

_____

_____

_____

Who is Mr. Victor? Look at the phrase marked by quotation marks on line 119. Who do you think might have said these words?

_____

_____

_____

_____

Finding the wires is an important **detail**. What is the purpose of these wires?

_____

_____

_____

_____

Academic Vocabulary

What *effect*, or result, does the discovery of the wires have on Mami?

_____

_____

_____

and the other one had left his fingerprints on my arm. After I locked up the pen, I watched Liberty wander back slowly to his house and actually go inside, turn around, and stick his little head out the door. He'd always avoided that ugly doghouse before. I walked back to my own house, head down, to find my parents and tell them what I had seen.

Overnight, it seemed, Mister Victor moved in. He ate all his meals with us, stayed 'til late, and when he had to leave, someone from the embassy was left behind "to keep an eye on things." **A**

120   Now, when Papi and Mister Victor talked or when the *tíos*[5] came over, they all went down to the back of the property near Liberty's pen to talk. Mami had found some wires in the study, behind the portrait of Papi's great-grandmother fanning herself with a painted fan. The wires ran behind a screen and then out a window, where there was a little box with lots of other wires coming from different parts of the house. **B**

Mami explained that it was no longer safe to talk in the house about certain things. But the only way you knew what things those were was when Mami leveled her eyes on you as

130   if she were pressing the off button on your mouth. She did this every time I asked her what was going on. **C**

"Nothing," she said stiffly, and then she urged me to go outside and play. Forgotten were the admonitions to go study or I would flunk out of fifth grade. To go take a bath or the *microbios*[6] might kill me. To drink my milk or I would grow up stunted and with no teeth. Mami seemed absent and tense and always in tears. Papi was right—she was too nervous, poor thing.

I myself was enjoying a heyday of liberty. Several times I even got away with having one of Mister Victor's Coca-Colas

140   for breakfast instead of my boiled milk with a beaten egg, which Liberty was able to enjoy instead.

"You love that dog, don't you?" Mister Victor asked me one day. He was standing by the pen with Papi waiting for the uncles.

---

5. *tíos:* Spanish for "uncles."
6. *microbios:* Spanish for "germs."

He had a funny accent that sounded like someone making fun of
Spanish when he spoke it.

I ran Liberty through some of the little tricks I had taught
him, and Mister Victor laughed. His face was full of freckles—so
that it looked as if he and Liberty were kin. I had the impression that God had spilled a lot of his colors when he was making
150 American things.

Soon the uncles arrived and the men set to talking. I wandered into the pen and sat beside Liberty with my back to the
house and listened. The men were speaking in English, and I had
picked up enough of it at school and in my parents' conversations
to make out most of what was being said. They were planning
some hunting expedition for a goat with guns to be delivered by
Mister Charlie. Papi was going to have to leave the goat to the
others because his tennis shoes were missing. Though I understood the words—or thought I did—none of it made sense. I
160 knew my father did not own a pair of tennis shoes, we didn't
know a Mister Charlie, and who ever heard of hunting a goat? **D**

As Liberty and I sat there with the sun baking the tops of
our heads, I had this sense that the world as I knew it was about
to end. The image of the two men in mirror glasses flashed
through my head. So as not to think about them, I put my arm
around Liberty and buried my face in his neck.

Late one morning Mami gave my sisters and me the news. Our
visa had come. Mister Victor had arranged everything, and
that very night we were going to the United States of America!
170 Wasn't that wonderful! She flashed us a bright smile, as if someone were taking her picture.

We stood together watching her, alarmed at this performance of happiness when really she looked like she wanted to
cry. All morning aunts had been stopping by and planting big
kisses on our foreheads and holding our faces in their hands
and asking us to promise we would be very good. Until now, we
hadn't a clue why they were so worked up.

Mami kept smiling her company smile. She had a little job
for each of us to do. There would not be room in our bags for

The conversation in this
paragraph is very strange,
and confuses the narrator.
Why do you think the men
are talking in code? What
does this tell us about their
situation?

_____

_____

_____

_____

_____

_____

A READING FOCUS

Underline the **details** in lines 167–181 that tell us how Mami really feels about the family's departure.

B LITERARY FOCUS

Circle two sentences in lines 182–186 that show the **conflict** between the narrator and Mami.

C LITERARY FOCUS

How does Tía Mimi help to resolve the **conflict** between the narrator and Mami?

_____

_____

_____

_____

_____

_____

_____

180 everything. We were to pick the one toy we wanted to take with us to the United States. **A**

I didn't even have to think twice about my choice. It had suddenly dawned on me we were leaving, and that meant leaving *everything* behind. "I want to take Liberty."

Mami started shaking her head no. We could not take a dog into the United States of America. That was not allowed. **B**

"Please," I begged with all my might. "Please, please, Mami, please." Repetition sometimes worked—each time you said the word, it was like giving a little push to the yes that was having a

190 hard time rolling out of her mouth.

"I said no!" The bright smile on Mami's face had grown dimmer and dimmer. "*N–O.*" She spelled it out for me in case I was confusing no with another word like yes. "I said a toy, and I mean a toy."

I burst into tears. I was not going to the United States unless I could take Liberty! Mami shook me by the shoulders and asked me between clenched teeth if I didn't understand we had to go to the United States or else. But all I could understand was that a world without Liberty would break my heart. I was inconsolable.

200 Mami began to cry.

Tía[7] Mimi took me aside. She had gone to school in the States and always had her nose in a book. In spite of her poor taste in how to spend her free time, I still loved her because she had smart things to say. Like telling Mami that punishment was not the way to make kids behave. "I'm going to tell you a little secret," she offered now. "You're going to find liberty when you get to the United States."

"Really?" I asked.

She hesitated a minute, and then she gave me a quick nod.

210 "You'll see what I mean," she said. And then, giving me a pat on the butt, she added, "Come on, let's go pack. How about taking that wonderful book I got you on the Arabian Nights?" **C**

---

7. **tía:** Spanish for "aunt."

© Raul Touzon/National Geographic/Getty Images

D QUICK CHECK

What is it time for the narrator and her family to do?

_____

_____

_____

_____

_____

_____

_____

Late in the night someone comes in and shakes us awake. "It's time!"

Half asleep, we put on our clothes, hands helping our arms to go into the right sleeves, buttoning us up, running a comb through our hair.

We were put to sleep hours earlier because the plane had not come in.

220   But now it's time. **D**

"Go sit by the door," we are ordered, as the hands, the many hands that now seem to be in control, finish with us. We file out of the bedroom, one by one, and go sit on the bench where packages are set down when Mami comes in from shopping. There is much rushing around. Mister Victor comes by and pats us on the head like dogs. "We'll have to wait a few more minutes," he says.

In that wait, one sister has to go to the bathroom. Another wants a drink of water. I am left sitting with my baby sister, who is dozing with her head on my shoulder. I lay her head down on

230   the bench and slip out.

Through the dark patio down the path to the back of the yard I go. Every now and then a strange figure flashes by. I have said good-bye to Liberty a dozen times already, but there is something else I have left to do.

Sitting on the bench, I had an image again of those two men in mirror glasses. After we are gone, they come onto the property. They smash the picture of Papi's great-grandmother fanning herself. They knock over the things on the coffee table as if they

_____

_____

_____

_____

_____

_____

B **LANGUAGE COACH**

The word _resort_ has **multiple meanings**. Which meaning of the word is being used here?

_____

_____

_____

_____

C **LITERARY ANALYSIS**

The word _liberty_ has appeared regularly throughout this story. How do you think the narrator's understanding of the word has changed?

_____

_____

_____

_____

_____

_____

_____

240 don't know any better. They throw the flowered cushions on the floor. They smash the windows. And then they come to the back of the property and they find Liberty.

Quickly, because I hear calling from the big house, I slip open the door of the pen. Liberty is all over me, wagging his tail so it beats against my legs, jumping up and licking my face.

"Get away!" I order sharply, in a voice he is not used to hearing from me. I begin walking back to the house, not looking around so as not to encourage him. I want him to run away before the gangsters come. A

He doesn't understand and keeps following me. Finally I
250 have to resort to Mami's techniques. B I kick him, softly at first, but then, when he keeps tagging behind me, I kick him hard. He whimpers and dashes away toward the front yard, disappearing in areas of darkness, then reappearing when he passes through lighted areas. At the front of the house, instead of turning toward our secret place, he keeps on going straight down the drive, through the big gates, to the world out there.

He will beat me to the United States is what I am thinking as I head back to the house. I will find Liberty there, like Tía Mimi says. But I already sense it is a different kind of liberty my aunt
260 means. All I can do is hope that when we come back—as Mami has promised we will—my Liberty will be waiting for me here. C

Applying Your Skills

Liberty

VOCABULARY DEVELOPMENT

DIRECTIONS: Write vocabulary words from the Word Box on the correct blanks to complete the paragraph. One word will not be used.

Word Box

elect

distracted

admonitions

impression

inconsolable

resort

In the story "Liberty," the narrator's family must (1) _____ to leaving their homeland because of the political situation there. Because of the family's worries, Mami is (2) _____ and does not pay as much attention as usual to her daughters. Mami and Papi (3) _____ to leave the country with their family as quickly as possible, for their own safety. Although the narrator is very sad, almost (4) _____, about leaving, she gets the (5) _____ that she will find liberty when she arrives in the United States.

LITERARY FOCUS: SETTING AND CONFLICT

The author never states the **setting** of the story. Instead, she gives the reader clues as to where the story takes place.

DIRECTIONS: On the lines below, write three details from the story that help to show the reader where the story takes place.

1. _____

2. _____

3. _____

READING FOCUS: ANALYZING DETAILS

DIRECTIONS: Study the chart of **details** and their meanings that you made as you read this story. Use it to help you answer the following questions on a separate sheet of paper:

1. What is the political situation in the narrator's homeland?

2. Why do the two strange men in dark glasses visit the family's house?

3. How does Mami feel about the family going to the United States?

4. How does the narrator feel about going to the United States?

5. What happens to Liberty at the end of the story?

SKILLS FOCUS

Literary Skills
Understand the relationship between setting and conflict.

Reading Skills
Analyze details.

The Great Escape

INFORMATIONAL TEXT FOCUS: MAIN IDEA

When you read informational texts, two important questions to ask are "What is the writer trying to say?" and "Why is the author making that point?" The answers to those questions will tell you the writer's **main idea**, or central point, and the reason he or she wrote the article. Authors use a variety of details to help you understand the main idea, such as facts, quotations, and numbers.

Tips for Finding the Main Idea

- Read the article's title to see if it provides a clue.

- Read the article's introduction to see if it states the main idea.

- Scan the headings of the article to get an idea of its important points.

- Reread the article's conclusion to see if the writer has repeated the main idea there.

SELECTION VOCABULARY

neutral (NOO TRUHL) *adj.*: not taking sides.

  In times of war, some countries choose to remain neutral.

prowled (PROWLD) *v.*: hunted; stalked.

  German guards prowled through the camp to stop escapes.

pursued (PUHR SOOD) *v.*: followed; chased.

  Thousands of Germans pursued the escaped prisoners.

WORD STUDY

DIRECTIONS: Each of the vocabulary words above contains a letter that is not pronounced, or is silent. Underline the silent letters. Then, read the list of words below. Circle all of the words that contain silent letters. You can use a dictionary to help you.

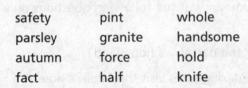

safety	pint	whole
parsley	granite	handsome
autumn	force	hold
fact	half	knife

THE GREAT ESCAPE

by Thomas Fleming

> **BACKGROUND**
>
> The article below is from *Boys Life* magazine. It tells the story of one of the most famous real-life escapes in the last century. During The Great Escape of World War II, 76 captured men from many different countries escaped a Nazi prisoner-of-war (POW) camp in Poland.

The seven hundred fliers in the prisoner of war camp called Stalag Luft III came from many countries—the United States, England, Canada, Poland, Czechoslovakia, Australia, South Africa. They had two things in common. All had been shot down fighting Germany during World War II in the early 1940s.

And all were determined to escape. **A**

They had tried to escape from many other camps and had been caught. That was why these prisoners had ended up in Stalag Luft III, deep in eastern Germany. It was supposed to be
10 escape-proof.

Two nine-foot-high barbed wire fences surrounded the camp. Between the fences were big towers equipped with search-lights and machine guns. The prisoners called the towers "goon boxes." Day and night specially trained groups of Germans, whom the fliers called "ferrets," prowled inside the camp, looking for escape activity.

Anyone the ferrets caught planning an escape was sent to "the cooler"—a block of solitary sonfinement[1] cells where the prisoner would live on nothing but bread and water. **B**

A **VOCABULARY**

Word Study

The word *determined* means "having one's mind made up." How does the next paragraph show that these prisoners were determined?

_____

_____

_____

_____

_____

B **READING FOCUS**

What background does the author give about the camp?

---

1. **solitary confinement:** imprisonment in a cell isolated from all other prisoners.

"The Great Escape" by **Thomas Fleming** from *Boys' Life*, March 1997. Copyright © 1997 by Thomas Fleming. Reproduced by permission of the author.

The "Escape Genius" section describes Roger Bushell. Underline the sentence that explains why he wanted the tunnels to be so deep.

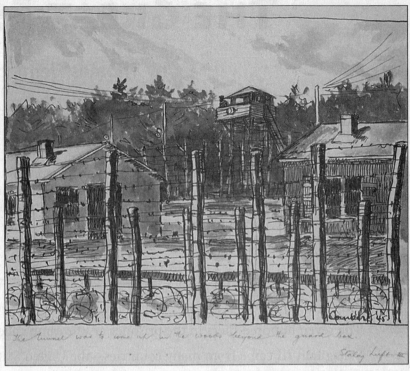

The tunnel was to come up in the woods beyond the guard box.

Stalag Luft III

© Australian War Memorial Negative Number ART 34781.021

The Escape Genius

20   The Germans seemed to have thought of everything. But they did not count on facing Roger Bushell. This South African was an escape genius. He was called Big X by the rest of the prisoners. He transformed Stalag Luft III into the "X Organization," announcing to his fellow prisoners that they were going to pull off the greatest escape in history.

Big X's plan called for the prisoners to start three tunnels—called Tom, Dick and Harry. The men cut trapdoors through the stone floors of three huts and inserted removable slabs made from stolen concrete. "Tunnel rats" dropped through the trap-
30   doors and began digging.

Big X wanted deep tunnels. If they were too shallow, the Germans would be able to hear the men working in them. So, despite the danger of the tunnels collapsing and burying them alive, the tunnel rats went down thirty feet before they started for the fences. **A**

The Escape Factory

The tunnels were only the beginning. "I want each escaping man to be equipped with a set of forged documents that will fool the German police," Big X said. "I want them to be wearing civilian clothes or fake German uniforms. I want them to have com-
40 passes and maps that will help them reach the borders of neutral countries." **B**

The X Organization spotted weaklings among the ferrets and bribed them with chocolate from their Red Cross aid packages. **C** Soon they had ink and pens, a camera and a set of official documents. A forgery factory ran day and night.

In other huts prisoners created civilian clothes by cutting and reshaping prisoners' uniforms, the linings of winter coats and other pieces of cloth. An Australian flight lieutenant ran a factory that made two hundred compasses out of melted phonograph
50 records. The compass needles were slices of magnetized razor blades.

An engineering factory built air pumps so the tunnel rats could breathe. The engineers also made small flatbed trolleys from wooden bed boards. They even stole light bulbs and wiring for the tunnels.

The diggers lay on their stomachs in the two-foot-wide tunnels and filled boxed on the trolleys with sand. Other prisoners poured the sand into bags made from towels—bags that could be inserted under a man's pants.
60 Fifty Americans worked as sand carriers. They were called "penguins" because they had to spend most of their time outside, walking up and down, waiting for the right moment to pull a string on the bags and let the sand run out.

All around the camp were dozens of "stooges" who signaled when a ferret approached. This gave the forgers, tailors, penguins and the others time to hide their work or take cover. Thirty feet underground, the tunnel rats kept digging.

B VOCABULARY

Selection Vocabulary
The word *neutral* means "not taking sides." Why would escaping prisoners try to go to a neutral country?

_____

_____

_____

C LANGUAGE COACH

Some letters, when pronounced together, blend to make one sound; for example, the *ti* in *nation* is pronounced as a *sh* sound. Circle one word in this sentence with two letters that blend to make one sound when pronounced. Which letters blend, and what sound do they make together?

_____

_____

B **QUICK CHECK**

List the main reason that the prisoners had to escape on this night. Circle the name of the man who decided to go on with the escape.

_____

_____

_____

_____

_____

_____

_____

Pretending Defeat

Then disaster struck. The Germans discovered the trapdoor for Tom, the longest tunnel. The diggers had gotten past the wire fence and were only one hundred feet from the woods around the camp. Big X ordered a halt to all digging for more than a month. He wanted the Germans to think they had given up.

Then Big X ordered an all-out push in Harry. Soon they were under the wire and—they thought—into the woods. It was time for "the great escape." Big X was hoping to spring no fewer that 250 men. Not even a six-inch snowfall was going to stop them. **A**

At 9 P.M. on March 24, 1944, the breakout began. Men wearing German uniforms, business suits and tattered workers' outfits crowded into the hut containing Harry's trapdoor. At the other end, the tunnel rats finished the thirty-foot shaft to the surface.

They finally broke through and stared around in horror. They were ten feer short of the trees!

After a frantic conference, Big X decided they had to keep going. All their forged documents were dated. If they dug another ten feet and waited a month for the next moonless night, the forgery factory would have to do its work all over again. **B**

Australian War Memorial Negative Number ART34781.017

© Australian War Memorial Negative
Number ART34781.016

C VOCABULARY

Word Study

Startled means "surprised; scared." Why was the guard startled?

_____

_____

_____

_____

_____

_____

90
They stretched a rope from the hole to the trees. The first man out lay in the trees and pulled the rope to signal when the guard in the nearest goon box was not looking. Over the next seven hours, seventy-six men scuttled through the woods towards freedom.

It was almost dawn when a German sentry patrolling outside the barbed wire discovered the hole. The guard raised his rifle to shoot the man crawling out. The rope controller leaped from the woods crying: "*Nicht schiessen!*" ("Don't shoot!"). The startled guard's shot went wild. C

By this time Big X and his friends were far away from Stalag Luft III.

A **READING FOCUS**

How does this sentence support the **main idea** of this article that the escape was successful?

_____

_____

B **QUICK CHECK**

How many men finally escaped?

_____

_____

_____

_____

100   The German dictator, Adolf Hitler, was furious. He ordered one of the biggest manhunts in history. More than 70,000 policemen and troops pursued the fugitives. Big X's plan to humiliate the Germans and make them worry about escapees—and not the war front—was successful. **A**

      But only three men—Peter Bergsland, Jens Mueller and Bram van der Stok—made it to freedom. Fifty of the captured men, including Big X, were shot by the German secret police, the Gestapo, at Hitler's order. This was an outrageous violation of the rules of war. The bodies were cremated to hide the murders. **B**

Jens Muller. Courtesy of Jonathan F. Vance, Canada Research Chair, The University of Western Ontario.

Peter Bergsland. Courtesy of Jonathan F. Vance, Canada Research Chair, The University of Western Ontario.

Bram van der Stok. Courtesy of the Ian Le Sueur Collection.

Map depicting Germany and its surroundings during World War II.

110   The rest of the escapers were returned to Stalag Luft III and other camps for long stays in the cooler. A year later, Allied tanks[2] freed the survivors as Germany surrendered.

      After the war, the British sent a team of investigators to Germany. They tracked down those who had carried out Hitler's order. Twenty-one were hanged for murder, seventeen received prison terms.

      What had the great escape accomplished? One writer summed it up this way: It proved that "there is nothing that can stop a group of men, regardless of race, creed, color or national-
120   ity, from achieving a goal once they agree to what that goal is."

C VOCABULARY

Academic Vocabulary
Authors use various methods to *convey*, or communicate, key points in a story. The last sentence of this article includes a quotation. What is the impact of this sentence?

---

2. **Allied tanks:** tanks belonging to the Allied counties (including the United States, Great Britain, France, and Russia), those countries battling the Axis powers (Germany, Italy, and Japan) in World War II.

The Great Escape   49

Skills Practice

The Great Escape

USE A CHART

DIRECTIONS: Use the chart below to record information from the article that might help you identify the main idea.

Main Idea Chart	
Text Feature	**Description**
Title	
Headings	
Key words that are repeated	
Conclusion	

Applying Your Skills

The Great Escape

VOCABULARY DEVELOPMENT

DIRECTIONS: Write the vocabulary words from the Word Box on the correct blanks to complete the paragraph.

Word Box

neutral

prowled

pursued

The article "The Great Escape" tells the story of a brave group of prisoners-of-war during World War II. These airmen had been captured by the Germans and were being held in a prison camp where guards (1) _____ the camp looking for escapers. Like many prisoners-of-war, they hoped to escape and flee to a (2) _____ country where they would be safe. After their escape, they were (3) _____ by German police and soldiers.

INFORMATIONAL TEXT FOCUS: MAIN IDEA

To express the **main idea** of a story or article, an author might use a variety of details, including facts, quotations, and numbers.

DIRECTIONS: Read the following list of important details from the article. Based on these details and the information in your Main Idea Chart, determine the **main idea** of the article and write it on the lines below.

- The airmen who planned the escape were of many different nationalities.

- They planned an escape for 250 men.

- The tunnels they dug were very deep.

- The men had to come up with creative solutions for many problems, including removing the dirt from their tunnels, forging documents, and ventilating and lighting the tunnels.

- On the night of the escape, many things went wrong, but the men still carried on with their attempt.

_____

_____

_____

_____

Informational Text Skills
Use details from an article to determine the main idea.

Skills Review

Collection 1

VOCABULARY REVIEW

DIRECTIONS: Read the sentences below and insert the correct vocabulary word from the Word Box into the blank. Some words will not be used.

Word Box

admonitions
convey
disarming
distracted
effect
elect
excerpt
impression
imprudent
inconsolable
invariably
neutral
outcome
prowled
pursued
receding
resort
support
surmounted

1. I have made up my mind; I do not _____ to eat that cake.

2. Throughout the evening she seemed tired and _____, barely able to pay attention to a word I said to her.

3. They asked me to settle their argument, but I was determined to stay _____.

4. Just as it is impossible to know the future, it is impossible to predict the _____ of this story.

5. He ignored my _____ and jumped into the freezing water.

6. Barking furiously, the angry terrier _____ the chattering squirrel.

7. Her words clearly _____ her anger and frustration with the situation.

8. After you give your opinion, list three pieces of evidence that _____ it.

9. Her harsh words made a lasting _____ on her brother—in fact, he never forgave her.

10. I have such bad luck; _____, every time I go on vacation, my car breaks down.

Skills Review

Collection 1

LANGUAGE COACH

Several of this collection's vocabulary words are homographs, which are words that have **multiple meanings**, but are always spelled the same. Homographs may or may not have different pronunciations. Some common homographs are listed below.

DIRECTIONS: Write two sentences for each homograph, using a different meaning of the word in each sentence. You may use a dictionary to help you find the new meanings of the words.

1. bow _____

_____

_____

2. contract _____

_____

_____

3. lead _____

_____

_____

4. rose _____

_____

_____

5. upset _____

_____

_____

WRITING ACTIVITY

Many stories start with a short introduction which is made up of a few paragraphs that present a story's setting, its main character, and his or her conflict.

DIRECTIONS: On a separate sheet of paper, write a short introduction for one of the stories in this collection.

Collection

2

Character

Literary and Academic Vocabulary for Collection 2

observation (AHB zur VAY shuhn) *n.:* statement based on what one sees.

After reading the story, Anna made the observation that the writing was very funny.

incident (IHN suh DUHNT) *n.:* something that took place; event.

The incident that took place on the bridge had a major impact on Paul's future.

complex (KAHM plehks) *adj.:* having more than one part or aspect; complicated.

Although the old man's words are simple, the emotions behind the words are complex.

significant (sihg NIHF uh kuhnt) *adj.:* important.

The old man says very little, but what he says is significant and helps to reveal his character.

characters (KAR ihk tuhrz) *n.:* the people in a story, poem, or play.

The characters in the story seem very real.

protagonist (proh TAG uh nihst) *n.:* the main character in a story or play.

The story's protagonist struggles to help his family overcome poverty.

antagonist (an TAG uh nihst) *n.:* a character who conflicts with the story's protagonist, trying to prevent the protagonist from reaching his or her goals.

Throughout the story, the antagonist causes more suffering for the family.

Preparing to Read

Thank You, M'am

by Langston Hughes

LITERARY FOCUS: CHARACTER AND DIALOGUE

- Writers often develop **characters** by telling us how they look and act. In "Thank You, M'am," two characters, an older woman and a boy, meet in an unusual way. The characters reveal, or show, themselves to each other and to the reader through **dialogue**, or conversation. As you read, notice what these characters say to each other—and what they don't say.

- As you read, look for other details that bring the characters to life. For example, what do the characters' actions and appearances tell you about them? What does the setting tell you about one of the characters?

READING FOCUS: MAKING INFERENCES

An **inference** is an educated guess—a guess based on evidence. When you **infer**, or make an inference, you use details in the text and your own experience to guess about something you don't know for sure.

For example, the writer may say, "When Mr. Green called on the new girl in class, she smiled." The writer doesn't tell you directly that the new girl is pleased. Based on your own experience, however, you can probably *infer* that she is happy to be called on.

To make an inference:

- Look for details in the text.

- Relate the details to what you know about life.

- Make a careful guess.

Make inferences as you read "Thank You, M'am." Look for clues that reveal important information about the characters. Then, read on to see how the characters develop. You might use a chart like this one to record your inferences:

SKILLS FOCUS

Literary Skills
Understand how character traits are revealed through dialogue.

Reading Skills
Make inferences.

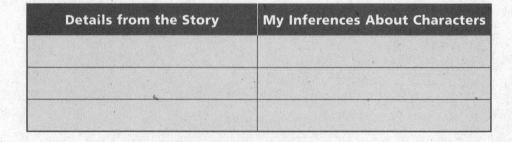

Details from the Story	My Inferences About Characters

Vocabulary Development

Thank You, M'am

SELECTION VOCABULARY

permit (PUR MIHT) *v.:* allow.
> *The old woman would not permit the boy to commit a crime.*

frail (FRAYL) *adj.:* thin and weak; delicate.
> *The underfed boy looked frail and scared.*

barren (BAR UHN) *adj.:* empty; deserted.
> *Everyone had gone home by midnight, and the streets were barren.*

WORD STUDY

DIRECTIONS: An antonym is a word with the opposite definition of another word. For example, *happy* is an antonym of *sad*. Match the vocabulary words in the left column with their antonyms in the right column.

1. _____ permit   a. full
2. _____ frail   b. deny
3. _____ barren   c. strong

THANK YOU, M'AM

Langston Hughes

A LANGUAGE COACH

Shoulder has **multiple meanings**. As a noun, it refers to a body part. What does *shoulder* mean as a verb?

B LITERARY FOCUS

You have just met the two main **characters** of this story. Underline the details that tell you what the boy does here. Circle the sentences that tell you how the woman reacts.

She was a large woman with a large purse that had everything in it but a hammer and nails. It had a long strap, and she carried it slung across her shoulder. **A** It was about eleven o'clock at night, dark, and she was walking alone, when a boy ran up behind her and tried to snatch her purse. The strap broke with the sudden single tug the boy gave it from behind. But the boy's weight and the weight of the purse combined caused him to lose his balance. Instead of taking off full blast as he had hoped, the boy fell on his back on the sidewalk and his legs flew up. The
10 large woman simply turned around and kicked him right square in his blue-jeaned sitter. Then she reached down, picked the boy up by his shirt front, and shook him until his teeth rattled. **B**

"Thank You, M'am" from *Short Stories* by Langston Hughes. Copyright © 1996 by Ramona Bass and Arnold Rampersad. All rights reserved. Reprinted by permission of **Hill and Wang, a division of Farrar, Straus and Giroux, LLC.**

After that the woman said, "Pick up my pocketbook, boy, and give it here."

She still held him tightly. But she bent down enough to permit him to stoop and pick up her purse. Then she said, "Now ain't you ashamed of yourself?"

Firmly gripped by his shirt front, the boy said, "Yes'm."

The woman said, "What did you want to do it for?"

20 The boy said, "I didn't aim to."

She said, "You a lie!"

By that time two or three people passed, stopped, turned to look, and some stood watching.

"If I turn you loose, will you run?" asked the woman.

"Yes'm," said the boy.

"Then I won't turn you loose," said the woman. She did not release him.

"Lady, I'm sorry," whispered the boy.

"Um-hum! Your face is dirty. I got a great mind to wash
30 your face for you. Ain't you got nobody home to tell you to wash your face?"

"No'm," said the boy. **C** **D**

"Then it will get washed this evening," said the large woman starting up the street, dragging the frightened boy behind her.

He looked as if he were fourteen or fifteen, frail and willow-wild, in tennis shoes and blue jeans.

The woman said, "You ought to be my son. I would teach you right from wrong. Least I can do right now is to wash your face. Are you hungry?" **E**

40 "No'm," said the being-dragged boy. "I just want you to turn me loose."

"Was I bothering *you* when I turned that corner?" asked the woman.

"No'm."

"But you put yourself in contact with *me*," said the woman. "If you think that that contact is not going to last awhile, you

Word Study

The boy answers the woman's questions with "Yes'm" and "No'm." The term *m'am* is a contraction of "madam," a polite way of addressing a woman. Why do you think the boy is trying to be polite?

_____

_____

_____

_____

D LITERARY FOCUS

In lines 13–32, the woman speaks roughly to the boy. Circle everything the boy says in response. What do these lines of **dialogue** suggest about the boy's feelings?

_____

_____

_____

_____

E LITERARY FOCUS

Underline the words in this paragraph that tell you what the woman plans to do. What do these words reveal, or show, about the personality of this **character**?

_____

_____

_____

_____

Word Study

In this paragraph we see Mrs. Jones *drag* Roger up the street. *Drag* and *pull* are synonyms, or words with similar meanings. If the writer had used *pull* instead of *drag,* would Mrs. Jones have seemed as bold? Explain.

_____

_____

_____

_____

_____

B READING FOCUS

What can you **infer,** or guess, about Roger from what he says about himself here?

_____

_____

_____

C READING FOCUS

Roger says "M'am?" because he is surprised at Mrs. Jones's response. **Infer** what he might have expected her to say.

_____

_____

_____

_____

_____

got another thought coming. When I get through with you, sir, you are going to remember Mrs. Luella Bates Washington Jones."

Sweat popped out on the boy's face and he began to struggle.

50 Mrs. Jones stopped, jerked him around in front of her, put a half nelson about his neck, and continued to drag him up the street. When she got to her door, she dragged the boy inside, down a hall, and into a large kitchenette-furnished room at the rear of the house. She switched on the light and left the door open. The boy could hear other roomers laughing and talking in the large house. Some of their doors were open, too, so he knew he and the woman were not alone. The woman still had him by the neck in the middle of her room. **A**

She said, "What is your name?"

60 "Roger," answered the boy.

"Then, Roger, you go to that sink and wash your face," said the woman, whereupon she turned him loose—at last. Roger looked at the door—looked at the woman—looked at the door—*and went to the sink.*

"Let the water run until it gets warm," she said. "Here's a clean towel."

"You gonna take me to jail?" asked the boy, bending over the sink.

"Not with that face, I would not take you nowhere," said 70 the woman. "Here I am trying to get home to cook me a bite to eat, and you snatch my pocketbook! Maybe you ain't been to your supper either, late as it be. Have you?"

"There's nobody home at my house," said the boy. **B**

"Then we'll eat," said the woman. "I believe you're hungry—or been hungry—to try to snatch my pocketbook."

"I want a pair of blue suede shoes," said the boy.

"Well, you didn't have to snatch *my* pocketbook to get some suede shoes," said Mrs. Luella Bates Washington Jones. "You could've asked me."

80 "M'am?" **C**

The water dripping from his face, the boy looked at her. There was a long pause. A very long pause. After he had dried

© Underwood & Underwood/Corbis

his face and not knowing what else to do, dried it again, the boy turned around, wondering what next. The door was open. He could make a dash for it down the hall. He could run, run, run, *run*!

The woman was sitting on the daybed. After a while she said, "I were young once and I wanted things I could not get." **D**

There was another long pause. The boy's mouth opened.
90 Then he frowned, not knowing he frowned.

The woman said, "Um-hum! You thought I was going to say *but,* didn't you? You thought I was going to say, *but I didn't snatch people's pocketbooks.* Well, I wasn't going to say that." Pause. Silence. "I have done things, too, which I would not tell you, son—neither tell God, if He didn't already know. Everybody's got something in common. **E** So you set down while I fix us something to eat. You might run that comb through your hair so you will look presentable."

In another corner of the room behind a screen was a gas
100 plate and an icebox. Mrs. Jones got up and went behind the screen. The woman did not watch the boy to see if he was going

D **LITERARY ANALYSIS**

What does this sentence tell you about Mrs. Jones?

_____

_____

_____

_____

_____

E **LITERARY ANALYSIS**

Mrs. Jones avoids saying, "but I didn't snatch people's pocketbooks." Why doesn't she say this?

_____

_____

_____

_____

_____

_____

A **VOCABULARY**

Academic Vocabulary

Roger's question is more *complex*, or complicated, than it may seem at first. Why does Roger offer to go to the store?

_____

_____

_____

_____

B **LITERARY FOCUS**

Examine the **dialogue** in this paragraph. What do you think Mrs. Jones is trying to teach Roger?

_____

_____

_____

_____

C **VOCABULARY**

Selection Vocabulary

The stoop is described as *barren*, which means "empty" or "deserted." How could the word also be used to describe Roger's feelings?

_____

_____

_____

_____

D **LITERARY ANALYSIS**

At the end of the story, why is it difficult for the boy to thank Mrs. Jones?

_____

_____

_____

_____

110 to run now, nor did she watch her purse, which she left behind her on the daybed. But the boy took care to sit on the far side of the room, away from the purse, where he thought she could easily see him out of the corner of her eye if she wanted to. He did not trust the woman not to trust him. And he did not want to be mistrusted now.

"Do you need somebody to go the store," asked the boy, "maybe to get some milk or something?" **A**

"Don't believe I do," said the woman, "unless you just want sweet milk yourself. I was going to make cocoa out of this canned milk I got here."

120 "That will be fine," said the boy.

She heated some lima beans and ham she had in the icebox, made the cocoa, and set the table. The woman did not ask the boy anything about where he lived, or his folks, or anything else that would embarrass him. Instead, as they ate, she told him about her job in a hotel beauty shop that stayed open late, what the work was like, and how all kinds of women came in and out, blondes, redheads, and Spanish. Then she cut him a half of her ten-cent cake.

"Eat some more, son," she said.

130 When they were finished eating, she got up and said, "Now here, take this ten dollars and buy yourself some blue suede shoes. And next time, do not make the mistake of latching onto *my* pocketbook *nor nobody else's*—because shoes got by devilish ways will burn your feet. I got to get my rest now. But from here on in, son, I hope you will behave yourself." **B**

She led him down the hall to the front door and opened it. "Good night! Behave yourself, boy!" she said, looking out into the street as he went down the steps.

The boy wanted to say something other than "Thank you, m'am" to Mrs. Luella Bates Washington Jones, but although his lips moved, he couldn't even say that as he turned at the foot of the barren stoop and looked up at the large woman in the door. **C** Then she shut the door. **D**

Applying Your Skills

Thank You, M'am

VOCABULARY DEVELOPMENT

DIRECTIONS: Write vocabulary words from the Word Box on the correct blanks to complete the sentences. Each word will be used once.

Word Box

permit

barren

frail

1. The stoop felt especially _____ as Roger stood there all alone.

2. Roger was surprised by how strong Mrs. Jones was; she certainly was not _____.

3. Mrs. Jones would not _____ Roger to thank her for her help.

LITERARY FOCUS: CHARACTER AND DIALOGUE

DIRECTIONS: By closely analyzing, or examining, the **dialogue** of the **characters**, we can find deeper meaning in their words. Pick three meaningful quotes from the story and write them on a separate sheet of paper. Analyze the quotes and discuss what the dialogue tells you about the story and characters. One example is provided below.

Quote: Mrs. Jones: "Eat some more, son."

Analysis: Mrs. Jones is concerned for Roger. Although they just met, she calls him "son" as a term of affection.

READING FOCUS: MAKING INFERENCES

DIRECTIONS: In this story, we learn a lot about the characters through their actions. Complete the chart below by selecting parts of the story from which you can **make inferences**, or guess, about the characters' nature.

Action	Inference about this character
"Mrs. Jones stopped, put a half nelson about his neck, and continued to drag him up the street."	Mrs. Jones is tough, but caring. She is determined to teach Roger a lesson.
1.	2.
3.	4.

SKILLS FOCUS

Literary Skills
Understand deeper messages that characters convey through dialogue.

Reading Skills
Make inferences from the story about the nature of characters.

Preparing to Read

American History

by Judith Ortiz Cofer

LITERARY FOCUS: ROUND AND FLAT CHARACTERS

Main characters in stories are usually **round characters**, with many sides to their personalities. By contrast, we learn very little about **flat characters**, who might only have one or two personality traits. These characters are often **minor characters** who have less importance in a story.

Flat or Round?   In "American History," the narrator (Elena) is a round character. Use the chart below to keep track of characters' personality traits to determine if they are round or flat.

Character	Traits	Round or Flat?
Elena		
Elena's mother		
Gail		
Eugene		
Eugene's mother		

READING FOCUS: MAKING INFERENCES ABOUT CHARACTERS

Often, you need to determine a character's personality by **making inferences**, or educated guesses, based on the character's words, thoughts, and actions.

Use the Skill   As you read, record your inferences about the narrator in a chart like the one below to help you understand her personality.

Narrator's Words, Thoughts, and Actions	My Inferences About the Narrator
Line 38: felt a burning on her cheeks	embarrassed; hurt; cares what others think
Line 163: felt sad for Eugene	

SKILLS FOCUS

Literary Skills
Determine round and flat characters.

Reading Skills
Make inferences about characters.

Vocabulary Development

American History

SELECTION VOCABULARY

discreet (DIHS KREET) *adj.:* careful; showing good judgment.
> *Elena was so discreet about her feelings for Eugene that even her best friends were clueless.*

infatuated (IHN FACH OO AYT IHD) *adj.:* carried away by shallow or foolish love.
> *Elena's mother thinks her daughter is infatuated with the boy next door.*

vigilant (VIHJ UH LUHNT) *adj.:* watchful.
> *Elena's mother became increasingly vigilant about Elena's comings and goings, often locking the front door to prevent her from going out.*

elation (EE LAY SHUHN) *n.:* great joy.
> *Elena had a feeling of elation when the boy she admired smiled at her.*

solace (SAHL IHS) *n.:* comfort; easing of grief.
> *In the awful days that followed, Elena's mother went from friend to friend, seeking the solace she needed from her grief.*

WORD STUDY

DIRECTIONS: Select the correct vocabulary word to complete each sentence. Not every word will be used.

1. Elena experienced _____ when she did well on the test.

2. The girl was _____ with the neighbor she liked.

3. Elena's parents were _____, or careful, when discussing secretive matters.

4. People looked to each other for _____ when the president was killed.

AMERICAN HISTORY

by Judith Ortiz Cofer

© Elmtree Images/Alamy

A **LITERARY ANALYSIS**

Circle the tragic event mentioned here. What effect did this event have on the people of El Building?

_____

_____

_____

_____

_____

Slight adaptation of "American History" from *The Latin Deli: Prose and Poetry* by Judith Ortiz Cofer. Copyright © 1993 by Judith Ortiz Cofer. Reprinted by permission of **The University of Georgia Press**.

I once read in a "Ripley's Believe It or Not" column that Paterson, New Jersey, is the place where the Straight and Narrow (streets) intersect. The Puerto Rican tenement known as El Building was one block up on Straight. It was, in fact, the corner of Straight and Market; not "at" the corner, but *the* corner. At almost any hour of the day, El Building was like a monstrous jukebox, blasting out salsas[1] from open windows as the residents, mostly new immigrants just up from the island, tried to drown out whatever they were currently enduring with loud music. But the day

10 President Kennedy was shot, there was a profound silence in El Building; even the abusive tongues of viragoes,[2] the cursing of the unemployed, and the screeching of small children had been somehow muted. President Kennedy was a saint to these people.

A In fact, soon his photograph would be hung alongside the

---

1. **salsas** (SAL SAHS) *n.:* lively dance music from Latin America.
2. **viragoes** (VIH RAH GOHS) *n.:* quarrelsome women.

Sacred Heart and over the spiritist altars[3] that many women kept in their apartments. He would become part of the hierarchy of martyrs[4] they prayed to for favors that only one who had died for a cause would understand.

On the day that President Kennedy was shot, my ninth-grade class had been out in the fenced playground of Public School Number 13. We had been given "free" exercise time and had been ordered by our PE teacher, Mr. DePalma, to "keep moving." That meant that the girls should jump rope and the boys toss basketballs through a hoop at the far end of the yard. He in the meantime would "keep an eye" on us from just inside the building.

It was a cold gray day in Paterson. The kind that warns of early snow. I was miserable, since I had forgotten my gloves and my knuckles were turning red and raw from the jump rope. I was also taking a lot of abuse from the black girls for not turning the rope hard and fast enough for them.

"Hey, Skinny Bones, pump it, girl. Ain't you got no energy today?" Gail, the biggest of the black girls who had the other end of the rope yelled, "Didn't you eat your rice and beans and pork chops for breakfast today?" **B** **C**

The other girls picked up the "pork chop" and made it into a refrain: "Pork chop, pork chop, did you eat your pork chop?" They entered the double ropes in pairs and exited without tripping or missing a beat. I felt a burning on my cheeks and then my glasses fogged up so that I could not manage to coordinate the jump rope with Gail. The chill was doing to me what it always did: entering my bones, making me cry, humiliating me. I hated the city, especially in winter. I hated Public School Number 13. I hated my skinny, flat-chested body, and I envied the black girls, who could jump rope so fast that their legs became a blur. They always seemed to be warm, while I froze.

---

3. **the Sacred Heart . . . altars:** The Sacred Heart is an image depicting the wounded heart of Jesus, often encircled by a crown of thorns. "Spiritist altars" most likely refers to memorials for dead relatives.
4. **hierarchy** (HY UHR AHR KEE) **of martyrs** (MAHRT UHRZ): *Hierarchy* means "ranking in order of importance." Martyrs are people who have suffered or died rather than give up their faith or principles.

B QUICK CHECK

Circle the words the girls say to taunt Elena, the narrator. What are they making fun of?

_____

_____

_____

C READING FOCUS

Based on how she treats Elena, what **inferences** can you make about Gail?

_____

_____

_____

_____

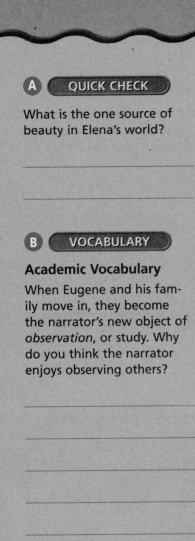

B VOCABULARY

Academic Vocabulary

When Eugene and his fam-
ily move in, they become
the narrator's new object of
observation, or study. Why
do you think the narrator
enjoys observing others?

_____

_____

_____

_____

_____

_____

_____

There was only one source of beauty and light for me that
school year—the only thing I had anticipated at the start of the
semester. That was seeing Eugene. **A** In August, Eugene and
his family had moved into the only house on the block that had
a yard and trees. I could see his place from my window in El
Building. In fact, if I sat on the fire escape I was literally suspended above Eugene's backyard. It was my favorite spot to read
my library books in the summer. Until that August the house
had been occupied by an old Jewish couple. Over the years I
had become part of their family, without their knowing it, of
course. I had a view of their kitchen and their backyard, and
though I could not hear what they said, I knew when they were
arguing, when one of them was sick, and many other things. I
knew all this by watching them at mealtimes. I could see their
kitchen table, the sink, and the stove. During good times, he sat
at the table and read his newspapers while she fixed the meals.
If they argued, he would leave and the old woman would sit and
stare at nothing for a long time. When one of them was sick, the
other would come and get things from the kitchen and carry
them out on a tray. The old man had died in June. The last week
of school I had not seen him at the table at all. Then one day I
saw that there was a crowd in the kitchen. The old woman had
finally emerged from the house on the arm of a stocky middle-
aged woman, whom I had seen there a few times before, maybe
her daughter. Then a man had carried out suitcases. The house
had stood empty for weeks. I had had to resist the temptation to
climb down into the yard and water the flowers the old lady had
taken such good care of.

By the time Eugene's family moved in, the yard was a tan-
gled mass of weeds. The father had spent several days mowing,
and when he finished, from where I sat I didn't see the red, yellow, and purple clusters that meant flowers to me. I didn't see this
family sit down at the kitchen table together. **B** It was just the
mother, a redheaded, tall woman who wore a white uniform—a
nurse's, I guessed it was; the father was gone before I got up in
the morning and was never there at dinner time. I only saw him

on weekends, when they sometimes sat on lawn chairs under the oak tree, each hidden behind a section of the newspaper; and there was Eugene. He was tall and blond, and he wore glasses. I liked him right away because he sat at the kitchen table and read books for hours. That summer, before we had even spoken one word to each other, I kept him company on my fire escape.

Once school started, I looked for him in all my classes, but PS 13 was a huge, overpopulated place and it took me days and many discreet questions to discover that Eugene was in honors classes for all his subjects, classes that were not open to me because English was not my first language, though I was a straight-A student. **C** **D** After much maneuvering I managed to "run into him" in the hallway where his locker was—on the other side of the building from mine—and in study hall at the library, where he first seemed to notice me but did not speak, and finally, on the way home after school one day when I decided to approach him directly, though my stomach was doing somersaults.

I was ready for rejection, snobbery, the worst. But when I came up to him, practically panting in my nervousness, and blurted out: "You're Eugene. Right?" He smiled, pushed his glasses up on his nose, and nodded. I saw then that he was blushing deeply. Eugene liked me, but he was shy. I did most of the talking that day. **E** He nodded and smiled a lot. In the weeks that followed, we walked home together. He would linger at the corner of El Building for a few minutes, then walk down to his two-story house. It was not until Eugene moved into that house that I noticed that El Building blocked most of the sun and that the only spot that got a little sunlight during the day was the tiny square of earth the old woman had planted with flowers.

I did not tell Eugene that I could see inside his kitchen from my bedroom. I felt dishonest, but I liked my secret sharing of his evenings, especially now that I knew what he was reading since we chose our books together at the school library.

One day my mother came into my room as I was sitting on the windowsill staring out. In her abrupt way she said: "Elena,

90

100

110

C VOCABULARY

Selection Vocabulary
After reading this sentence, what do you think the word *discreet* means?

_____

_____

_____

D LITERARY ANALYSIS

How does Elena's background keep her apart from Eugene, even at school?

_____

_____

_____

E LITERARY FOCUS

To prove that Elena is a **round character**, list some of her personality traits that you've learned so far.

_____

_____

_____

The Latin word *fatuus* means "foolish." Something that is fatuous (FA CHOO UHS) is "silly" or "idiotic." In what way might someone who is infatuated with someone else display silliness or idiocy?

_____

_____

_____

_____

B **VOCABULARY**

Selection Vocabulary

Elena's mother is always watching her. Knowing this, what do you think *vigilant* means?

_____

_____

_____

you are acting 'moony.'" "Enamorada" was what she really said, that is—like a girl stupidly infatuated. **A** Since I had turned

120   fourteen, my mother had been more vigilant than ever. **B** She acted as if I was going to go crazy or explode or something if she didn't watch me and nag me all the time about being a señorita[5] now. She kept talking about virtue, morality, and other subjects that did not interest me in the least. My mother was unhappy in Paterson, but my father had a good job at the bluejeans factory in Passaic and soon, he kept assuring us, we would be moving to our own house there. Every Sunday we drove out to the suburbs of Paterson, Clifton, and Passaic, out to where people mowed grass on Sundays in the summer and where children

130   made snowmen in the winter from pure white snow, not like the gray slush of Paterson, which seemed to fall from the sky in that hue. I had learned to listen to my parents' dreams, which were spoken in Spanish, as fairy tales, like the stories about life in the island paradise of Puerto Rico before I was born. I had been to the island once as a little girl, to Grandmother's funeral, and all I remembered was wailing women in black, my mother becoming hysterical and being given a pill that made her sleep two days, and me feeling lost in a crowd of strangers all claiming to be my aunts, uncles, and cousins. I had actually been glad to return to

140   the city. We had not been back there since then, though my parents talked constantly about buying a house on the beach someday, retiring on the island—that was a common topic among the residents of El Building. As for me, I was going to go to college and become a teacher.

But after meeting Eugene I began to think of the present more than of the future. What I wanted now was to enter that house I had watched for so many years. I wanted to see the other rooms where the old people had lived and where the boy spent his time. Most of all I wanted to sit at the kitchen table with

150   Eugene like two adults, like the old man and his wife had done,

---

5.   **señorita** (SEH NYUH REE TUH) *n.*: Spanish for "unmarried woman."

maybe drink some coffee and talk about books. I had started reading *Gone with the Wind*. I was enthralled by it, with the daring and the passion of the beautiful girl living in a mansion, and with her devoted parents and the slaves who did everything for them. I didn't believe such a world had ever really existed, and I wanted to ask Eugene some questions since he and his parents, he had told me, had come up from Georgia, the same place where the novel was set. His father worked for a company that had transferred him to Paterson. His mother was very unhappy,
160 Eugene said, in his beautiful voice that rose and fell over words in a strange, lilting way. The kids at school called him "the Hick" and made fun of the way he talked. I knew I was his only friend so far, and I liked that, though I felt sad for him sometimes. "Skinny Bones and the Hick" was what they called us at school when we were seen together.

The day Mr. DePalma came out into the cold and asked us to line up in front of him was the day that President Kennedy was shot. **C** Mr. DePalma, a short, muscular man with slicked-down black hair, was the science teacher, PE coach, and discipli-
170 narian at PS 13. He was the teacher to whose homeroom you got assigned if you were a troublemaker, and the man called out to break up playground fights and to escort violently angry teenagers to the office. And Mr. DePalma was the man who called your parents in for "a conference."

That day, he stood in front of two rows of mostly black and Puerto Rican kids, brittle from their efforts to "keep moving" on a November day that was turning bitter cold. Mr. DePalma, to our complete shock, was crying. Not just silent adult tears, but really sobbing. There were a few titters from the back of the line
180 where I stood shivering. **D**

"Listen," Mr. DePalma raised his arms over his head as if he were about to conduct an orchestra. His voice broke, and he covered his face with his hands. His barrel chest was heaving. Someone giggled behind me.

C QUICK CHECK

Circle the tragic event that is mentioned in this sentence.

D READING FOCUS

Underline details in this paragraph that describe Mr. DePalma's reaction to the president's death. What **inferences** can you make about Mr. DePalma?

_____

_____

_____

_____

LITERARY ANALYSIS

How has the mood in the neighborhood suddenly changed?

_____

_____

_____

_____

_____

B **VOCABULARY**

Selection Vocabulary

Elena is excited about spending time with Eugene. Knowing this, what do you think *elation* means?

_____

_____

_____

_____

_____

C **READING FOCUS**

Why does Elena feel conflicted, and what can you **infer** about her from her feelings?

_____

_____

_____

_____

_____

_____

"Listen," he repeated, "something awful has happened." A strange gurgling came from his throat, and he turned around and spat on the cement behind him.

"Gross," someone said, and there was a lot of laughter.

"The president is dead, you idiots. I should have known
190 that wouldn't mean anything to a bunch of losers like you kids. Go home." He was shrieking now. No one moved for a minute or two, but then a big girl let out a "Yeah!" and ran to get her books piled up with the others against the brick wall of the school building. The others followed in a mad scramble to get to their things before somebody caught on. It was still an hour to the dismissal bell.

A little scared, I headed for El Building. There was an eerie feeling on the streets. I looked into Mario's drugstore, a favorite hangout for the high school crowd, but there were only a couple
200 of old Jewish men at the soda bar talking with the short-order cook in tones that sounded almost angry, but they were keeping their voices low. Even the traffic on one of the busiest intersections in Paterson—Straight Street and Park Avenue—seemed to be moving slower. There were no horns blasting that day. At El Building, the usual little group of unemployed men was not hanging out on the front stoop making it difficult for women to enter the front door. No music spilled out from open doors in the hallway. When I walked into our apartment, I found my mother sitting in front of the grainy picture of the television set. **A**
210   She looked up at me with a tear-streaked face and just said: "Dios mío,"[6] turning back to the set as if it were pulling at her eyes. I went into my room.

Though I wanted to feel the right thing about President Kennedy's death, I could not fight the feeling of elation that stirred in my chest. **B** Today was the day I was to visit Eugene in his house. He had asked me to come over after school to study for an American history test with him. **C** We had also planned to walk to the public library together. I looked down into his

_____

6. **dios mío** (DEE OHS MEE OH): Spanish for "Oh, my God."

© Time Life Pictures *and* © 2007 Corbis/Jupiterimages

220

yard. The oak tree was bare of leaves and the ground looked gray with ice. The light through the large kitchen window of his house told me that El Building blocked the sun to such an extent that they had to turn lights on in the middle of the day. I felt ashamed about it. **D** But the white kitchen table with the lamp hanging just above it looked cozy and inviting. I would soon sit there, across from Eugene, and I would tell him about my perch just above his house. Maybe I should.

In the next thirty minutes I changed clothes, put on a little pink lipstick, and got my books together. Then I went in to tell my mother that I was going to a friend's house to study. I did not

230

expect her reaction.

"You are going out *today*?" The way she said "today" sounded as if a storm warning had been issued. It was said in utter disbelief. Before I could answer, she came toward me and held my elbows as I clutched my books.

D VOCABULARY

Academic Vocabulary
Elena paints a sad picture in lines 219–223. Recall a time when a *significant* event saddened your day.

A LITERARY FOCUS

What do you know about Elena's mother's personality so far? Do you think she is a **round character** or a **flat character**? Explain.

_____

_____

_____

_____

_____

_____

_____

_____

_____

_____

"Hija,[7] the president has been killed. We must show respect. He was a great man. Come to church with me tonight."

She tried to embrace me, but my books were in the way. My first impulse was to comfort her, she seemed so distraught, but I had to meet Eugene in fifteen minutes.

240 "I have a test to study for, Mama. I will be home by eight."

"You are forgetting who you are, Niña.[8] I have seen you staring down at that boy's house. You are heading for humiliation and pain." My mother said this in Spanish and in a resigned tone that surprised me, as if she had no intention of stopping me from "heading for humiliation and pain." I started for the door. She sat in front of the TV holding a white handkerchief to her face. **A**

I walked out to the street and around the chain-link fence that separated El Building from Eugene's house. The yard was neatly edged around the little walk that led to the door. It always

250 amazed me how Paterson, the inner core of the city, had no apparent logic to its architecture. Small, neat single residences like this one could be found right next to huge, dilapidated apartment buildings like El Building. My guess was that the little houses had been there first, then the immigrants had come in droves, and the monstrosities had been raised for them—the Italians, the Irish, the Jews, and now us, the Puerto Ricans and the blacks. The door was painted a deep green: verde, the color of hope. I had heard my mother say it: verde-esperanza.

I knocked softly. A few suspenseful moments later the door

260 opened just a crack. The red, swollen face of a woman appeared. She had a halo of red hair floating over a delicate ivory face—the face of a doll—with freckles on the nose. Her smudged eye makeup made her look unreal to me, like a mannequin[9] seen through a warped store window.

"What do you want?" Her voice was tiny and sweet sounding, like a little girl's, but her tone was not friendly.

---

7. **hija** (EE HAH) *n.:* Spanish for "daughter."
8. **niña** (NEE NYUH) *n.:* Spanish for "girl."
9. **mannequin** (MAN UH KIHN) *n.:* life-size model of a person.

"I'm Eugene's friend. He asked me over. To study." I thrust out my books, a silly gesture that embarrassed me almost immediately.

270 "You live there?" She pointed up to El Building, which looked particularly ugly, like a gray prison, with its many dirty windows and rusty fire escapes. The woman had stepped halfway out and I could see that she wore a white nurse's uniform with "St. Joseph's Hospital" on the name tag.

"Yes. I do."

She looked intently at me for a couple of heartbeats, then said as if to herself, "I don't know how you people do it." **B** Then directly to me: "Listen. Honey. Eugene doesn't want to study with you. He is a smart boy. Doesn't need help. You understand me.

280 I am truly sorry if he told you you could come over. He cannot study with you. It's nothing personal. You understand? We won't be in this place much longer, no need for him to get close to people—it'll just make it harder for him later. Run back home now." **C**

I couldn't move. I just stood there in shock at hearing these things said to me in such a honey-drenched voice. I had never heard an accent like hers, except for Eugene's softer version. It was as if she were singing me a little song.

"What's wrong? Didn't you hear what I said?" She seemed
290 very angry, and I finally snapped out of my trance. I turned away from the green door and heard her close it gently.

Our apartment was empty when I got home. My mother was in someone else's kitchen, seeking the solace she needed. **D** Father would come in from his late shift at midnight. I would hear them talking softly in the kitchen for hours that night. They would not discuss their dreams for the future, or life in Puerto Rico, as they often did; that night they would talk sadly about the young widow and her two children, as if they were family. For the next few days, we would observe luto in our apartment;
300 that is, we would practice restraint and silence—no loud music

B READING FOCUS

What **inferences** can you make about Eugene's mother based on her dialogue with Elena?

_____

_____

_____

_____

_____

_____

C QUICK CHECK

Summarize what happens in this scene between Elena and Eugene's mother in your own words.

_____

_____

_____

_____

D VOCABULARY

Selection Vocabulary

The word *solace* means "comfort." Rewrite this sentence in your own words.

_____

_____

_____

_____

_____

While the nation grieves for the loss of its president, Elena must deal with another kind of grief. What bitter lesson has Elena learned?

_____

_____

_____

_____

_____

_____

_____

_____

or laughter. Some of the women of El Building would wear black for weeks.

That night, I lay in my bed trying to feel the right thing for our dead president. But the tears that came up from a deep source inside me were strictly for me. When my mother came to the door, I pretended to be sleeping. Sometime during the night, I saw from my bed the streetlight come on. It had a pink halo around it. I went to my window and pressed my face to the cool glass. Looking up at the light, I could see the white snow falling
310   like a lace veil over its face. I did not look down to see it turning gray as it touched the ground below.

Applying Your Skills

American History

Word Box

- discreet
- infatuated
- vigilant
- elation
- solace

VOCABULARY DEVELOPMENT

DIRECTIONS: Write a one-paragraph summary of the story using all the vocabulary words listed in the Word Box.

LITERARY FOCUS: ROUND AND FLAT CHARACTERS

DIRECTIONS: Remember that writers really allow readers to get to know **round characters**, while they only identify a few traits of **flat characters**. Use the chart you completed on page 64 to help you rank the characters below in order of most round (1) to least round, or flat (5).

_____ Elena   _____ Eugene

_____ Elena's mother   _____ Eugene's mother

_____ Gail

READING FOCUS: MAKING INFERENCES ABOUT CHARACTERS

DIRECTIONS: In the story, Elena tells us about some of the characters directly. For instance, she describes how Eugene looks and acts. Other times we have to **make inferences**, or educated guesses, about the characters based on their words and actions. Fill in the chart below with inferences about the characters based on each detail from each story that is given.

SKILLS FOCUS

Literary Skills
Determine round and flat characters.

Reading Skills
Make inferences about characters.

Action	Inference about this character
After struggling to break the news to the children, Mr. DePalma finally says, "The president is dead, you idiots."	1.
When Eugene and Elena first meet, Eugene just smiles and nods.	2.
When Elena visits to study, Eugene's mother turns her away, saying, "He is a smart boy. Doesn't need help."	3.

Preparing to Read

An Interview with Dave Eggers
from Writing

INFORMATIONAL TEXT FOCUS: MAIN IDEA, AUDIENCE, AND PURPOSE

A **primary source** is a firsthand account in which a writer presents his or her experiences, opinions, and ideas. The informational text you are about to read is a primary source about helping others by sharing a passion for writing.

In order to get the most out of a primary source, ask yourself the following questions:

- **Audience** Who is this written for?
- **Purpose** Why does the author want me to know this?
- **Main Idea** What is the main point the author is trying to tell me?

SELECTION VOCABULARY

unconventional (UHN KUHN VEHN SHUN UHL) *adj.*: not done in the usual or accepted way.
Compared to other ways of cooking eggs, Betty's was unconventional.

enabled (EHN AY BUHLD) *v.*: to make able or allow; provide with means, opportunity, power, or authority.
The success of Eggers's book enabled him to pursue other writing projects.

WORD STUDY

When you don't know the meaning of a word, you can often find hints in its context, the words or sentences that surround it.

DIRECTIONS: Underline any clues in the sentences below that would help explain the meanings of *unconventional* and *enabled*.

1. I've never seen a movie like it; the plot was completely *unconventional*.

2. The money he earned as a lawyer *enabled* him to fulfill his dream of opening a bakery.

3. Her strength and speed *enabled* her to set a new world record for the long jump.

4. The Victorian writer, feminist, and philosopher Mary Wollstonecraft lived an *unconventional* life, at odds with the commonly held values of her time.

SKILLS FOCUS

Informational Text Skills
Analyze primary sources based on their audience, purpose, and main idea.

AN INTERVIEW WITH DAVE EGGERS

from Writing

> **BACKGROUND**
> Dave Eggers is an author, editor, and publisher who has also created a number of drop-in tutoring organizations around the country. In the following interview from *Writing*, Eggers talks about his passion for writing and the organization he founded.

© AP Images/Susan Ragan

A VOCABULARY

Selection Vocabulary
The word *unconventional* means "not done in the usual or accepted way." Based on this definition, what do you think the word *conventional* means?

_____

_____

_____

A "Staggering Genius" Talks About Writing, Fame, and . . . Trout

When Dave Eggers was 21, he lost his parents to cancer. Each died within five weeks of the other, leaving Eggers to raise his 7-year-old brother, Christopher, or "Toph," on his own. A few years later, Eggers published his story in a highly unconventional, funny-sad memoir called *A Heartbreaking Work of Staggering Genius* (2000). **A** The title hints at the self-mocking tone of the book, but it's not kidding—at least not totally. Critics called

10   Eggers "refreshingly honest," "an original new voice," and oh, yes, "a staggering genius."

From "A 'Staggering Genius' Talks About Writing, Fame, and ...Trout An Interview With Dave Eggers" from *Writing Magazine*, vol. 27, no. 4, January 2005. Copyright © 2005 by Weekly Reader Corporation. All rights reserved. Reproduced by permission of **Weekly Reader**.

A ⬤ VOCABULARY

Selection Vocabulary

The word *enabled* appears in line 13. It means "to make able; provide with means, opportunity, power." Underline the things in this paragraph that the success of Eggers' first book enabled him to do.

B ⬤ READING FOCUS

Based on the first question the interviewer asks, who do you think is the intended **audience** for this interview?

_____

_____

_____

_____

C ⬤ QUICK CHECK

Eggers says that as a child he wanted to be a cartoonist. What does he say started his interest in writing?

_____

_____

_____

_____

The success of his first book, which he refers to as *AHWOSG*, enabled Eggers to pursue a number of writing projects, including the creation of the superhip online literary journal *McSweeney's* (**www.mcsweeneys.net**). **A** He has written several novels; edits an annual anthology of nonfiction, *The Best American Nonrequired Reading;* and recently published a book of short stories, *How We Are Hungry*. He also founded 826 Valencia, a writing center for kids in San Francisco. Recently, *Writing*
20 caught up with Eggers and tossed him a few questions.

Writing: First, let's talk a little about you. What kind of student were you in school? **B**

Dave Eggers: I guess I always liked school. I wasn't all about school—I didn't go running to the bus stop every day—but I did well in school, and I had a string of great teachers and enjoyed my time there. English and art were my favorite subjects, and I would take after-school art classes to learn more. I wanted to be a cartoonist.

Writing: When and why did you start writing?

30 **Eggers:** At various points—fifth grade, seventh grade, eighth grade—we were asked to create books, where we would write and illustrate them and spend a lot of time making them look official and spiffy, and I remember those books sparking in me an interest in writing. I still wanted, first and foremost, to be a comic-book artist, but I was doing well in English classes and started thinking I could combine my interest in art and in writing. It wasn't until college, though—not until my junior year—that I really thought about writing for a living. I studied painting for three years in college and switched to the
40 journalism program my last year. **C**

Writing: So many people today seem to think fame is the ultimate goal of life. What's the deal with fame anyway?

Eggers: The aspect of being well known that's important is that sometimes you can use your fame to help people or to change those things that need changing. Because people read my books, I can sometimes raise money for good causes easier than I could when I was younger and not known. I can write

about an issue—like the need to pay teachers better—and people
will listen to me in a way they wouldn't have before I had some

50   success. I'm really happy that I can help that way. That's the
main upshot of any measure of fame. **D** **E**

Writing: A little about the writing process: How do you write?
Do you, like some writers, sit down and write for a set amount
of time very day? Or do you write only when inspiration hits?

Eggers: I write most days. Sometimes I write for about 10 hours
a day, sometimes only a few hours. Sometimes I sit at the computer and stall forever; sometimes the words shoot onto the page
at lightning speed. But I do write pretty much every day, even
weekends. And I usually write late at night, from about 10 P.M.

60   to 3 A.M.

Writing: Tell us about your work with 826 Valencia.

Eggers: 826 Valencia is a drop-in tutoring, writing, and publishing center in San Francisco. We help local students with writing-
related homework, and we teach classes in tons of different fields:
journalism, radio, film, poetry, and bookmaking—you name it.
We also publish student work in various collections that are then
sold in bookstores all over the city and on Amazon.

Writing: Why did you want to help young people learn to write?

Eggers: Over the years, I'd worked with the YMCA and other

70   groups, teaching middle school and high school students about
cartooning, writing, and publishing, and we always had a great
time. I learned a lot of what I know about writing and design
while I was in high school, so I think if we at 826 Valencia can
help aspiring writers when they're very young and if we can
introduce them to actual writers who have been successful, then
those students can get a clear idea of a writer's life, and how to get
from *A* to *Z*. I meet hundreds of students every year who could
be successful writers—as novelists, journalists, poets. Our goal
at 826 Valencia is to make sure these aspirants know that they

80   can actually do it and to give them as many tools as possible.
On the other hand, we also help tons of students who need assistance with the basics—lots of students new to this country who

D QUICK CHECK

When he speaks about
fame, Eggers says one thing
is important. Review this
paragraph and circle the
important thing. He also
gives two specific examples
of the benefits of fame.
Underline each example.

E READING FOCUS

Based on the marks you
just made, what do you
think is the **main idea** of
this paragraph about fame?

_____

_____

_____

A VOCABULARY

Academic Vocabulary

How does Eggers think 826 Valencia can have a *significant,* or important, impact on young peoples' lives?

_____

_____

_____

_____

_____

_____

_____

B VOCABULARY

Word Study

The present tense of the word *read* is pronounced "reed," while the past tense of the word is pronounced "rehd." You can figure out which verb tense is being used in a sentence by looking at the words around it. Write one sentence using *read* in the past tense and one using it in the present tense.

_____

_____

_____

_____

_____

_____

_____

are just learning English. So it varies, from the basics to the most advanced. That's what makes 826 Valencia a good place to be. **A**

Writing: A lot of people complain that kids today don't read. Some blame TV, computers, fast food. (Just kidding, but who knows?) What are your thoughts about it?

Eggers: I watched a whole lot of TV when I was growing up. I lived in a house where the TV was on most of the day and
90 night, but I still found a lot of time to read and I spent most of my time outside, running around in the woods. I think there's a balance— you have to get out there and see the world, learn from books, and also know what's happening via the TV, the Web, and other media. Any young person who's interested in writing should be reading (outside of school) about 10 books a year. That's only one a month—you could definitely read more— but 10 a year is a guideline. **B** I still keep track of my reading, making sure I'm reading a book every week or two. Again, it's part of the balance, because I still love TV.

100 *Writing*: What books would you recommend to young people?

Eggers: I recommend any book that grabs you, any book you can't put down. There are millions of books in the world, so I don't feel like we should spend too much time slogging our way through books we feel no connection to. I don't like Jane Austen very much. After reading a few of her books and feeling no particular connection to that world, I've decided I probably won't read any more. If you don't consider yourself a big reader, start by reading books about things you're interested in, like fishing. Maybe you're like LeBron James and you love trout,
110 but you don't like reading so much, because you think books are always about people in the 19th century eating cucumber sandwiches. So go find some books about trout and trout fishing, trout preparation, trout eating. The point is to begin to love books. I guarantee there are at least 100 books out there for everyone—100 books that will knock you over and change your life—so get started looking for those. (That doesn't mean you shouldn't finish the books you're reading in class. Your teachers

know why they're asking you to read a certain book. You have to trust them.) Sometimes a book will bore the life out of you for 120 50 pages, then get really interesting. You have to have patience, but if you're reading a book for fun and you're not having fun, maybe it's time to try something else. **C**

Dave's Advice for Young Writers

Wear a helmet. Write every day. Keep a journal—buy one small enough to keep in your pocket. Listen to people, to the way they talk. Get lost in the woods or in new neighborhoods, explore. Swim a lot. Come up with new and better names for llamas. Listen to a lot of music, loud. Read as much as you can. Watch *Time Bandits and Napoleon Dynamite.* Don't let any one person discourage you. Don't count on your friends' liking your work. 130 Maybe you like to write about zombies, and none of your friends are zombies—this doesn't mean there aren't thousands of people all over the world who are just dying (excuse the pun) to read your work about zombies. And when you write about zombies or anything else, try to describe them in ways never before done by humankind. A writer's job is to make the world new, to charge it full of new life, so you have to start over, from scratch; you can't rehash stories that have been told a hundred times. **D** You have to give readers something brand-spanking new. Especially if it involves trout. **E**

C READING FOCUS

Write the **main idea** of this paragraph on the lines below and underline at least two sentences from this paragraph that support it.

_____

_____

_____

D LANGUAGE COACH

The word origin of *rehash,* which means "to bring back in a slightly different form," is the French word *hacher,* which means "to cut up." How do these definitions help you to understand what Eggers is saying here?

_____

_____

_____

_____

E READING FOCUS

What is the **purpose** of Eggers' advice to young writers?

_____

_____

_____

An Interview with Dave Eggers

USE A TABLE

DIRECTIONS: Use the table below to record information from the interview that will help you analyze this **primary source**.

An Interview with Dave Eggers	
Audience	
Purpose	
Main Idea	

Applying Your Skills

An Interview with Dave Eggers

VOCABULARY DEVELOPMENT

DIRECTIONS: Write the vocabulary words from the Word Box on the correct blanks to complete the paragraph.

> ### Word Box
> unconventional
> enabled

The success of Dave Eggers' first book, *A Heartbreaking Work of Staggering Genius*, has (1) _____ him to pursue many different things. One that he is particularly passionate about is the drop-in tutoring and writing center, 826 Valencia. Eggers has a somewhat (2) _____ attitude toward his fame and success and feels that the most important part of fame is the good that it helps him to do.

INFORMATIONAL TEXT FOCUS: MAIN IDEA, AUDIENCE, AND PURPOSE

After reading this interview, you should have a clear idea of its **main idea** and its intended **audience** and **purpose**.

DIRECTIONS: Imagine that the interview was conducted for an audience of published writers, with the purpose of persuading them to volunteer as tutors for young people. On the lines labeled a), write a total of three sentences from the interview that would have to be different for this new audience and purpose. On the lines labeled b), re-write those sentences to fit the new circumstances.

1. a) _____
   _____
   b) _____
   _____

2. a) _____
   _____
   b) _____
   _____

3. a) _____
   _____
   b) _____
   _____

SKILLS FOCUS

Informational Text Skills
Identify audience, purpose and main idea in primary sources.

Skills Review

Collection 2

VOCABULARY REVIEW

DIRECTIONS: Read the sentences below and fill in the blanks with the correct vocabulary words from the Word Box. Not every word will be used.

Word Box
barren
complex
discreet
elation
enabled
frail
incident
infatuated
observation
permit
significant
solace
unconventional
vigilant

1. He trusted Laura with his secret because he knew that she would be _____ about what she said.

2. She was an unusual woman who led an adventurous and _____ life.

3. It was after midnight; everyone had gone home and the streets were _____.

4. The success of her business _____ her to retire early and dedicate her life to charitable work.

5. The time that Kristen fell in the pool was the funniest _____ of the summer.

6. Although he barely knows the girl who sits next to him in class, he is completely _____ with her.

7. The eighty-year-old woman is _____, but still energetic and alert.

8. I will always remember my graduation as a _____ moment in my life.

9. The novel's plot is _____, following four different families and their adventures.

10. After her mother's death, she found _____ in the company of her brothers and sisters.

Skills Review

Collection 2

LANGUAGE COACH

Some words can have **multiple meanings** depending on if you use them as a noun or a verb. The word *dance*, for example, can be used as a noun or a verb: you might bring your friends to the high school *dance* (noun), or you might *dance* to the music on the radio (verb). The italicized words in the sentences below also have more than one meaning. Determine whether each italized word is used as a noun or a verb and circle the correct answer.

1. Marin's letter *puzzles* me because I can't understand what she wrote.
   noun/verb

2. A *fly* landed on the old man's nose and surprised him.
   noun/verb

3. The *shot* I got from Dr. Syrup hurt a lot.
   noun/verb

4. At dinner, I accidentally spilled *pepper* all over Ingo.
   noun/verb

5. When you sort through the clothes, don't forget to *pair* all the socks.
   noun/verb

ORAL LANGUAGE AND WRITING ACTIVITY

DIRECTIONS: Think about one of your favorite hobbies or interests—playing a sport, drawing, reading, or writing, for example. Talk about your interest with a partner. Next, write down 10 questions to ask your partner about his or her interest. You might want to ask what they like about the interest, how it makes them feel, and why they would encourage others to pursue the interest. Take turns interviewing each other by asking the questions. Record your partner's answers. Then, write a paragraph summarizing what you learned in the interview.

Collection 3

Narrator and Voice

© Noma / Images.com

Literary and Academic Vocabulary for Collection 3

distinct (DIHS TIHNGKT) *adj.:* different; unique.

The narrator's description of Clara conveys a distinct tone.

impression (IHM PREHSH UHN) *n.:* overall effect.

The story's events leave readers with the impression that life in the narrator's household is unusual.

insight (IHN SYT) *n.:* clear understanding.

With a sudden insight, I realized that the narrator was unreliable.

portray (PAWR TRAY) *v.:* describe, show.

Would a different narrator portray the story's events differently?

narrator (NAR AY TUHR) *n.:* the person who tells a story.

The story's narrator hides some important facts.

omniscient (AHM NIHSH UHNT) *adj.:* all-knowing.

An omniscient narrator can tell readers what all the characters think and feel.

tone (TOHN) *n.:* the attitude a speaker or writer takes toward a subject, character, or audience.

The author of the book seemed to have an angry tone toward the main character.

voice (VOYS) *n.:* a writer's unique use of language and overall style.

The writer used a young voice to tell the story from the point of view of a 10-year-old boy.

Preparing to Read

The Interlopers

by Saki

LITERARY FOCUS: OMNISCIENT NARRATOR

A story's **omniscient narrator** knows everything that happens, and why. An omniscient narrator is not a character in the story but an outside observer who can tell you what each character is thinking and feeling.

- As you read "The Interlopers," pay special attention to the information the narrator gives you about the two characters' pasts.

- The narrator of "The Interlopers" makes us think that events are leading one way—up until the story's very end. Prepare to be surprised.

READING FOCUS: DRAWING CONCLUSIONS

While you read, think about what the author is saying and then **draw conclusions**, or make judgments. You can draw conclusions about the characters, or think about their actions to reach broader conclusions about human nature. As you read, look for details you can use to draw conclusions. Record the details and your conclusions in the chart below.

Story Details	My Conclusion
Ulrich and Georg have been enemies for years. The two families have been fighting over the land for generations.	Some people are enemies just because of family history, not because they actually dislike each other.

SKILLS FOCUS

Literary Skills
Recognize an omniscient narrator.

Reading Skills
Draw conclusions.

Vocabulary Development

The Interlopers

SELECTION VOCABULARY

disputed (DIHS PYOOT IHD) *adj.:* subject of an argument.
> *The disputed border caused conflict between the neighbors.*

marauders (MUH RAW DUHRZ) *n.:* people who roam around in search of loot, or goods to steal.
> *The man kept a sharp lookout for marauders who might be watching him, ready to rob him of his valuables.*

exasperation (EHG ZAS PUH RAY SHUHN) *n.:* great annoyance.
> *His exasperation at being captured was so great that he cursed aloud.*

condolences (KUHN DOH LUHNS IHZ) *n.:* expressions of sympathy.
> *When he heard about his enemy's death, he sent his condolences to the widow.*

reconciliation (REHK UHN SIHL EE AY SHUHN) *n.:* friendly end to a quarrel.
> *The fight could end in one of two ways—reconciliation or death.*

WORD STUDY

DIRECTIONS: By changing the ending of a word, we can change its part of speech. For example, *exasperate* and *reconcile* are verb forms of the vocabulary words *exasperation* and *reconciliation*, which are nouns.

Write four sentences below using each of these four words.

1. _____

   _____

2. _____

   _____

3. _____

   _____

4. _____

   _____

THE INTERLOPERS

by Saki

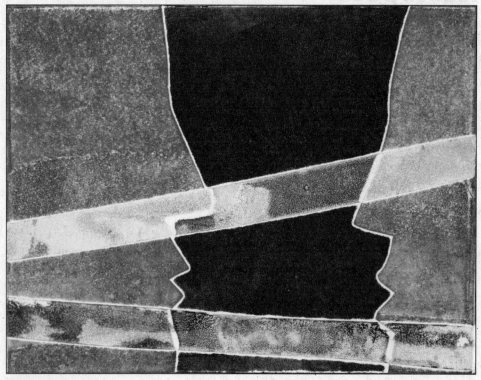

Face to Face by Jim Dandy © Images.com/Corbis

A (**VOCABULARY**)

Academic Vocabulary

How does the author *portray,* or describe, Ulrich von Gradwitz here?

_____

_____

_____

_____

_____

_____

In a forest of mixed growth somewhere on the eastern spurs of the Carpathians,[1] a man stood one winter night watching and listening, as though he waited for some beast of the woods to come within the range of his vision and, later, of his rifle. But the game for whose presence he kept so keen an outlook was none that figured in the sportsman's calendar as lawful and proper for the chase; Ulrich von Gradwitz patrolled the dark forest in quest of a human enemy. **A**

10 The forest lands of Gradwitz were of wide extent and well stocked with game; the narrow strip of precipitous woodland that lay on its outskirt was not remarkable for the game it harbored or the shooting it afforded, but it was the most jealously guarded of all its owner's territorial possessions. A famous lawsuit, in the days

---

1. **Carpathians** (KAHR PAY THEE UHNS): mountain range that starts in Slovakia and extends through Poland, Ukraine, and Romania.

of his grandfather, had wrested it from the illegal possession of a neighboring family of petty landowners; the dispossessed party had never acquiesced in the judgment of the courts, and a long series of poaching affrays[2] and similar scandals had embittered the relationships between the families for three generations. The neighbor feud had grown into a personal one since Ulrich had come to be head of
20 his family; if there was a man in the world whom he detested and wished ill to, it was Georg Znaeym, the inheritor of the quarrel and the tireless game snatcher and raider of the disputed border forest. **B** The feud might, perhaps, have died down or been compromised if the personal ill will of the two men had not stood in the way; as boys they had thirsted for one another's blood, as men each prayed that misfortune might fall on the other, and this wind-scourged winter night Ulrich had banded together his foresters to watch the dark forest, not in quest of four-footed quarry, but to keep a lookout for the prowling thieves whom he suspected of
30 being afoot from across the land boundary. The roebuck,[3] which usually kept in the sheltered hollows during a storm wind, were running like driven things tonight, and there was movement and unrest among the creatures that were wont to sleep through the dark hours. Assuredly there was a disturbing element in the forest, and Ulrich could guess the quarter from whence it came.

He strayed away by himself from the watchers whom he had placed in ambush on the crest of the hill and wandered far down the steep slopes amid the wild tangle of undergrowth, peering through the tree trunks and listening through the whistling and
40 skirling[4] of the wind and the restless beating of the branches for sight or sound of the marauders. If only on this wild night, in this dark, lone spot, he might come across Georg Znaeym, man to man, with none to witness—that was the wish that was uppermost in his thoughts. **C** And as he stepped round the trunk of a huge beech he came face to face with the man he sought.

---

2. **poaching affrays** (UH FRAYS): noisy quarrels or brawls about poaching, which means "fishing or hunting illegally on private property."
3. **roebuck** (ROH BUHK) *n.*: male (or males) of the roe deer, small deer that live in Europe and Asia.
4. **skirling** (SKURL ING) *v.* used as *n.*: shrill, piercing sound.

B **VOCABULARY**

Selection Vocabulary

The two families have been fighting over the forest borders for years. Knowing this, what do you think the word *disputed* means?

_____

_____

_____

C **VOCABULARY**

Word Study

In this sentence, underline the compound word, a word that is made up of two words. What does this compound word mean?

_____

_____

_____

_____

The two enemies stood glaring at one another for a long silent moment. Each had a rifle in his hand, each had hate in his heart and murder uppermost in his mind. **A** The chance had come to give full play to the passions of a lifetime. But a man
50 who has been brought up under the code of a restraining civilization cannot easily nerve himself to shoot down his neighbor in cold blood and without a word spoken, except for an offense against his hearth and honor. And before the moment of hesitation had given way to action, a deed of Nature's own violence overwhelmed them both. A fierce shriek of the storm had been answered by a splitting crash over their heads, and ere they could leap aside, a mass of falling beech tree had thundered down on them. **B** Ulrich von Gradwitz found himself stretched on the ground, one arm numb beneath him and the other held almost
60 as helplessly in a tight tangle of forked branches, while both legs were pinned beneath the fallen mass. His heavy shooting boots had saved his feet from being crushed to pieces, but if his fractures were not as serious as they might have been, at least it was evident that he could not move from his present position till someone came to release him. The descending twigs had slashed the skin of his face, and he had to wink away some drops of blood from his eyelashes before he could take in a general view of the disaster. At his side, so near that under ordinary circumstances he could almost have touched him, lay Georg Znaeym,
70 alive and struggling, but obviously as helplessly pinioned[5] down as himself. All round them lay a thick-strewn wreckage of splintered branches and broken twigs.

Relief at being alive and exasperation at his captive plight brought a strange medley of pious thank offerings and sharp curses to Ulrich's lips. **C** **D** Georg, who was nearly blinded with the blood which trickled across his eyes, stopped his struggling for a moment to listen, and then gave a short, snarling laugh.

"So you're not killed, as you ought to be, but you're caught, anyway," he cried, "caught fast. Ho, what a jest, Ulrich von
80 Gradwitz snared in his stolen forest. There's real justice for you!"

---

5. **pinioned** (PIHN YUHND) *v.* used as *adj.:* pinned, as if chained or tied up.

And he laughed again, mockingly and savagely.

"I'm caught in my own forest land," retorted Ulrich. "When my men come to release us, you will wish, perhaps, that you were in a better plight than caught poaching on a neighbor's land, shame on you."

Georg was silent for a moment; then he answered quietly:

"Are you sure that your men will find much to release? I have men, too, in the forest tonight, close behind me, and *they* will be here first and do the releasing. When they drag me out

90 from under these branches, it won't need much clumsiness on their part to roll this mass of trunk right over on the top of you. Your men will find you dead under a fallen beech tree. For form's sake I shall send my condolences to your family." **E** **F**

"It is a useful hint," said Ulrich fiercely. "My men had orders to follow in ten minutes' time, seven of which must have gone by already, and when they get me out—I will remember the hint. Only as you will have met your death poaching on my lands, I don't think I can decently send any message of condolence to your family."

100 "Good," snarled Georg, "good. We fight this quarrel out to the death, you and I and our foresters, with no cursed interlopers to come between us. **G** Death and damnation to you, Ulrich von Gradwitz."

"The same to you, Georg Znaeym, forest thief, game snatcher."

Both men spoke with the bitterness of possible defeat before them, for each knew that it might be long before his men would seek him out or find him; it was a bare matter of chance which party would arrive first on the scene.

Both had now given up the useless struggle to free them-

110 selves from the mass of wood that held them down; Ulrich limited his endeavors to an effort to bring his one partially free arm near enough to his outer coat pocket to draw out his wine flask. **H** Even when he had accomplished that operation, it was long before he could manage the unscrewing of the stopper or get

E **VOCABULARY**

Selection Vocabulary

Condolences comes from two Latin words: *com-*, a prefix meaning "with," and *dolere*, meaning "to grieve." Using this information and the clues in the text, what do you think *condolences* means?

_____

_____

_____

F **QUICK CHECK**

What do the enemies threaten to do to each other once they are rescued?

_____

_____

_____

G **VOCABULARY**

Word Study

Use a dictionary to find the definition of *interlopers*. Which definition applies to the word as it is used in this sentence?

_____

_____

_____

H **VOCABULARY**

Word Study

Circle the word in this sentence that restates the meaning of *endeavors*.

A READING FOCUS

Re-read this paragraph. What **conclusions** can you draw about Ulrich based on what he says to Georg?

_____

_____

_____

_____

_____

_____

_____

B LITERARY FOCUS

In this paragraph, the **omniscient narrator** reveals an important change in Ulrich's attitude. Circle the important change the narrator tells you about.

any of the liquid down his throat. But what a heaven-sent draft[6] it seemed! It was an open winter[7], and little snow had fallen as yet, hence the captives suffered less from the cold than might have been the case at that season of the year; nevertheless, the wine was warming and reviving to the wounded man, and he looked across with something like a throb of pity to where his enemy lay, just keeping the groans of pain and weariness from crossing his lips.

"Could you reach this flask if I threw it over to you?" asked Ulrich suddenly. "There is good wine in it, and one may as well be as comfortable as one can. Let us drink, even if tonight one of us dies." **A**

"No, I can scarcely see anything; there is so much blood caked round my eyes," said Georg; "and in any case I don't drink wine with an enemy."

Ulrich was silent for a few minutes and lay listening to the weary screeching of the wind. An idea was slowly forming and growing in his brain, an idea that gained strength every time that he looked across at the man who was fighting so grimly against pain and exhaustion. In the pain and languor that Ulrich himself was feeling, the old fierce hatred seemed to be dying down. **B**

"Neighbor," he said presently, "do as you please if your men come first. It was a fair compact. But as for me, I've changed my mind. If my men are the first to come, you shall be the first to be helped, as though you were my guest. We have quarreled like devils all our lives over this stupid strip of forest, where the trees can't even stand upright in a breath of wind. Lying here tonight, thinking, I've come to think we've been rather fools; there are better things in life than getting the better of a boundary dispute. Neighbor, if you will help me to bury the old quarrel, I—I will ask you to be my friend."

Georg Znaeym was silent for so long that Ulrich thought perhaps he had fainted with the pain of his injuries. Then he spoke slowly and in jerks.

---

6. **draft** _n._: drink.
7. **open winter**: mild winter.

"How the whole region would stare and gabble if we rode into the market square together. No one living can remember seeing a Znaeym and a von Gradwitz talking to one another in friendship. And what peace there would be among the forester folk if we ended our feud tonight. And if we choose to make peace among our people, there is none other to interfere, no interlopers from outside. . . . You would come and keep the Sylvester night[8] beneath my roof, and I would come and feast on some high day at your castle. . . . I would never fire a shot on your land, save when you invited me as a guest; and you should come and shoot with me down in the marshes where the wildfowl are. In all the countryside there are none that could hinder if we willed to make peace. I never thought to have wanted to do other than hate you all my life, but I think I have changed my mind about things too, this last half-hour. And you offered me your wine flask. . . . Ulrich von Gradwitz, I will be your friend." **C**

For a space both men were silent, turning over in their minds the wonderful changes that this dramatic reconciliation would bring about. **D** In the cold, gloomy forest, with the wind tearing in fitful gusts through the naked branches and whistling round the tree trunks, they lay and waited for the help that would now bring release and succor to both parties. And each prayed a private prayer that his men might be the first to arrive, so that he might be the first to show honorable attention to the enemy that had become a friend. **E**

The Forest with Red Earth, c.1891 (oil on canvas)
71 × 50 cm. © Musee des Beaux–Arts, Quimper, France/Bridgeman Art Library

---

8. **Sylvester night:** feast day honoring Saint Sylvester (Pope Sylvester I, d. 335), observed on December 31.

C QUICK CHECK

How have Georg's feelings toward Ulrich charged?

_____
_____
_____
_____

D LANGUAGE COACH

How many syllables are in the word *reconciliation*? On which syllable is the primary stress?

_____
_____

E LITERARY ANALYSIS

Earlier in the story, why did each man hope that his friends would be the first to arrive? What has changed?

_____
_____
_____
_____
_____
_____
_____
_____

A **LITERARY FOCUS**

The **omniscient narrator** doesn't reveal who is coming toward the men. What effect does this lack of information create?

_____

_____

_____

_____

B **QUICK CHECK**

Underline the one word that reveals the story's surprise ending.

C **LITERARY ANALYSIS**

Why is it fitting that the two men, who were hunting each other in the forest that winter night, are discovered by wolves rather than by rescuers?

_____

_____

_____

_____

_____

_____

_____

_____

Presently, as the wind dropped for a moment, Ulrich broke the silence.

"Let's shout for help," he said; "in this lull our voices may carry a little way."

"They won't carry far through the trees and undergrowth," said Georg, "but we can try. Together, then."

The two raised their voices in a prolonged hunting call.

190   "Together again," said Ulrich a few minutes later, after listening in vain for an answering halloo.

"I heard something that time, I think," said Ulrich.

"I heard nothing but the pestilential[9] wind," said Georg hoarsely.

There was silence again for some minutes, and then Ulrich gave a joyful cry.

"I can see figures coming through the wood. They are following in the way I came down the hillside."

Both men raised their voices in as loud a shout as they

200   could muster.

"They hear us! They've stopped. Now they see us. They're running down the hill toward us," cried Ulrich.

"How many of them are there?" asked Georg.

"I can't see distinctly," said Ulrich; "nine or ten."

"Then they are yours," said Georg; "I had only seven out with me."

"They are making all the speed they can, brave lads," said Ulrich gladly.

"Are they your men?" asked Georg. "Are they your men?" he

210   repeated impatiently, as Ulrich did not answer. **A**

"No," said Ulrich with a laugh, the idiotic chattering laugh of a man unstrung with hideous fear.

"Who are they?" asked Georg quickly, straining his eyes to see what the other would gladly not have seen.

"_Wolves._" **B** **C**

---

9. **pestilential** (PEHS TIH LEHN SHUHL) _adj._: Strictly speaking, _pestilential_ means "deadly; causing disease; harmful." Here, Georg uses the word to mean "cursed."

Applying Your Skills

The Interlopers

VOCABULARY DEVELOPMENT

DIRECTIONS: Write vocabulary words from the Word Box on the correct blanks to complete the sentences. Not every word will be used.

Word Box

disputed
marauders
exasperation
condolences
reconciliation

1. After years of fighting, a _____ took place between the enemies and they called a truce.

2. To protect his land, Ulrich patrolled the woods for _____.

3. Georg's _____ reached new highs when he found himself trapped with his enemy.

4. Ulrich's wife received countless _____ at her husband's funeral.

LITERARY FOCUS: OMNISCIENT NARRATOR

DIRECTIONS: Look over the text of "The Interlopers" again and put brackets around four different parts of the story in which the **omniscient narrator** reveals one of the characters' thoughts or feelings.

READING FOCUS: DRAWING CONCLUSIONS

DIRECTIONS: Complete the chart by **drawing conclusions** from the details listed below. Your conclusions might describe what the characters are like, human nature, or the author's intention in writing the detail.

Story details	Conclusions
While trapped under the tree, both men swear "death and damnation" upon each other.	
Georg comments that "the whole region would stare" if he and Ulrich became friends.	
After spotting the approaching wolves, Ulrich releases an "idiotic chattering laugh."	

SKILLS FOCUS

Literary Skills
Understand how an omniscient narrator changes a story.

Reading Skills
Use details from the story to draw broader conclusions.

The Cask of Amontillado

by Edgar Allan Poe

LITERARY FOCUS: UNRELIABLE NARRATOR

Some stories are told by a first-person narrator. In such stories, all the action is explained from the point of view of the narrator. When you see the pronoun "I" being used by the narrator, you know the story is written using the first person point of view. Sometimes a writer will purposely use a narrator who does not always tell the truth. An **unreliable narrator** may not know the whole truth or may lie on purpose. A narrator's actions, statements, **voice** (style of speaking), **diction** (word choice), and **tone** (attitude) will provide you with clues about his or her reliability.

READING FOCUS: DRAWING CONCLUSIONS

When you read, you act like a detective. You gather evidence and **draw conclusions**, or make judgments, based on that evidence. To decide if the narrator of Poe's story is reliable, look closely at everything the narrator says and does. Then, examine what his enemy, Fortunato, does. What details show the narrator is unreliable?

Use the Skill As you read, keep track of specific details to help you draw conclusions about the narrator of this story.

SKILLS FOCUS

Literary Skills
Understand the characteristics of an unreliable narrator.

Reading Skills
Use details to draw conclusions.

What the narrator says	What the narrator does	What Fortunato does
Fortunato has injured him a thousand times.	He hides his feelings from Fortunato.	He happily accompanies the narrator back to the palazzo.
He vows to get back at his enemy.		

Vocabulary Development

The Cask of Amontillado

SELECTION VOCABULARY

impunity (IHM PYOO NUH TEE) *n.:* freedom from punishment or harm.
> *He thinks he can do what he wants because he knows that he has impunity.*

retribution (REHT RUH BYOO SHUHN) *n.:* punishment for something done.
> *I seek retribution for the wrongs done against me.*

impose (IHM POHZ) *v.:* (used with *upon*) take advantage of.
> *Please do not impose upon me by asking for such a difficult favor.*

implore (IHM PLAWR) *v.:* to beg.
> *I implore you to give up this unnecessary feud.*

obstinate (AHB STUH NIHT) *adj.:* stubborn.
> *The men waited in obstinate silence, each one refusing to speak first.*

WORD STUDY

DIRECTIONS: Sometimes people confuse words that start with the same letters. Create short sentences to help you remember the meanings of words that are easily confused. The sentences can even be silly if that's what helps you remember. Use a dictionary to look up the meanings of any words you do not know.

1. impatient _____

_____

2. impossible _____

_____

3. implore _____

_____

THE CASK OF AMONTILLADO

by Edgar Allan Poe

> ### BACKGROUND
> Hundreds of years ago, Christians in Italy buried their dead in catacombs, or underground tunnels. Later, wealthy families built private catacombs under their homes. The catacombs were cool and dark, which made them good for burial and storing fine wines such as amontillado (UH MAHN TEE YAH DOH). This story takes place during Carnival, a celebration that comes before Lent—the season when Christians give up various pleasures. During Carnival, people wear costumes and dance in the streets.

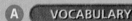

A **VOCABULARY**

Selection Vocabulary
The word *impunity* means "freedom from punishment or harm." Re-write the sentence in which it appears using your own words.

_____

_____

_____

The thousand injuries of Fortunato I had borne as best I could; but when he ventured upon insult, I vowed revenge. You, who so well know the nature of my soul, will not suppose, however, that I gave utterance to a threat. At length I would be avenged; this was a

10   point definitively settled—but the very definitiveness with which it was resolved precluded the idea of risk. I must not only punish, but punish with impunity. **A** A wrong is unredressed[1] when retribution overtakes its redresser. It is equally unredressed when the avenger fails to make himself felt as such to him who has done the wrong.

It must be understood that neither by word nor deed had I given Fortunato cause to doubt my goodwill. I continued,

© Jim Zuckerman/Alamy

---

1.   **unredressed**: not set right; uncorrected..

as was my wont, to smile in his face, and he did not perceive that
20 my smile *now* was at the thought of his immolation[2]. **B**

He had a weak point—this Fortunato—although in other
regards he was a man to be respected and even feared. He prided
himself on his connoisseurship in wine. Few Italians have the
true virtuoso spirit. For the most part their enthusiasm is adopted
to suit the time and opportunity—to practice imposture upon
the British and Austrian millionaires. In painting and gemmary,
Fortunato, like his countrymen, was a quack—but in the matter of
old wines he was sincere. In this respect I did not differ from him
materially: I was skillful in the Italian vintages myself and bought
30 largely whenever I could. **C**

It was about dusk, one evening during the supreme madness
of the carnival season, that I encountered my friend. He accosted
me with excessive warmth, for he had been drinking much. The
man wore motley.[3] He had on a tight-fitting parti-striped dress,
and his head was surmounted by the conical cap and bells. I was
so pleased to see him that I thought I should never have done
wringing his hand. **D**

I said to him, "My dear Fortunato, you are luckily met. How
remarkably well you are looking today! But I have received a
40 pipe[4] of what passes for amontillado, and I have my doubts."

"How?" said he. "Amontillado? A pipe? Impossible! And in
the middle of the carnival!"

"I have my doubts," I replied; "and I was silly enough
to pay the full amontillado price without consulting you in the
matter. You were not to be found, and I was fearful of losing a
bargain."

"Amontillado!"

"I have my doubts."

"Amontillado!"

50 "And I must satisfy them."

"Amontillado!"

---

2. **immolation:** destruction
3. **motley:** multicolored costume worn by a clown or jester.
4. **pipe:** barrel.

B LITERARY FOCUS

What do you learn about
the **narrator** when he smiles
at the thought of Fortunato's
death?

_____

_____

_____

C QUICK CHECK

According to this paragraph,
what is one similarity
between the narrator
and Fortunato?

_____

_____

_____

_____

D READING FOCUS

Draw a conclusion as to why
the narrator is happy to see
Fortunato.

_____

_____

_____

_____

"As you are engaged, I am on my way to Luchesi. If anyone has a critical turn, it is he. He will tell me—"

"Luchesi cannot tell amontillado from sherry."

"And yet some fools will have it that his taste is a match for your own."

"Come, let us go."

"Whither?"

"To your vaults."

60 "My friend, no; I will not impose upon your good nature. I perceive you have an engagement. Luchesi—"

"I have no engagement; come."

"My friend, no. It is not the engagement, but the severe cold with which I perceive you are afflicted. The vaults are insufferably damp. They are encrusted with niter."[5]

"Let us go, nevertheless. The cold is merely nothing. Amontillado! You have been imposed upon. And as for Luchesi, he cannot distinguish sherry from amontillado."

Thus speaking, Fortunato possessed himself of my arm.
70 Putting on a mask of black silk and drawing a roquelaure[6] closely about my person, I suffered him to hurry me to my *palazzo*.[7] A

There were no attendants at home; they had absconded to make merry in honor of the time. B I had told them that I should not return until the morning and had given them explicit orders not to stir from the house. These orders were sufficient, I well knew, to ensure their immediate disappearance, one and all, as soon as my back was turned.

I took from their sconces two flambeaux[8] and, giving one to Fortunato, bowed him through several suites of rooms to the
80 archway that led into the vaults. I passed down a long and winding staircase, requesting him to be cautious as he followed. We came at length to the foot of the descent and stood together on the damp ground of the catacombs of the Montresors.

---

5. **niter:** salt deposits.
6. **roquelaure** (RAHK UH LOHR): heavy knee-length cape.
7. **palazzo** (PAH LAHT SOH): Italian for "palace."
8. **sconces:** wall fixtures that hold flambeaux (FLAHM BOHZ), candlesticks or flaming pieces of wood.

The gait of my friend was unsteady, and the bells upon his cap jingled as he strode.

"The pipe," said he.

"It is farther on," said I; "but observe the white web-work which gleams from these cavern walls."

He turned toward me, and looked into my eyes with two 90 filmy orbs that distilled the rheum[9] of intoxication.

"Niter?" he asked, at length.

"Niter," I replied. "How long have you had that cough?"

"Ugh! ugh! ugh!—ugh! ugh! ugh!—ugh! ugh! ugh!—ugh! ugh! ugh!—ugh! ugh! ugh!"

My poor friend found it impossible to reply for many minutes. **C**

"It is nothing," he said, at last.

"Come," I said, with decision, "we will go back; your health is precious. You are rich, respected, admired, beloved; you are 100 happy, as once I was. You are a man to be missed. For me it is no matter. We will go back; you will be ill, and I cannot be responsible. Besides, there is Luchesi—" **D**

"Enough," he said; "the cough is a mere nothing; it will not kill me. I shall not die of a cough."

"True—true," I replied; "and, indeed, I had no intention of alarming you unnecessarily—but you should use all proper caution. A draft of this Médoc[10] will defend us from the damps."

Here I knocked off the neck of a bottle which I drew from a long row of its fellows that lay upon the mold.

110 "Drink," I said, presenting him the wine.

He raised it to his lips with a leer. He paused and nodded to me familiarly, while his bells jingled.

"I drink," he said, "to the buried that repose around us."

"And I to your long life."

He again took my arm, and we proceeded.

"These vaults," he said, "are extensive."

9. **rheum** (ROOM): watery discharge.
10. **Médoc** (MAY DOHK): type of red wine.

C LITERARY FOCUS

The **narrator** refers to Fortunato as "my poor friend." What clues suggest that the narrator means the opposite of what he says?

_____

_____

_____

_____

_____

_____

D LITERARY FOCUS

Do you think the **narrator** means what he says in this paragraph? Why or why not?

_____

_____

_____

_____

_____

_____

_____

_____

_____

_____

_____

_____

_____

_____

_____

_____

_____

_____

_____

"The Montresors," I replied, "were a great and numerous family."

"I forget your arms."[11]

120 "A huge human foot d' or, in a field azure; the foot crushes a serpent rampant whose fangs are embedded in the heel."[12]

"And the motto?"

"*Nemo me impune lacessit.*"[13]

"Good!" he said. **A**

The wine sparkled in his eyes and the bells jingled. My own fancy grew warm with the Médoc. We had passed through walls of piled bones, with casks and puncheons[14] intermingling, into the inmost recesses of the catacombs. I paused again, and this time I made bold to seize Fortunato by an arm above the elbow.

130 "The niter!" I said. "See, it increases. It hangs like moss upon the vaults. We are below the river's bed. The drops of moisture trickle among the bones. Come, we will go back ere it is too late. Your cough—" **B**

"It is nothing," he said; "let us go on. But first, another draft of the Médoc."

I broke and reached him a flagon of de Grave.[15] He emptied it at a breath. His eyes flashed with a fierce light. He laughed and threw the bottle upward with a gesticulation I did not understand.

140 I looked at him in surprise. He repeated the movement—a grotesque one.

"You do not comprehend?" he said.

"Not I," I replied.

"Then you are not of the brotherhood."

"How?"

---

11. **arms:** coat of arms, a group of symbols used to represent a family.
12. **foot d'or...heel:** The Montresor coat of arms shows a huge golden foot against a blue background, with the foot crushing a snake that is rearing up and biting the heel.
13. **Nemo me impune lacessit** (NAY MOH MAY IHM POO NAY LAH KAY SIHT): Latin for "nobody attacks me without punishment."
14. **puncheons:** large wine casks.
15. **flagon of de Grave:** a bottle containing wine from the Graves region of France.

"You are not of the Masons."[16]

"Yes, yes," I said, "yes, yes."

"You? Impossible! A Mason?"

"A Mason," I replied.

150   "A sign," he said.

"It is this," I answered, producing a trowel[17] from beneath the folds of my roquelaure. Ⓒ

"You jest," he exclaimed, recoiling a few paces. "But let us proceed to the amontillado."

"Be it so," I said, replacing the tool beneath the cloak and again offering him my arm. He leaned upon it heavily. We continued our route in search of the amontillado. We passed through a range of low arches, descended, passed on, and, descending again, arrived at a deep crypt in which the foulness of the air

160   caused our flambeaux rather to glow than flame.

At the most remote end of the crypt there appeared another less spacious. Its walls had been lined with human remains, piled to the vault overhead, in the fashion of the great catacombs of Paris. Three sides of this interior crypt were still ornamented in this manner. From the fourth the bones had been thrown down and lay promiscuously upon the earth, forming at one point a mound of some size. Within the wall thus exposed by the displacing of the bones, we perceived a still interior recess, in depth about four feet, in width three, in height six or seven.

170   It seemed to have been constructed for no especial use within itself, but formed merely the interval between two of the colossal supports of the roof of the catacombs and was backed by one of their circumscribing walls of solid granite.

It was in vain that Fortunato, uplifting his dull torch, endeavored to pry into the depth of the recess. Its termination the feeble light did not enable us to see.

---

16. **Masons:** Freemasons, a secret society of people who believe in brotherhood, giving to the poor, and helping one another. Members use secret signs and gestures to recognize one another.

17. **trowel:** flat tool with a pointed blade, especially used by a mason, a person who builds with stone or concrete. The Freemasons probably began as associations of stoneworkers.

C   **READING FOCUS**

Why might Montresor be carrying a trowel? What **conclusion** can you draw about his plans?

_____

_____

_____

_____

_____

_____

_____

_____

_____

_____

_____

The Cask of Amontillado   **107**

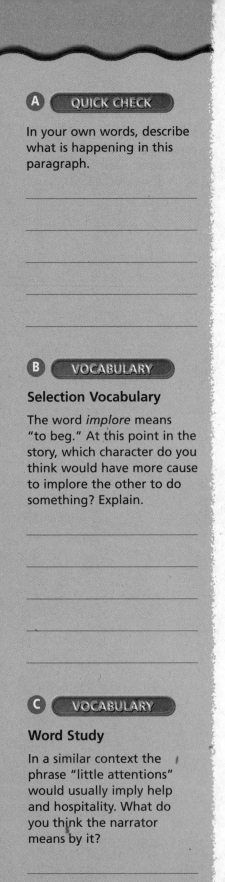

A **QUICK CHECK**

In your own words, describe what is happening in this paragraph.

_____

_____

_____

_____

_____

B **VOCABULARY**

Selection Vocabulary

The word _implore_ means "to beg." At this point in the story, which character do you think would have more cause to implore the other to do something? Explain.

_____

_____

_____

_____

_____

_____

C **VOCABULARY**

Word Study

In a similar context the phrase "little attentions" would usually imply help and hospitality. What do you think the narrator means by it?

_____

_____

_____

_____

"Proceed," I said; "herein is the amontillado. As for Luchesi—"

"He is an ignoramus," interrupted my friend, as he stepped unsteadily forward, while I followed immediately at his heels. In an instant he had reached the extremity of the niche, and finding his progress arrested by the rock, stood stupidly bewildered. A moment more and I had fettered him to the granite. In its surface were two iron staples, distant from each other about two feet horizontally. From one of these depended a short chain, from the other a padlock. Throwing the links about his waist, it was but the work of a few seconds to secure it. He was too much astounded to resist. Withdrawing the key, I stepped back from the recess. **A**

"Pass your hand," I said, "over the wall; you cannot help feeling the niter. Indeed it is _very_ damp. Once more let me implore you to return. **B** No? Then I must positively leave you. But I must first render you all the little attentions in my power." **C**

"The amontillado!" ejaculated my friend, not yet recovered from his astonishment.

"True," I replied; "the amontillado."

As I said these words, I busied myself among the pile of bones of which I have before spoken. Throwing them aside, I soon uncovered a quantity of building stone and mortar. With these materials and with the aid of my trowel, I began vigorously to wall up the entrance of the niche.

I had scarcely laid the first tier of the masonry when I discovered that the intoxication of Fortunato had in a great measure worn off. The earliest indication I had of this was a low moaning cry from the depth of the recess. It was _not_ the cry of a drunken man. There was then a long and obstinate silence. I laid the second tier, and the third, and the fourth; and then I heard the furious vibrations of the chain. The noise lasted for several minutes, during which, that I might hearken to it with the more satisfaction, I ceased my labors and sat down upon the bones. When at last the clanking subsided, I resumed the trowel and finished without interruption the fifth, the sixth, and the seventh tier. The wall was now nearly upon a level with my breast. I again paused and, holding the flambeaux over the mason-work, threw a few feeble rays upon the figure within. **D**

A succession of loud and shrill screams, bursting suddenly from the throat of the chained form, seemed to thrust me violently back. For a brief moment I hesitated—I trembled. Unsheathing my rapier,[18] I began to grope with it about the recess; but the thought of an instant reassured me. I placed my hand upon the solid fabric of the catacombs and felt satisfied. I reapproached the wall; I replied to the yells of him who clamored. I reechoed—I aided—I surpassed them in volume and in strength. I did this, and the clamorer grew still.

It was now midnight, and my task was drawing to a close. I had completed the eighth, the ninth, and the tenth tier. I had finished a portion of the last and the eleventh; there remained but a single stone to be fitted and plastered in. I struggled with its weight; I placed it partially in its destined position. But now there came from out the niche a low laugh that erected the hairs upon my head. It was succeeded by a sad voice, which I had difficulty in recognizing as that of the noble Fortunato. The voice said—

"Ha! ha! ha!—he! he! he!—a very good joke indeed—an excellent jest. We will have many a rich laugh about it at the *palazzo*—he! he! he!—over our wine—he! he! he!"

"The amontillado!" I said.

"He! he! he!—he! he! he!—yes, the amontillado. But is it not getting late? Will not they be awaiting us at the *palazzo*—the Lady Fortunato and the rest? Let us be gone."

"Yes," I said, "let us be gone."

"*For the love of God, Montresor!*"

"Yes," I said, "for the love of God!"

But to these words I hearkened in vain for a reply. I grew impatient. I called aloud—

"Fortunato!"

No answer. I called again—

"Fortunato!"

---

18. **rapier** (RAY PEE UHR): long, thin sword.

Draw a conclusion about Montresor's state of mind when he stops his work to enjoy Fortunato's cries.

_____

_____

_____

_____

_____

_____

_____

A **LITERARY FOCUS**

Do you think the **unreliable narrator** is telling us the truth about why his "heart grew sick"? Explain.

_____

_____

_____

_____

_____

_____

_____

_____

B **VOCABULARY**

Academic Vocabulary

After reading the entire story, write a few sentences describing the *impression*, or overall effect, that the writer leaves you with about the narrator.

_____

_____

_____

_____

_____

_____

© Scala/Art Resource, NY

No answer still. I thrust a torch through the remaining aperture and let it fall within. There came forth in return only a jingling of the bells. My heart grew sick—on account of the dampness of the catacombs. **A** I hastened to make an end of my labor. I forced the last stone into its position; I plastered it up. Against the new masonry I reerected the old rampart[19] of bones. For the half of a century no mortal has disturbed them. *In pace requiescat.*[20] **B**

---

19. **rampart:** wall built for protection or defense.
20. **In pace requiescat** (IHN PAH CHAY RAY KWEE EHS KAHT): Latin for "May he rest in peace."

250

Applying Your Skills

The Cask of Amontillado

VOCABULARY DEVELOPMENT

DIRECTIONS: Write vocabulary words from the Word Box on the correct blanks to complete the paragraph. Not all words will be used.

Word Box

impunity

retribution

impose

implore

obstinate

The Cask of Amontillado is a disturbing tale of (1) _____. Montresor firmly believes that the only real revenge is achieved with (2) _____, so he plans carefully to avoid punishment for his crime. He is single-minded and (3) _____ in his quest for revenge. Fortunato seems to sense that it would be useless to (4) _____ Montresor to release him.

LITERARY FOCUS: UNRELIABLE NARRATOR

DIRECTIONS: Read the quotations from story listed below. In the middle column, write *Yes* if you think Montresor, **the unreliable narrator**, is telling the truth in that quote or *No* if he is not. Then give your reasons in the third column.

Quotation	Is it the truth?	Why or why not?
. . . he did not perceive that my smile *now* was at the thought of his immolation.		
I was so pleased to see him that I thought I should never have done wringing his hand.		
My heart grew sick—on account of the dampness of the catacombs.		

READING FOCUS: DRAWING CONCLUSIONS

DIRECTIONS: Use the chart of details that you made as you read this story to help you think of traits that describe each character. Answer these questions on a separate sheet of paper:

1. Which of Fortunato's character traits make him fall for Montresor's plan?

2. Which of Montresor's character traits make him a good narrator for this story?

3. How does Montresor use his knowledge of Fortunato to lure his victim farther and farther in the catacombs?

SKILLS FOCUS

Literary Skills
Understand how to identify an unreliable narrator.

Reading Skills
Use details to help you draw conclusions.

Readings About Poe's Death

INFORMATIONAL TEXT FOCUS: SYNTHESIZING SOURCES—DRAWING CONCLUSIONS

When you research a subject, you read many different sources carefully. Then, you need to **synthesize** the information from these sources, putting all the pieces together to see the big picture. Follow these steps to synthesize information:

1. **Find the main idea.** Identify each writer's main idea, or central point. If you run into a difficult passage, **paraphrase** it, or restate it in your own words.

2. **Look for supporting evidence.** Look for the facts, statistics, examples, and quotations the author uses to support his or her point.

3. **Compare and contrast.** Look for similarities and differences between your sources. Then, try **making connections,** or relating what you've just read about to similar ideas you've encountered in the past.

4. **Put it together.** Finally, synthesize the sources. How do they relate to each other? Do the sources have similar or different main ideas?

SELECTION VOCABULARY

insensible (IHN SEHN SUH BUHL) *adj.:* not fully conscious or aware.
When the doctor arrived, he found Poe insensible.

imposing (IHM POH ZIHNG) *adj.:* large and impressive-looking.
The old stone hospital's appearance is imposing.

conspicuous (KUHN SPIHK YOO UHS) *adj.:* obvious, noticeable.
The investigating doctor found the lack of tests conspicuous.

chronic (KRAHN IHK) *adj.:* Frequently occurring.
Poe was known for his chronic drinking.

WORD STUDY

DIRECTIONS: Match the words with their synonyms, or words that have the same meaning.

_____ 1. chronic   **a.** unconscious

_____ 2. insensible   **b.** grand

_____ 3. imposing   **c.** habitual

Informational Text Skills
Learn to synthesize information from several sources by focusing on the main idea and pieces of supporting evidence.

POE'S FINAL DAYS

from Edgar A. Poe: Mournful and Never-Ending Remembrance by Kenneth Silverman

BACKGROUND

This biography traces the last few days of Edgar Allan Poe's life. He had just parted from Elmira Shelton, to whom he had recently been engaged. Shelton lived in Richmond, Virginia, and Poe set out from there for Baltimore, Maryland, with plans to go to New York City. He never completed his journey.

In the early morning of September 27, a Thursday, Poe began the first leg of his return to the North, setting out from Richmond for Baltimore on the 4 A.M. steamer,[1] with a trunk containing some clothing, books, and manuscripts.

No reliable evidence exists about what happened to or within Poe between that time and October 3, a week later, when a printer named Joseph Walker saw him at Gunner's Hall, a Baltimore tavern, strangely dressed and semiconscious. **A**

It was Election Day for members of Congress, and like other local watering holes[2] the tavern served as a polling place. Poe seemed to Walker "rather the worse for wear" and "in great distress." Apparently flooded with drink, he may also have been ill from exposure. Winds and soaking rains the day before had sent Baltimoreans prematurely hunting up overcoats and seeking charcoal fires for warmth. . . . Poe managed to tell Walker that he knew Joseph Evans Snodgrass, the Baltimore editor and physician with whom he had often corresponded while living in Philadelphia. As it happened, Walker had worked as a typesetter

A **READING FOCUS**

Based on the first two paragraphs and the article title, what do you think is the **main idea** of this piece?

_____

_____

_____

_____

_____

_____

_____

---

1. **steamer** (STEE MUHR): steamship, or ship driven by steam power.
2. **watering holes:** informal for "bars, taverns."

Excerpt (retitled "Poe's Final Days") from *Edgar A. Poe: Mournful and Never-Ending Remembrance* by Kenneth Silverman. Copyright © 1991 by Kenneth Silverman. Reproduced by permission of **HarperCollins Publishers**.

B VOCABULARY

Selection Vocabulary

If you don't know the meaning of the word *insensible,* try breaking it into its parts. The prefix *in-* means "not." Look up the word *sensible.* Which definition makes up part of the word *insensible* as it is used here? Explain your answer.

_____

_____

_____

_____

_____

C  VOCABULARY

Word Study

What does the word *admitted* mean in this sentence? Does *admitted* have the same meaning in the sentence, "Poe admitted to close friends that he drank too much?"

_____

_____

_____

_____

20 for Snodgrass's *Saturday Visitor*. He sent Snodgrass a dire note, warning that Poe needed "immediate assistance."

When Snodgrass arrived at Gunner's Hall, he found Poe sitting in an armchair, surrounded by onlookers. Poe had a look of "vacant stupidity." He wore neither vest nor tie, his dingy trousers fit badly, his shirt was crumpled, his cheap hat soiled. Snodgrass thought he must be wearing castoff clothing, having been robbed or cheated of his own. **A** He ordered a room for Poe at the tavern, where he might stay comfortably until his relatives in Baltimore could be notified. Just then, however, one of them arrived—Henry Herring, Poe's uncle by marriage, who

30 somehow had also learned of his condition. A lumber dealer now nearly sixty years old, he had wed Muddy's[3] sister, and spent time with Poe during his early days in Baltimore and later when both families lived in Philadelphia. But he refused now to take over his care, saying that on former occasions, when drunk, Poe had been abusive and ungrateful. Instead, he suggested sending Poe to a hospital. A carriage was called for. Poe had to be carried into it, Snodgrass said—insensible, muttering. **B**

Through the chilly wet streets Poe was driven to the hospital of Washington Medical College, set on the highest

40 ground of Baltimore. An imposing five-story building with vaulted gothic windows, it afforded both public wards and private rooms, advertised as being spacious, well ventilated, and directed by an experienced medical staff. Admitted at five in the afternoon, Poe was given a private room, reportedly in a section reserved for cases involving drunkenness. **C** He was attended by the resident physician, Dr. John J. Moran, who apparently had living quarters in the hospital together with his wife. Moran had received his medical degree from the University of Maryland four years earlier and was now only about twenty-six years

50 old. But he knew the identity of his patient—a "*great* man," he wrote of Poe, to whose "rarely gifted mind are we indebted for

---

3. **Muddy's:** Muddy was Poe's nickname for Maria Clemm, his aunt and mother-in-law. Poe had married his cousin, Virginia Clemm.

many of the brightest thoughts that adorn our literature." He as well as the medical students, nurses, and other physicians—all considered Poe, he said, "an object of unusual regard."

According to Moran and his wife, Poe reached the hospital in a stupor,[4] unaware of who or what had brought him there. He remained thus "unconscious" until three o'clock the next morning, when he developed a tremor[5] of the limbs and what Moran called "a busy, but not violent or active delirium."[6] His face was pale and he was drenched in sweat. He talked constantly, Moran said, addressing "spectral[7] and imaginary objects on the walls." Apparently during Poe's delirium, his cousin Neilson Poe came to the hospital, having been contacted by Dr. Moran. A lawyer and journalist involved in Whig politics, Neilson was just Poe's age. In happier circumstances Poe would not have welcomed the visit. Not only had Neilson offered Virginia[8] and Muddy a home apart from him; his cousin also, he believed, envied his literary reputation. Years before he had remarked that he considered "the little dog," as he called Neilson, the "bitterest enemy I have in the world." The physicians anyway thought it inadvisable for Neilson to see Poe at the moment, when "very excitable." Neilson sent some changes of linen and called again the next day, to find Poe's condition improved. **D**

Poe being quieted, Moran began questioning him about his family and about where he lived, but found his answers mostly incoherent. Poe did not know what had become of his trunk or when he had left Richmond, but said he had a wife there, as Moran soon learned was untrue. He said that his "degradation," as Moran characterized it, made him feel like sinking into the ground. **E** Trying to rouse Poe's spirits, Moran told him he wished to contribute in every way to his comfort,

---

4. **stupor** (STOO PUHR): dull, half-conscious state.
5. **tremor** (TREHM UHR): involuntary trembling, especially from a physical illness.
6. **delirium** (DIH LIHR EE UHM): irrational, raving behavior, often caused by high fever.
7. **spectral** (SPEHK TRUHL): ghostly; unreal.
8. **Virginia:** Poe's wife, Virginia Clemm. She died of tuberculosis in 1847.

D **READING FOCUS**

Briefly **paraphrase** this paragraph in three to five sentences. Be sure to include the **main idea** in your version of the paragraph.

_____

_____

_____

_____

_____

_____

_____

_____

_____

_____

E **LANGUAGE COACH**

An **antonym** is a word with the opposite meaning of another word. Circle the word in this sentence that is an antonym of *improvement*.

How does Poe's behavior at the hospital support the **main idea** of this selection?

_____

_____

_____

_____

_____

_____

and hoped Poe would soon be enjoying the company of his friends. . . . **A**

Then Poe seemed to doze, and Moran left him briefly. On returning he found Poe violently delirious, resisting the efforts of two nurses to keep him in bed. From Moran's description, Poe seems to have raved a full day or more, through Saturday evening, October 6, when he began repeatedly calling out someone's name. It may have been that of a Baltimore family named Reynolds or, more likely, the name of his uncle-in-law Henry Herring. Moran later said that he sent for the Herring family, but that only one of Herring's two daughters came to the hospital. Poe continued deliriously calling the name until three o'clock on Sunday morning. Then his condition changed. Feeble from his exertions he seemed to rest a short time and then, Moran reported, "quietly moving his head he said '*Lord help my poor Soul*' and expired!"

The cause of Poe's death remains in doubt. Moran's account of his profuse perspiration, trembling, and hallucinations indicates delirium tremens, *mania à potu*.[9] Many others who had known Poe, including the professionally trained Dr. Snodgrass, also attributed his death to a lethal amount of alcohol. Moran later vigorously disputed this explanation, however, and some Baltimore newspapers gave the cause of death as "congestion of the brain" or "cerebral inflammation."[10] Although the terms were sometimes used euphemistically[11] in public announcements of deaths from disgraceful causes, such as alcoholism, they may in this case have come from the hospital staff itself. According to Moran, one of its senior physicians diagnosed Poe's condition as encephalitis, a brain inflammation, brought on by "exposure." This explanation is consistent with the prematurely wintry

---

9. **delirium tremens, *mania à potu*:** *Delirium tremens* refers to an alcoholic state in which the victim behaves irrationally and sometimes violently, hallucinates (sees imaginary things), and trembles. *Mania à potu* is a Latin phrase meaning "madness from drinking."
10. **"congestion of the brain" or "cerebral inflammation":** These are terms for conditions of the brain caused by injury or infection.
11. **euphemistically** (YOO FUH MIHS TUH KLEE): in a manner meant to hide or substitute for something unpleasant or offensive.

© Rebekah F. Owens, Westminster Preservation Trust, Inc.

weather at the time, with Snodgrass's account of Poe's partly clad condition, and with Elmira Shelton's recollection that on leaving Richmond Poe already had a fever. Both explanations may have been correct: Poe may have become too drunk to care about protecting himself against the wind and rain. **B**

B **READING FOCUS**

Why doesn't Moran believe that Poe died of alcohol poisoning? Write your answer below and underline all of the **supporting evidence** in the paragraph.

POE'S DEATH IS REWRITTEN AS CASE OF RABIES, NOT TELLTALE ALCOHOL

from The New York Times, September 15, 1996

BACKGROUND

One of the ways doctors keep up with medical advances in their field is by attending medical conferences. While attending such a conference, Dr. R. Michael Benitez from Baltimore came up with a new theory about Poe's death.

A READING FOCUS

After reading the first page of this article, what do you think is its **main idea**?

_____

_____

_____

_____

_____

_____

_____

Edgar Allan Poe did not die drunk in a gutter in Baltimore but rather had rabies, a new study suggests.

The researcher, Dr. R. Michael Benitez, a cardiologist[1] who practices a block from Poe's grave, says it is true that the writer was seen in a bar on Lombard Street in October 1849, delirious and possibly wearing somebody else's soiled clothes.

But Poe was not drunk, said Dr. Benitez, an assistant professor of medicine at the University of Maryland Medical Center. "I think Poe is much maligned[2] in that respect," he added.

10 The writer entered Washington College Hospital comatose,[3] Dr. Benitez said, but by the next day was perspiring heavily, hallucinating, and shouting at imaginary companions. The next day, he seemed better but could not remember falling ill. **A**

---

1. **cardiologist** (KAHR DEE AH LUH JIHST): doctor who specializes in diseases of the heart.
2. **maligned** (MUH LYND): falsely accused of bad conduct; slandered.
3. **comatose** (KAH MUH TOHS): deeply unconscious and unable to be wakened.

On his fourth day at the hospital, Poe again grew confused and belligerent,[4] then quieted down and died.

That is a classic case of rabies, the doctor said. His study is in the September issue of *The Maryland Medical Journal*.

20 In the brief period when he was calm and awake, Poe refused alcohol and could drink water only with great difficulty. Rabies victims frequently exhibit hydrophobia, or fear of water, because it is painful to swallow. **B**

There is no evidence that a rabid animal had bitten Poe. About one fourth of rabies victims reportedly cannot remember being bitten. After an infection, the symptoms can take up to a year to appear. But when the symptoms do appear, the disease is a swift and brutal killer. Most patients die in a few days. **C**

Poe "had all the features of encephalitic rabies," said Dr. Henry Wilde, who frequently treats rabies at Chulalongkorn
30 University Hospital in Bangkok, Thailand.

Although it has been well established that Poe died in the hospital, legend has it that he succumbed in the gutter, a victim of his debauched[5] ways.

The legend may have been fostered by his doctor, who in later years became a temperance advocate[6] and changed the details to make an object lesson of Poe's death. **D**

The curator of the Edgar Allan Poe House and Museum in Baltimore, Jeff Jerome, said that he had heard dozens of tales but that "almost everyone who has come forth with a theory has
40 offered no proof."

Some versions have Poe unconscious under the steps of the Baltimore Museum before being taken to the hospital. Other accounts place him on planks between two barrels outside a tavern on Lombard Street. In most versions, Poe is wearing someone else's clothes, having been robbed of his suit.

---

4. **belligerent** (BUH LIHJ UHR UHNT): angry and aggressive or ready to start a fight.
5. **debauched** (DIH BAWCHT): characterized by extreme indulgence in pleasures.
6. **temperance advocate**: someone who believes that people should not drink alcohol.

B READING FOCUS

Compare and contrast this article with "Poe's Final Days." Underline each event that appears in both articles. Below, list the differences between the two accounts.

_____
_____
_____
_____

C READING FOCUS

Paraphrase this paragraph and state its **main idea**.

_____
_____
_____
_____
_____
_____
_____

D VOCABULARY

Academic Vocabulary

Recall that *portray* means "describe or show." How does the author portray Poe's doctor here?

_____
_____
_____

A **READING FOCUS**

What **supporting evidence** does Mr. Jerome offer for Dr. Benitez's theory?

_____

_____

_____

_____

_____

_____

_____

B **VOCABULARY**

Selection Vocabulary

The word *conspicuous* means "obvious; noticeable." Use *conspicuous* in a sentence.

_____

_____

_____

_____

_____

_____

Poe almost surely did not die of alcohol poisoning or withdrawal, Mr. Jerome said. The writer was so sensitive to alcohol that a glass of wine would make him violently ill for days. Poe may have had problems with alcohol as a younger man, Mr. Jerome said, but by the time he died at forty he almost always avoided it. **A**

Dr. Benitez worked on Poe's case as part of a clinical pathologic conference. Doctors are presented with a hypothetical[7] patient and a description of the symptoms and are asked to render a diagnosis.

Dr. Benitez said that at first he did not know that he had been assigned Poe, because his patient was described only as "E. P., a writer from Richmond." But by the time he was scheduled to present his findings a few weeks later, he had figured out the mystery. "There was a conspicuous lack in this report of things like CT scans and MRI's,"[8] the doctor said. **B** "I started to say to myself, 'This doesn't look like it's from the 1990s.' Then it dawned on me that E. P. was Edgar Poe."

50

60

---

7. **hypothetical** (HY PUH THEHT UH KUHL): theoretical; not actual.
8. **CT scans and MRI's**: medical tests that use modern technology. Both tests produce an image of a cross-section of soft tissue such as the brain.

IF ONLY POE HAD SUCCEEDED WHEN HE SAID NEVERMORE TO DRINK

from **The New York Times, September 23, 1996**

BACKGROUND

To comment on a publication's article or to challenge it, a reader may choose to write a letter to the editor. Letters to the editor are printed in a later publication. In response to the previous article, Burton R. Pollin and Robert E. Benedetto wrote a letter disputing Dr. Benitez's theory.

To the Editor:

Dr. R. Michael Benitez, an assistant professor of medicine at Maryland University Medical Center, is wrong to ascribe[1] the death of Edgar Allan Poe to rabies through animal infection rather than to the traditionally maintained cause of alcoholism (news article, September 15). **C**

Poe was found outside a Baltimore saloon in an alcoholic stupor on October 3, 1849, and died four days later. Dr. John J. Moran's account of his final days is given in a letter to Poe's aunt and mother-in-law, Maria Clemm, a New York Herald article in 1875, and a book by Moran in 1885. Supplementary accounts of Poe's alcoholic condition came from Joseph Walker, a Baltimore printer who first found him; Dr. Joseph Snodgrass, an editor well known to Poe; and two of Poe's relatives. None of these confirm Dr. Benitez's statement that "Poe was not drunk." Evidence of Poe's chronic binges is strewn through his letters, in

C **READING FOCUS**

This paragraph states the **main idea** of the letter. **Paraphrase** this paragraph.

_____

_____

_____

_____

_____

_____

_____

---

1. **ascribe** (UH SKRYB): assign or attribute something to a cause.

A VOCABULARY

Selection Vocabulary

The word *chronic* means "frequently occurring." Underline the evidence given in support of the claim that Poe suffered from chronic drinking.

B QUICK CHECK

What new facts about rabies are presented in this letter?

_____

_____

_____

_____

_____

_____

C READING FOCUS

Compare and contrast this article to the two previous pieces. Which account of Poe's death does this letter support?

_____

_____

_____

_____

periodic admissions of "recoveries" and promises to his wife, Virginia, and her mother to "reform." **A**

20   Dr. Benitez admits the primary weakness of his theory— lack of evidence of a bite or scratch. In those days, rabies was well known as to causes and symptoms, including itching and other sensations that could affect an entire limb or side of the body. How could Moran and his staff ignore such symptoms in a patient? **B**

    And what of Poe's cat, dearly loved but left behind in the Bronx over three months earlier? Guiltless was the pet Caterina, who, uninfected and showing no sign of rabies, died of starvation when deserted by Clemm after Poe's death.

    In short, there is no need to whitewash[2] the self-destructive

30 behavior of this literary genius and major American poet, critic, and teller of tales.

    Burton R. Pollin

    Robert E. Benedetto

    Bronxville, New York

    September 20, 1996

The writers are, respectively, professor emeritus of English, City University of New York, and an associate film professor at the University of South Carolina. **C**

---

2.   **whitewash** (HWYT WAHSH): cover up the faults or defects of something; give a favorable appearance to something.

© The Granger Collection, New York

Applying Your Skills

Readings About Poe's Death

VOCABULARY DEVELOPMENT

DIRECTIONS: Write the vocabulary words from the Word Box on the correct blanks to complete the paragraph.

Word Box

insensible

imposing

conspicuous

chronic

Although these sources disagree on many things, they all confirm that shortly before his death, Edgar Allan Poe was found (1) _____ in a Baltimore tavern. None of the authors disputes the fact that when he appeared in the tavern, Poe's clothing was (2) _____ for its poor condition and fit, nor do any authors disagree on the fact that he was an important and (3) _____ literary figure of his time. The main point of disagreement among these three sources is whether Poe had a (4) _____ drinking problem and whether that problem caused his death.

INFORMATIONAL TEXT FOCUS: SYNTHESIZING SOURCES—DRAWING CONCLUSIONS

DIRECTIONS: Now it is time to **synthesize** the information found in these three articles. Use this chart to fill in the **main idea** and some **supporting evidence** from each source. Then, look at the pieces of supporting evidence you listed. Are any of them repeated in more than one source? Circle any evidence that appears more than once. Do any pieces of evidence directly contradict each other? Underline any evidence that does.

	Poe's Final Days	Poe's Death Is Rewritten . . .	If Only Poe Had Succeeded . . .
Main Idea:			
Support:			
Support:			
Support:			

SKILLS FOCUS

Informational Text Skills
Synthesize sources by studying the main ideas and supporting evidence.

Skills Review

Collection 3

VOCABULARY REVIEW

DIRECTIONS: Use context clues to figure out the meaning of the boldfaced vocabulary word in each sentence. Circle the letter next to the correct meaning.

1. After Jan's mother died, all of her friends visited her to offer their **condolences**.

   a. help

   b. money

   c. sympathy

   d. books

2. After being the victim of her brother's many pranks, Susan decided that she must have **retribution** and began planning a prank of her own.

   a. a break

   b. revenge

   c. a vacation

   d. help

3. He was the only club member who was not at the meeting, and his absence was **conspicuous**.

   a. obvious

   b. boring

   c. interesting

   d. tiring

4. On my hands and knees, I **implore** you to stop this foolish fight and forgive each other.

   a. ask

   b. tell

   c. ignore

   d. beg

Skills Review

Collection 3

LANGUAGE COACH

Sometimes you can find words you already know inside of larger words. The word *happy,* for example, is part of the word *unhappy.* These word parts can give clues about what the larger word means.

DIRECTIONS: In the words below, underline any familiar words, or word parts. Cross out any words whose word parts do NOT help you to understand the meaning of the word. Two examples have been done for you. You may use a dictionary to check your work.

un<u>able</u>   ~~chair~~   sadness   battery   endanger

bread   recreate   joyful   unlucky   fantastic

WRITING ACTIVITY

The type of narrator an author uses makes a big difference in how readers experience a story.

DIRECTIONS: Retell any 25 lines from *The Cask of Amontillado* using a third-person narrator. A third-person narrator is not one of the characters in the story, such as the narrator for "The Interlopers." Try to create a similar atmosphere, or feeling, to the one Poe used. As you write, think about why Poe might have chosen to use a first-person narrator. Do you think the atmosphere is easier or harder to recreate with a third-person narrator?

Collection

4

Symbolism and Irony

© Images.com/Corbis

Literary and Academic Vocabulary for Collection 4

imply (IHM PLY) *v.:* suggest; hint at.

Did the writer mean to imply that love is always doomed?

associate (UH SOH SHEE AYT) *v.:* mentally make a link.

I associate budding trees with the idea of warmth and promise.

literal (LIHT UHR UHL) *adj.:* based on the actual words in their ordinary meaning.

To find out the moral of a fairytale, sometimes you have to look beyond the literal meaning.

symbolic (SIHM BAH LIHK) *adj.:* serving as a symbol.

In the story, the boy's bike is symbolic of his wish to explore other lands.

symbol (SIHM BUHL) *n.:* an ordinary object, event, person, or animal that is used to represent something else.

The roses are a symbol of his love.

allegory (A LUH GAWR EE) *n.:* a story in which the characters, setting, and action stand for something beyond themselves.

The novel Animal Farm, *in which the animals represent different political philosophies, is a well-known allegory.*

irony (AHY RUH NEE) *n.:* the difference between what we expect and what actually happens.

The irony of the situation was that he stole the money she had already planned to give him.

ambiguity (AM BIH GYOO UH TEE) *n.:* uncertainty; ability to be understood more than one way.

The story's end is full of ambiguity; the reader is never entirely sure what happened to the characters.

The Scarlet Ibis

by James Hurst

LITERARY FOCUS: SYMBOLS AND THEME

A **symbol** is a person, a place, a thing, or an event that stands both for itself and for something beyond itself. In literature, symbols add deeper meaning to a work. Sometimes a symbol is associated with a particular character. For example, in "The Scarlet Ibis," you'll notice similarities between one character and an exotic bird. A symbolic connection such as this can deepen your understanding of a story and its characters.

Writers use **theme** to share their ideas on a subject. A theme is the central idea within a work of literature, and it is not usually stated directly. It is up to the reader to think about a story's symbols and other elements to make an educated guess about its theme.

READING FOCUS: ANALYZING DETAILS

In most stories you will encounter **details** about characters, plot, and setting. Some details may seem irrelevant at first, but they can develop more meaning later in the story. As you read "The Scarlet Ibis," keep track of small details—like colors, seasons, or the weather—and think about what deeper meanings they may hint at. One example is provided below.

Detail: "summer was dead but autumn had not yet been born"

Deeper meaning: Nature is mirroring the characters. The author could be talking about life and death.

SKILLS FOCUS

Literary Skills
Recognize symbols to determine a story's theme.

Reading Skills
Analyze details to find deeper meaning.

Vocabulary Development

The Scarlet Ibis

SELECTION VOCABULARY

imminent (IHM IH NEHNT) *adj.:* near; about to happen.
>   *When thunder boomed and the sky darkened, they could tell the storm was imminent.*

iridescent (IHR IH DEH SEHNT) *adj.:* rainbowlike; displaying a shifting range of colors.
>   *The bird's wings glowed with iridescent color.*

infallibility (IHN FAL UH BIHL IH TEE) *n.:* inability to make a mistake.
>   *Because of his belief in his infallibility, the narrator never doubted the success of his project.*

reiterated (REE IHT UH RAY TEHD) *v.:* repeated.
>   *Several times, the narrator reiterated his desire to teach Doodle to swim.*

mar (MAHR) *v.:* damage; spoil.
>   *The storm could mar the cotton and other crops.*

WORD STUDY

Directions: Match the vocabulary words in the first column with the best synonyms, or words with similar meaning, from the second column.

_____ **1.** imminent   **a.** ruin

_____ **2.** iridescent   **b.** perfection

_____ **3.** infallibility   **c.** unavoidable

_____ **4.** mar   **d.** colorful

THE SCARLET IBIS

by James Hurst

> **BACKGROUND**
> The following story is set in the American South during the early 1900s toward the end of World War I. Note the references to the battles being fought far from this peaceful Southern setting.

"The Scarlet Ibis" by James R. Hurst from *The Atlantic Monthly*, July 1960. Copyright © 1960 by **James R. Hurst**. Reproduced by permission of the author.

It was in the clove of seasons, summer was dead but autumn had not yet been born, that the ibis lit in the bleeding tree. **A** The flower garden was stained with rotting brown magnolia petals, and ironweeds grew rank[1] amid the purple phlox. The five o'clocks by the chimney still marked time, but the oriole nest in the elm was untenanted and rocked back and forth like an empty cradle. The last graveyard flowers were blooming, and their smell drifted across the cotton field and through every room of our house, speaking softly the names of our dead.

10   It's strange that all this is still so clear to me, now that that summer has long since fled and time has had its way. A grindstone stands where the bleeding tree stood, just outside the kitchen door, and now if an oriole sings in the elm, its song seems to die up in the leaves, a silvery dust. The flower garden is prim, the house a gleaming white, and the pale fence across the yard stands straight and spruce. But sometimes (like right now), as I sit in the cool, green-draped parlor, the grindstone begins to turn, and time with all its changes is ground away—and I remember Doodle.

20   Doodle was just about the craziest brother a boy ever had. Of course, he wasn't a crazy crazy like old Miss Leedie, who was in love with President Wilson and wrote him a letter every day, but was a nice crazy, like someone you meet in your dreams. He

---

1. rank (RANGK): thick and wild. *Rank* can also mean "smelly."

was born when I was six and was, from the outset, a disappointment. He seemed all head, with a tiny body which was red and shriveled like an old man's. Everybody thought he was going to die—everybody except Aunt Nicey, who had delivered him. She said he would live because he was born in a caul[2] and cauls were made from Jesus' nightgown. Daddy had Mr. Heath, the carpenter, build a little mahogany coffin for him. But he didn't die, and when he was three months old, Mama and Daddy decided they might as well name him. They named him William Armstrong, which was like tying a big tail on a small kite. Such a name sounds good only on a tombstone. **B**

I thought myself pretty smart at many things, like holding my breath, running, jumping, or climbing the vines in Old Woman Swamp, and I wanted more than anything else someone to race to Horsehead Landing, someone to box with, and someone to perch with in the top fork of the great pine behind the barn, where across the fields and swamps you could see the sea. I wanted a brother. **C** But Mama, crying, told me that even if William Armstrong lived, he would never do these things with

---

2. **caul** (KAWL): membrane (thin, skinlike material) that sometimes covers a baby's head at birth.

© James Randklev/Photographer's Choice/Getty Images

B VOCABULARY

Word Study

A *compound word* is a word made up of two or more words. *Tombstone,* made up of the words *tomb* and *stone,* means "a stone marker on a tomb or grave." Circle another compound word in this paragraph. Write down what you think it means, then look up the word in a dictionary to check your answer.

_____

_____

_____

C QUICK CHECK

In your own words, what does the narrator want?

_____

_____

_____

_____

_____

_____

_____

_____

_____

Academic Vocabulary

What does the description in this sentence *imply*, or suggest, about Doodle?

_____

_____

_____

_____

_____

me. He might not, she sobbed, even be "all there." He might, as long as he lived, lie on the rubber sheet in the center of the bed in the front bedroom where the white marquisette[3] curtains billowed out in the afternoon sea breeze, rustling like palmetto fronds.[4]

It was bad enough having an invalid brother, but having one who possibly was not all there was unbearable, so I began to 50 make plans to kill him by smothering him with a pillow.

However, one afternoon as I watched him, my head poked between the iron posts of the foot of the bed, he looked straight at me and grinned. I skipped through the rooms, down the echoing halls, shouting, "Mama, he smiled. He's all there! He's all there!" and he was. **A**

When he was two, if you laid him on his stomach, he began to try to move himself, straining terribly. The doctor said that with his weak heart this strain would probably kill him, but it didn't. Trembling, he'd push himself up, turning first red, then 60 a soft purple, and finally collapse back onto the bed like an old worn-out doll. **B** I can still see Mama watching him, her hand pressed tight across her mouth, her eyes wide and unblinking. But he learned to crawl (it was his third winter), and we brought him out of the front bedroom, putting him on the rug before the fireplace. For the first time he became one of us.

As long as he lay all the time in bed, we called him William Armstrong, even though it was formal and sounded as if we were referring to one of our ancestors, but with his creeping around on the deerskin rug and beginning to talk, something had to 70 be done about his name. It was I who renamed him. When he crawled, he crawled backward, as if he were in reverse and couldn't change gears. If you called him, he'd turn around as if he were going in the other direction, then he'd back right up to you to be picked up. Crawling backward made him look like a doodlebug[5] so I began to call him Doodle, and in time even

---

3. **marquisette** (MAHR KUH ZEHT): a thin, netlike fabric.
4. **palmetto fronds:** fanlike leaves of a palm tree.
5. **doodlebug** (DOO DUHL BUG): larva of a type of insect that moves backward.

Mama and Daddy thought it was a better name than William Armstrong. Only Aunt Nicey disagreed. She said caul babies should be treated with special respect since they might turn out to be saints. **C** Renaming my brother was perhaps the kindest

80 thing I ever did for him, because nobody expects much from someone called Doodle.

Although Doodle learned to crawl, he showed no signs of walking, but he wasn't idle. He talked so much that we all quit listening to what he said. It was about this time that Daddy built him a go-cart, and I had to pull him around. At first I just paraded him up and down the piazza,[6] but then he started crying to be taken out into the yard and it ended up by my having to lug him wherever I went. If I so much as picked up my cap, he'd start crying to go with me, and Mama would call from wherever she

90 was, "Take Doodle with you."

He was a burden in many ways. The doctor had said that he mustn't get too excited, too hot, too cold, or too tired and that he must always be treated gently. A long list of don'ts went with him, all of which I ignored once we got out of the house. To discourage his coming with me, I'd run with him across the ends of the cotton rows and careen him around corners on two wheels. Sometimes I accidentally turned him over, but he never told Mama. His skin was very sensitive, and he had to wear a big straw hat whenever he went out. When the going got rough and

100 he had to cling to the sides of the go-cart, the hat slipped all the way down over his ears. He was a sight. **D** Finally, I could see I was licked. Doodle was my brother, and he was going to cling to me forever, no matter what I did, so I dragged him across the burning cotton field to share with him the only beauty I knew, Old Woman Swamp. I pulled the go-cart through the sawtooth fern, down into the green dimness where the palmetto fronds whispered by the stream. I lifted him out and set him down in the soft rubber grass beside a tall pine. His eyes were round with

---

6. **piazza** (PEE AHT SUH): large covered porch.

C QUICK CHECK

Why doesn't Aunt Nicey like Doodle's nickname?

_____

_____

_____

_____

D READING FOCUS

Analyze **details** in this paragraph. In your own words, describe the narrator and his brother as they might look to an observer.

_____

_____

_____

_____

_____

_____

_____

A QUICK CHECK

Re-read lines 108–112, and underline the details that help you learn Doodle's character traits.

B LITERARY ANALYSIS

What is the narrator saying about the relationship between love and cruelty?

_____

_____

_____

_____

_____

_____

wonder as he gazed about him, and his little hands began to
stroke the rubber grass. Then he began to cry.

"For heaven's sake, what's the matter?" I asked, annoyed.

"It's so pretty," he said. "So pretty, pretty, pretty." **A**

After that day Doodle and I often went down into Old
Woman Swamp. I would gather wildflowers, wild violets,
honeysuckle, yellow jasmine, snakeflowers, and waterlilies, and
with wire grass we'd weave them into necklaces and crowns.
We'd bedeck ourselves with our handiwork and loll about thus
beautified, beyond the touch of the everyday world. Then when
the slanted rays of the sun burned orange in the tops of the
pines, we'd drop our jewels into the stream and watch them float
away toward the sea.

There is within me (and with sadness I have watched it
in others) a knot of cruelty borne by the stream of love, much
as our blood sometimes bears the seed of our destruction, and
at times I was mean to Doodle. **B** One day I took him up to
the barn loft and showed him his casket, telling him how we
all had believed he would die. It was covered with a film of Paris
green[7] sprinkled to kill the rats, and screech owls had built a nest
inside it.

Doodle studied the mahogany box for a long time, then
said, "It's not mine."

"It is," I said. "And before I'll help you down from the loft,
you're going to have to touch it."

"I won't touch it," he said sullenly.

"Then I'll leave you here by yourself," I threatened, and
made as if I were going down.

Doodle was frightened of being left. "Don't go leave me,
Brother," he cried, and he leaned toward the coffin. His hand,
trembling, reached out, and when he touched the casket, he
screamed. A screech owl flapped out of the box into our faces,
scaring us and covering us with Paris green. Doodle was para-
lyzed, so I put him on my shoulder and carried him down the

---

7. **Paris green** _n._: poisonous green powder used to kill insects.

ladder, and even when we were outside in the bright sunshine, he clung to me, crying, "Don't leave me. Don't leave me." **C**

When Doodle was five years old, I was embarrassed at having a brother of that age who couldn't walk, so I set out to teach him.

We were down in Old Woman Swamp and it was spring and the sick-sweet smell of bay flowers hung everywhere like a
150   mournful song. "I'm going to teach you to walk, Doodle," I said.

He was sitting comfortably on the soft grass, leaning back against the pine. "Why?" he asked.

I hadn't expected such an answer. "So I won't have to haul you around all the time."

"I can't walk, Brother," he said.

"Who says so?" I demanded.

"Mama, the doctor—everybody."

"Oh, you can walk," I said, and I took him by the arms and stood him up. He collapsed onto the grass like a half-empty flour
160   sack. It was as if he had no bones in his little legs. **D**

"Don't hurt me, Brother," he warned.

"Shut up. I'm not going to hurt you. I'm going to teach you to walk." I heaved him up again, and again he collapsed.

This time he did not lift his face up out of the rubber grass. "I just can't do it. Let's make honeysuckle wreaths."

"Oh yes you can, Doodle," I said. "All you got to do is try. Now come on," and I hauled him up once more.

It seemed so hopeless from the beginning that it's a miracle I didn't give up. But all of us must have something or someone
170   to be proud of, and Doodle had become mine. I did not know then that pride is a wonderful, terrible thing, a seed that bears two vines, life and death. **E** Every day that summer we went to the pine beside the stream of Old Woman Swamp, and I put him on his feet at least a hundred times each afternoon. Occasionally I too became discouraged because it didn't seem as if he was trying, and I would say, "Doodle, don't you want to learn to walk?"

He'd nod his head, and I'd say, "Well, if you don't keep trying, you'll never learn." Then I'd paint for him a picture of us

---

C LITERARY ANALYSIS

Why do you think the narrator shows Doodle the coffin? What might this event foreshadow, or tell us about the future?

_____

_____

_____

_____

D LITERARY ANALYSIS

What is the narrator saying about Doodle?

_____

_____

_____

_____

E QUICK CHECK

In your own words, what is the narrator saying about pride?

_____

_____

_____

_____

_____

A LITERARY FOCUS

Why do you think the narrator uses a cardinal as a **symbol** for hope?

_____

_____

_____

_____

_____

B VOCABULARY

Selection Vocabulary

The word *imminent* means "near" or "about to happen." What happened to make success seem imminent rather than unreachable?

_____

_____

_____

_____

_____

as old men, white-haired, him with a long white beard and me

180   still pulling him around in the go-cart. This never failed to make him try again.

Finally, one day, after many weeks of practicing, he stood alone for a few seconds. When he fell, I grabbed him in my arms and hugged him, our laughter pealing through the swamp like a ringing bell. Now we knew it could be done. Hope no longer hid in the dark palmetto thicket but perched like a cardinal in the lacy toothbrush tree, brilliantly visible. **A** "Yes, yes," I cried, and he cried it too, and the grass beneath us was soft and the smell of the swamp was sweet.

190   With success so imminent, we decided not to tell anyone until he could actually walk. **B** Each day, barring rain, we sneaked into Old Woman Swamp, and by cotton-picking time Doodle was ready to show what he could do. He still wasn't able to walk far, but we could wait no longer. Keeping a nice secret is very hard to do, like holding your breath. We chose to reveal all on October eighth, Doodle's sixth birthday, and for weeks ahead we mooned around the house, promising everybody a most spectacular surprise. Aunt Nicey said that, after so much talk, if we produced anything less tremendous than the Resurrection,[8]

200   she was going to be disappointed.

At breakfast on our chosen day, when Mama, Daddy, and Aunt Nicey were in the dining room, I brought Doodle to the door in the go-cart just as usual and had them turn their backs, making them cross their hearts and hope to die if they peeked. I helped Doodle up, and when he was standing alone I let them look. There wasn't a sound as Doodle walked slowly across the room and sat down at his place at the table. Then Mama began to cry and ran over to him, hugging him and kissing him. Daddy hugged him too, so I went to Aunt Nicey, who was thanks-pray-

210   ing in the doorway, and began to waltz her around. We danced together quite well until she came down on my big toe with her brogans,[9] hurting me so badly I thought I was crippled for life.

8. **Resurrection:** reference to the Christian belief that Jesus rose from the dead after his burial.
9. **brogans** (BROH GUHNZ): heavy, ankle-high shoes.

Doodle told them it was I who had taught him to walk, so everyone wanted to hug me, and I began to cry.

"What are you crying for?" asked Daddy, but I couldn't answer. They did not know that I did it for myself; that pride, whose slave I was, spoke to me louder than all their voices; and that Doodle walked only because I was ashamed of having a crippled brother. **C**

220 Within a few months Doodle had learned to walk well and his go-cart was put up in the barn loft (it's still there) beside his little mahogany coffin. Now, when we roamed off together, resting often, we never turned back until our destination had been reached, and to help pass the time, we took up lying. From the beginning Doodle was a terrible liar, and he got me in the habit. Had anyone stopped to listen to us, we would have been sent off to Dix Hill. **D**

My lies were scary, involved, and usually pointless, but Doodle's were twice as crazy. People in his stories all had wings 230 and flew wherever they wanted to go. His favorite lie was about a boy named Peter who had a pet peacock with a ten-foot tail. Peter wore a golden robe that glittered so brightly that when he walked through the sunflowers they turned away from the sun to face him. When Peter was ready to go to sleep, the peacock spread his magnificent tail, enfolding the boy gently like a closing go-to-sleep flower, burying him in the gloriously iridescent, rustling vortex.[10] Yes, I must admit it. Doodle could beat me lying.

Doodle and I spent lots of time thinking about our future. 240 We decided that when we were grown, we'd live in Old Woman Swamp and pick dog's-tongue[11] for a living. Beside the stream, he planned, we'd build us a house of whispering leaves and the swamp birds would be our chickens. All day long (when we weren't gathering dog's-tongue) we'd swing through the cypresses on the rope vines, and if it rained we'd huddle beneath an

---

10. **vortex** (VAWR TEHKS): something resembling a whirlpool.
11. **dog's-tongue**: wild vanilla plant.

C QUICK CHECK

Is the narrator describing pride as something wonderful or something terrible? Explain.

_____

_____

_____

_____

D LITERARY ANALYSIS

Dix Hill is a state mental hospital in Raleigh, North Carolina. What does the narrator mean by this statement?

_____

_____

_____

_____

The word *infallibility* means "inability to make a mistake" or "absolute trustworthiness." It comes from the Latin word *fallere*, meaning "to deceive." How are the two definitions related?

_____

_____

_____

_____

_____

_____

B LITERARY ANALYSIS

Do you think the narrator's "development program" is a good idea? Explain.

_____

_____

_____

_____

_____

_____

_____

_____

_____

umbrella tree and play stickfrog. Mama and Daddy could come and live with us if they wanted to. He even came up with the idea that he could marry Mama and I could marry Daddy. Of course, I was old enough to know this wouldn't work out, but the picture
250 he painted was so beautiful and serene that all I could do was whisper yes, yes.

Once I had succeeded in teaching Doodle to walk, I began to believe in my own infallibility and I prepared a terrific development program for him, unknown to Mama and Daddy, of course. **A** I would teach him to run, to swim, to climb trees, and to fight. He, too, now believed in my infallibility, so we set the deadline for these accomplishments less than a year away, when, it had been decided, Doodle could start to school.

That winter we didn't make much progress, for I was in
260 school and Doodle suffered from one bad cold after another. But when spring came, rich and warm, we raised our sights again. **B** Success lay at the end of summer like a pot of gold, and our campaign got off to a good start. On hot days, Doodle and I went down to Horsehead Landing, and I gave him swimming lessons or showed him how to row a boat. Sometimes we descended into the cool greenness of Old Woman Swamp and climbed the rope vines or boxed scientifically beneath the pine where he had learned to walk. Promise hung about us like leaves, and wherever we looked, ferns unfurled and birds broke
270 into song.

That summer, the summer of 1918, was blighted.[12] In May and June there was no rain and the crops withered, curled up, then died under the thirsty sun. One morning in July a hurricane came out of the east, tipping over the oaks in the yard and splitting the limbs of the elm trees. That afternoon it roared back out of the west, blew the fallen oaks around, snapping their roots and tearing them out of the earth like a hawk at the entrails[13]

---

12. **blighted** (BLY TIHD): suffering from conditions that destroy or prevent growth.
13. **entrails** (EHN TRAYLZ): inner organs; guts.

of a chicken. Cotton bolls were wrenched from the stalks and lay like green walnuts in the valleys between the rows, while the

280 cornfield leaned over uniformly so that the tassels touched the ground. Doodle and I followed Daddy out into the cotton field, where he stood, shoulders sagging, surveying the ruin. When his chin sank down onto his chest, we were frightened, and Doodle slipped his hand into mine. Suddenly Daddy straightened his shoulders, raised a giant knuckly fist, and with a voice that seemed to rumble out of the earth itself began cursing heaven, hell, the weather, and the Republican party.[14] Doodle and I, prodding each other and giggling, went back to the house, knowing that everything would be all right. **C**

290 And during that summer, strange names were heard through the house: Château-Thierry, Amiens, Soissons, and in her blessing at the supper table, Mama once said, "And bless the Pearsons, whose boy Joe was lost in Belleau Wood."[15]

So we came to that clove of seasons. School was only a few weeks away, and Doodle was far behind schedule. He could barely clear the ground when climbing up the rope vines, and his swimming was certainly not passable. We decided to double our efforts, to make that last drive and reach our pot of gold. I made him swim until he turned blue and row until he couldn't

300 lift an oar. Wherever we went, I purposely walked fast, and although he kept up, his face turned red and his eyes became glazed. Once, he could go no further, so he collapsed on the ground and began to cry. **D**

"Aw, come on, Doodle," I urged. "You can do it. Do you want to be different from everybody else when you start school?"

"Does it make any difference?"

"It certainly does," I said. "Now, come on," and I helped him up.

---

14. **Republican party**: At this time, most southern farmers were loyal Democrats.
15. **Château-Thierry** (SHAH TOH TEE ER EE), **Amiens** (AH MEE AN), **Soissons** (SWAH SOHN), **Belleau** (BEH LOH) **Wood**: World War I battle sites in France.

C LITERARY FOCUS

If the blighted summer, including the violent hurricane, is a **symbol** of what is to come, what might lie in Doodle's future?

_____

_____

_____

D READING FOCUS

Underline the **details** in this paragraph that suggest Doodle is becoming increasingly ill and weak. Based on these details, what do you predict will happen to Doodle?

_____

_____

_____

_____

A QUICK CHECK

In your own words, explain what the narrator means in this sentence.

_____

_____

_____

_____

B VOCABULARY

Selection Vocabulary

The word *reiterated* means "repeated." Why does Doodle repeat himself?

_____

_____

_____

_____

As we slipped through the dog days,[16] Doodle began to look feverish, and Mama felt his forehead, asking him if he felt ill. At night he didn't sleep well, and sometimes he had nightmares, crying out until I touched him and said, "Wake up, Doodle. Wake up."

It was Saturday noon, just a few days before school was to start. I should have already admitted defeat, but my pride wouldn't let me. The excitement of our program had now been gone for weeks, but still we kept on with a tired doggedness. It was too late to turn back, for we had both wandered too far into a net of expectations and had left no crumbs behind. **A**

Daddy, Mama, Doodle, and I were seated at the dining-room table having lunch. It was a hot day, with all the windows and doors open in case a breeze should come. In the kitchen Aunt Nicey was humming softly. After a long silence, Daddy spoke. "It's so calm, I wouldn't be surprised if we had a storm this afternoon."

"I haven't heard a rain frog," said Mama, who believed in signs, as she served the bread around the table.

"I did," declared Doodle. "Down in the swamp."

"He didn't," I said contrarily.

"You did, eh?" said Daddy, ignoring my denial.

"I certainly did," Doodle reiterated, scowling at me over the top of his iced-tea glass, and we were quiet again. **B**

Suddenly, from out in the yard came a strange croaking noise. Doodle stopped eating, with a piece of bread poised ready for his mouth, his eyes popped round like two blue buttons. "What's that?" he whispered.

I jumped up, knocking over my chair, and had reached the door when Mama called, "Pick up the chair, sit down again, and say excuse me."

By the time I had done this, Doodle had excused himself and had slipped out into the yard. He was looking up into the bleeding tree. "It's a great big red bird!" he called.

---

16. **dog days** *n.:* hot days in July and August, named after the Dog Star (Sirius), which rises and sets with the sun during this period.

© age fotostock/SuperStock

C **LITERARY FOCUS**

Re-read lines 340–351. In what ways is the bird a **symbol** of Doodle?

_____

_____

_____

_____

_____

_____

The bird croaked loudly again, and Mama and Daddy came out into the yard. We shaded our eyes with our hands against the hazy glare of the sun and peered up through the still leaves. On the topmost branch a bird the size of a chicken, with scarlet feathers and long legs, was perched precariously. Its wings hung down loosely, and as we watched, a feather dropped away and floated slowly down through the green leaves.

350   "It's not even frightened of us," Mama said.

"It looks tired," Daddy added. "Or maybe sick." **C**

Doodle's hands were clasped at his throat, and I had never seen him stand still so long. "What is it?" he asked.

Daddy shook his head. "I don't know, maybe it's—"

At that moment the bird began to flutter, but the wings were uncoordinated, and amid much flapping and a spray of flying feathers, it tumbled down, bumping through the limbs of the bleeding tree and landing at our feet with a thud. Its long, grace-ful neck jerked twice into an S, then straightened out, and the

360   bird was still. A white veil came over the eyes, and the long white beak unhinged. Its legs were crossed and its clawlike feet were delicately curved at rest. Even death did not mar its grace, for it lay on the earth like a broken vase of red flowers, and we stood around it, awed by its exotic beauty.

"It's dead," Mama said.

"What is it?" Doodle repeated.

A LITERARY ANALYSIS

Why is Doodle so fascinated by the scarlet ibis? Why does he take such pains to bury it?

_____

_____

_____

_____

_____

_____

_____

"Go bring me the bird book," said Daddy.

I ran into the house and brought back the bird book. As we watched, Daddy thumbed through its pages. "It's a scarlet ibis," he said, pointing to a picture. "It lives in the tropics—South America to Florida. A storm must have brought it here."

Sadly, we all looked back at the bird. A scarlet ibis! How many miles it had traveled to die like this, in our yard, beneath the bleeding tree.

"Let's finish lunch," Mama said, nudging us back toward the dining room.

"I'm not hungry," said Doodle, and he knelt down beside the ibis.

"We've got peach cobbler for dessert," Mama tempted from the doorway.

Doodle remained kneeling. "I'm going to bury him."

"Don't you dare touch him," Mama warned. "There's no telling what disease he might have had."

"All right," said Doodle. "I won't."

Daddy, Mama, and I went back to the dining-room table, but we watched Doodle through the open door. He took out a piece of string from his pocket and, without touching the ibis, looped one end around its neck. Slowly, while singing softly "Shall We Gather at the River," he carried the bird around to the front yard and dug a hole in the flower garden, next to the petunia bed. Now we were watching him through the front window, but he didn't know it. His awkwardness at digging the hole with a shovel whose handle was twice as long as he was made us laugh, and we covered our mouths with our hands so he wouldn't hear. **A**

When Doodle came into the dining room, he found us seriously eating our cobbler. He was pale and lingered just inside the screen door. "Did you get the scarlet ibis buried?" asked Daddy.

Doodle didn't speak but nodded his head.

"Go wash your hands, and then you can have some peach cobbler," said Mama.

"I'm not hungry," he said.

"Dead birds is bad luck," said Aunt Nicey, poking her head from the kitchen door. "Specially *red* dead birds!"

As soon as I had finished eating, Doodle and I hurried off to Horsehead Landing. Time was short, and Doodle still had a long way to go if he was going to keep up with the other boys when he started school. The sun, gilded with the yellow cast of autumn, still burned fiercely, but the dark green woods through which
410   we passed were shady and cool. When we reached the landing, Doodle said he was too tired to swim, so we got into a skiff and floated down the creek with the tide. Far off in the marsh a rail was scolding, and over on the beach locusts were singing in the myrtle trees. Doodle did not speak and kept his head turned away, letting one hand trail limply in the water.

After we had drifted a long way, I put the oars in place and made Doodle row back against the tide. Black clouds began to gather in the southwest, and he kept watching them, trying to pull the oars a little faster. When we reached Horsehead Landing,
420   lightning was playing across half the sky and thunder roared out, hiding even the sound of the sea. The sun disappeared and darkness descended, almost like night. Flocks of marsh crows flew by, heading inland to their roosting trees, and two egrets, squawking, arose from the oyster-rock shallows and careened away. **B**

Doodle was both tired and frightened, and when he stepped from the skiff he collapsed onto the mud, sending an armada[17] of fiddler crabs rustling off into the marsh grass. I helped him up, and as he wiped the mud off his trousers, he smiled at me ashamedly. He had failed and we both knew it, so we started back
430   home, racing the storm. We never spoke (what are the words that can solder[18] cracked pride?), but I knew he was watching me, watching for a sign of mercy. The lightning was near now, and from fear he walked so close behind me he kept stepping on my heels. The faster I walked, the faster he walked, so I began to run.

---

17. **armada** (AHR MAH DUH): group. *Armada* is generally used to mean "fleet, or group, of warships."
18. **solder** (SAHD UHR): patch or repair. Solder is a mixture of metals melted and used to repair metal parts.

B   **READING FOCUS**

Circle the **details** in this paragraph describing the approaching storm. What do you think the storm fore-shadows, or tells us about the future?

_____

_____

_____

_____

The Scarlet Ibis   **143**

Portrait of David by John, Augustus Edwin (1878–1961)
© Christie's Images/The Bridgeman Art Library International

The rain was coming, roaring through the pines, and then, like a bursting Roman candle, a gum tree ahead of us was shattered by a bolt of lightning. When the deafening peal of thunder had died, and in the moment before the rain arrived, I heard Doodle, who had fallen behind, cry out, "Brother, Brother, don't leave me! Don't leave me!" **A**

440

The knowledge that Doodle's and my plans had come to naught was bitter, and that streak of cruelty within me awakened. I ran as fast as I could, leaving him far behind with a wall of rain dividing us. The drops stung my face like nettles, and the wind flared the wet, glistening leaves of the bordering trees. Soon I could hear his voice no more. **B**

I hadn't run too far before I became tired, and the flood of childish spite evanesced[19] as well. I stopped and waited for Doodle. The sound of rain was everywhere, but the wind had died and it fell straight down in parallel paths like ropes hanging

450

---

19. **evanesced** (EH VUH NEHST): faded away; disappeared.

from the sky. As I waited, I peered through the downpour, but no one came. Finally I went back and found him huddled beneath a red nightshade bush beside the road. He was sitting on the ground, his face buried in his arms, which were resting on his drawn-up knees. "Let's go, Doodle," I said.

He didn't answer, so I placed my hand on his forehead and lifted his head. Limply, he fell backward onto the earth. He had been bleeding from the mouth, and his neck and the front of his shirt were stained a brilliant red.

460 "Doodle! Doodle!" I cried, shaking him, but there was no answer but the ropy rain. He lay very awkwardly, with his head thrown far back, making his vermilion[20] neck appear unusually long and slim. His little legs, bent sharply at the knees, had never before seemed so fragile, so thin.

I began to weep, and the tear-blurred vision in red before me looked very familiar. "Doodle!" I screamed above the pounding storm, and threw my body to the earth above his. For a long, long time, it seemed forever, I lay there crying, sheltering my fallen scarlet ibis from the heresy[21] of rain. **C D**

C READING FOCUS

What do the **details** in the description of Doodle in the last two paragraphs remind you of? Why do you think the writer makes this association?

_____

_____

_____

_____

D LITERARY FOCUS

What is the **theme** of this story?

_____

_____

_____

_____

_____

_____

_____

_____

_____

_____

_____

---

20. **vermilion** (VUHR MIHL YUHN): bright red.
21. **heresy** (HEHR EH SEE): here, mockery. *Heresy* generally means "denial of what is commonly believed to be true" or "rejection of an accepted religious teaching."

Skills Practice

The Scarlet Ibis

USE A TABLE

DIRECTIONS: In "The Scarlet Ibis," some of the people, places, things, and events stand for things beyond themselves. Complete the table below by identifying the **symbols** and their meanings in the selected passages. The first one has been done for you.

Story Passage	Symbol	Meaning
That winter we didn't make much progress, for I was in school and Doodle suffered one bad cold after another. But when spring came, rich and warm, we raised our sights again (lines 259–261).	spring	new start; rebirth
When Peter was ready to go to sleep, the peacock spread his magnificent tail, enfolding the boy gently like a closing go-to-sleep flower, burying him in the gloriously iridescent, rustling vortex (lines 234–237).	1.	2.
Sadly, we all looked back at the bird. A scarlet ibis! How many miles it had traveled to die like this, in our yard, beneath the bleeding tree (lines 372–374).	3.	4.

Applying Your Skills

The Scarlet Ibis

VOCABULARY DEVELOPMENT

DIRECTIONS: Write vocabulary words from the Word Box on the correct blanks to complete the sentences. Some words will not be used.

Word Box

imminent

iridescent

infallibility

reiterated

mar

As the sky darkened, the storm seemed (1) _____.

Our parents (2) _____ their instructions to stay inside.

I still wanted to play outside with Doodle, but I decided to go inside rather

than resist, which could possibly (3) _____ their opinion

of me.

LITERARY FOCUS: SYMBOL AND THEME

DIRECTIONS: Use the table you made on the previous page along with other **symbols** and details from the story to help you state the theme on the lines below.

_____

_____

_____

_____

_____

READING FOCUS: ANALYZING DETAILS

DIRECTIONS: Draw a chart like the one below onto another sheet of paper. In it, list **details** from the story that describe Doodle and the scarlet ibis. Then, explain any similarities between the two.

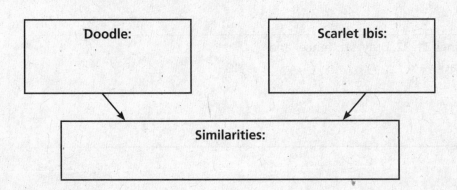

Literary Skills
Understand how symbols add deeper meaning to a story.

Reading Skills
Analyze story details.

Preparing to Read

The Gift of the Magi

by O. Henry

LITERARY FOCUS: SITUATIONAL IRONY

Sometimes the ending of a story turns out to be very different from what we had expected. Outcomes that are different from our expectations are examples of **situational irony**.

Use the skill   As you read "The Gift of the Magi," think about what Della and Jim were *expecting* to happen—and what *really* happens. In what way is the ending an example of **situational irony**?

READING FOCUS: ANALYZING DETAILS

Skilled writers write more interesting descriptions by using **details** to bring characters to life. For instance, instead of just saying that Della has nice hair, O. Henry writes: "Della's beautiful hair fell about her rippling and shining like a cascade of brown waters." While you read, consider the following questions when you encounter details:

- What do these details tell me about the characters?
- What could these details foreshadow, or hint, about what's coming in the story?

Track details   As you read, keep track of details and why they are important in a chart like the one below.

Details	Importance
Lines 1–7 and 32–40: saved pennies	shows how hard it is for Della to save money
Lines 31–32: gray cat, fence, and back yard	

SKILLS FOCUS

Literary Skills
Understand situational irony and the surprise ending.

Reading Skills
Analyze details.

Vocabulary Development

The Gift of the Magi

SELECTION VOCABULARY

agile (AJ UHL) *adj.:* moving with ease.
> *The dancer's movements were graceful and agile, like a cat's.*

prudence (PROO DUHNS) *n.:* caution; good judgment.
> *Della had tried to show prudence by saving money for months.*

scrutiny (SKROO TUH NEE) *n.:* close inspection.
> *Careful scrutiny of the jacket showed many worn spots.*

coveted (KUV IH TIHD) *v.:* used as *adj.:* longed for; desired.
> *Della's wishes were granted when she received the coveted gift.*

ardent (AHR DUHNT) *adj.:* passionate; extremely enthusiastic.
> *Della and Jim's love for each other is ardent.*

WORD STUDY

DIRECTIONS: Changing the ending of a word can change its part of speech and its meaning. The new word often has a meaning similar to the meaning of the original word. Look at the chart. All of the vocabulary words have been changed. Complete the chart by determining the words' parts of speech (noun, verb, adjective, adverb) and new definitions. If necessary, use a dictionary.

Altered Vocabulary Word	Part of Speech	Definition
agility	1.	2.
scrutinize	3.	4.
covetous	5.	6.
ardently	7.	8.

THE GIFT OF THE MAGI

by O. Henry

Man in a Flying Jacket, 1916, Philpot, Glyn Warren (1884–1937)/Private Collection/Bridgeman Art Gallery

> **BACKGROUND**
>
> The Magi referred to in the title of this story are the three "wise men" who, according to the Bible (Matthew 2:1–13), brought gifts to the infant Jesus. This story, first published in 1906, takes place in a time when people were paid much less than today, and things cost much less.

A **LITERARY ANALYSIS**

Why does Della flop down on the couch and howl?

_____

_____

_____

_____

B **VOCABULARY**

Word Study

The word *beggar* is usually used as a noun that means "a penniless person." Here it is used as a verb meaning "make useless." Why might the author have chosen to use this word?

_____

_____

_____

One dollar and eighty-seven cents. That was all. And sixty cents of it was in pennies. Pennies saved one and two at a time by bulldozing the grocer and the vegetable man and the butcher until one's cheeks burned with the silent imputation of parsimony[1] that such close dealing implied. Three times Della counted it. One dollar and eighty-seven cents. And the next day would be Christmas.

There was clearly nothing to do but flop down on the shabby little couch and howl. So Della did it. Which instigates the moral

10 reflection that life is made up of sobs, sniffles, and smiles, with sniffles predominating. **A**

While the mistress of the home is gradually subsiding from the first stage to the second, take a look at the home. A furnished flat[2] at $8 per week. It did not exactly beggar description, but it certainly had that word on the lookout for the mendicancy squad.[3] **B**

In the vestibule[4] below was a letter box into which no letter would go, and an electric button from which no mortal

---

1. **imputation** (IHM PYOO TAY SHUHN) of **parsimony** (PAHR SUH MOH NEE): suggestion of stinginess.
2. **flat** *n.:* apartment.
3. **mendicancy** (MEN DIH KUHN SEE) **squad:** police who arrested beggars and homeless people.
4. **vestibule** (VEHS TUH BYOOL) *n.:* small entrance hall.

finger could coax a ring. Also appertaining[5] thereunto was a card

20 bearing the name "Mr. James Dillingham Young."

The "Dillingham" had been flung to the breeze during a
former period of prosperity when its possessor was being paid
$30 per week. Now, when the income was shrunk to $20, the
letters of "Dillingham" looked blurred, as though they were
thinking seriously of contracting to a modest and unassuming
D. But whenever Mr. James Dillingham Young came home and
reached his flat above, he was called Jim and greatly hugged by
Mrs. James Dillingham Young, already introduced to you as
Della. Which is all very good. **C**

30 Della finished her cry and attended to her cheeks with the
powder rag. She stood by the window and looked out dully at
a gray cat walking a gray fence in a gray back yard. Tomorrow
would be Christmas Day and she had only $1.87 with which to
buy Jim a present. She had been saving every penny she could
for months, with this result. Twenty dollars a week doesn't go
far. Expenses had been greater than she had calculated. They
always are. Only $1.87 to buy a present for Jim. Her Jim. Many a
happy hour she had spent planning for something nice for him.
Something fine and rare and sterling—something just a little bit

40 near to being worthy of the honor of being owned by Jim. **D**

There was a pier glass[6] between the windows of the room.
Perhaps you have seen a pier glass in an $8 flat. A very thin and
very agile person may, by observing his reflection in a rapid
sequence of longitudinal strips, obtain a fairly accurate conception
of his looks. Della, being slender, had mastered the art. **E F**

Suddenly she whirled from the window and stood before
the glass. Her eyes were shining brilliantly, but her face had lost
its color within twenty seconds. Rapidly she pulled down her hair
and let it fall to its full length.

50 Now, there were two possessions of the James Dillingham
Youngs in which they both took a mighty pride. One was Jim's
gold watch that had been his father's and his grandfather's. The

---

5. **appertaining** (AP EHR TAYN ING) *v.* used as *adj.:* belonging.
6. **pier glass** *n.:* tall mirror hung between two windows.

C READING FOCUS

By **analyzing details** in this paragraph, what can you say about Jim and Della's relationship?

_____

_____

_____

_____

D QUICK CHECK

Why does Della want more money?

_____

_____

_____

E VOCABULARY

Selection Vocabulary
The word *agile* means "moving with ease." Underline words in this paragraph that may hint that Della is agile.

F LANGUAGE COACH

Now that you know what *agile* means, write a definition for the noun *agility*. Check your answer against a dictionary definition.

_____

_____

This paragraph names the two possessions that make Jim and Della proudest. Circle the word that names Jim's possession. Underline the word that names Della's. Why are the two items so important to the couple?

_____

_____

_____

_____

_____

_____

B **VOCABULARY**

Academic Vocabulary

Della's hair is *symbolic*, or representative, of her womanhood. Of what is Jim's watch *symbolic*? Why?

_____

_____

_____

_____

_____

_____

_____

other was Della's hair. Had the Queen of Sheba lived in the flat across the air shaft, Della would have let her hair hang out the window some day to dry just to depreciate Her Majesty's jewels and gifts. Had King Solomon been the janitor, with all his treasures piled up in the basement, Jim would have pulled out his watch every time he passed, just to see him pluck at his beard from envy. A B

60   So now Della's beautiful hair fell about her rippling and shining like a cascade of brown waters. It reached below her knee and made itself almost a garment for her. And then she did it up again nervously and quickly. Once she faltered for a minute and stood still while a tear or two splashed on the worn red carpet.

On went her old brown jacket; on went her old brown hat. With a whirl of skirts and with the brilliant sparkle still in her eyes, she fluttered out the door and down the stairs to the street.

Where she stopped, the sign read: "Mme. Sofronie. Hair
70   Goods of All Kinds." One flight up Della ran, and collected herself, panting. Madame, large, too white, chilly, hardly looked the "Sofronie."

"Will you buy my hair?" asked Della.

"I buy hair," said Madame. "Take yer hat off and let's have a sight at the looks of it."

Down rippled the brown cascade.

"Twenty dollars," said Madame, lifting the mass with a practiced hand.

"Give it to me quick," said Della.

80   Oh, and the next two hours tripped by on rosy wings. Forget the hashed metaphor. She was ransacking the stores for Jim's present.

She found it at last. It surely had been made for Jim and no one else. There was no other like it in any of the stores, and she had turned all of them inside out. It was a platinum fob chain,[7] simple and chaste in design, properly proclaiming its value by

---

7. **fob chain:** short chain meant to be attached to a pocket watch.

substance alone and not by meretricious[8] ornamentation—as all good things should do. It was even worthy of The Watch. As soon as she saw it she knew that it must be Jim's. It was like him. **C** Quietness and value—the description applied to both. Twenty-one dollars they took from her for it, and she hurried home with the 87 cents. With that chain on his watch, Jim might be properly anxious about the time in any company. Grand as the watch was, he sometimes looked at it on the sly on account of the old leather strap that he used in place of a chain.

When Della reached home, her intoxication gave way a little to prudence and reason. She got out her curling irons and lighted the gas and went to work repairing the ravages[9] made by generosity added to love. Which is always a tremendous task, dear friends—a mammoth task.

Within forty minutes her head was covered with tiny, close-lying curls that made her look wonderfully like a truant schoolboy. **D** She looked at her reflection in the mirror long, carefully, and critically.

"If Jim doesn't kill me," she said to herself, "before he takes a second look at me, he'll say I look like a Coney Island chorus girl. But what could I do—oh! what could I do with a dollar and eighty-seven cents?" **E**

At 7 o'clock the coffee was made and the frying pan was on the back of the stove hot and ready to cook the chops.

Jim was never late. Della doubled the fob chain in her hand and sat on the corner of the table near the door that he always entered. Then she heard his step on the stair away down on the first flight, and she turned white for just a moment. She had a habit of saying little silent prayers about the simplest everyday things, and now she whispered: "Please God, make him think I am still pretty."

The door opened and Jim stepped in and closed it. He looked thin and very serious. Poor fellow, he was only twenty-

---

8. **meretricious** (MEHR IH TRIHSH UHS) *adj.*: attractive in a cheap, flashy way.
9. **ravages** (RAV IHJ EHZ) *n.*: terrible damage.

C (QUICK CHECK)

Circle the item that Della buys for Jim.

D (VOCABULARY)

Selection Vocabulary

The word *prudence* means "good judgment." How does Della exercise prudence here?

_____

_____

_____

E (LITERARY ANALYSIS)

What reaction does Della think Jim will have to her short hair?

_____

_____

_____

_____

_____

_____

_____

A VOCABULARY

Academic Vocabulary

What is the author trying to *imply*, or suggest, about what Jim is feeling?

_____

_____

_____

_____

_____

120 two—and to be burdened with a family! He needed a new overcoat and he was without gloves.

Jim stepped inside the door, as immovable as a setter at the scent of quail. His eyes were fixed upon Della, and there was an expression in them that she could not read, and it terrified her. It was not anger, nor surprise, nor disapproval, nor horror, nor any of the sentiments that she had been prepared for. He simply stared at her fixedly with that peculiar expression on his face.

Della wriggled off the table and went for him.

"Jim, darling," she cried, "don't look at me that way. I had

130 my hair cut off and sold it because I couldn't have lived through Christmas without giving you a present. It'll grow out again—you won't mind, will you? I just had to do it. My hair grows awfully fast. Say 'Merry Christmas!' Jim, and let's be happy. You don't know what a nice—what a beautiful, nice gift I've got for you."

"You've cut off your hair?" asked Jim, laboriously, as if he had not arrived at that patent fact yet even after the hardest mental labor.

"Cut it off and sold it," said Della. "Don't you like me just

140 as well, anyhow? I'm me without my hair, ain't I?"

Jim looked about the room curiously.

"You say your hair is gone?" he said, with an air almost of idiocy. A

"You needn't look for it," said Della. "It's sold, I tell you—sold and gone, too. It's Christmas Eve, boy. Be good to me, for it went for you. Maybe the hairs on my head were numbered," she went on with a sudden serious sweetness, "but nobody could ever count my love for you. Shall I put the chops on, Jim?"

Out of his trance Jim seemed quickly to wake. He enfolded

150 his Della. For ten seconds let us regard with discreet scrutiny some inconsequential object in the other direction. Eight dollars a week or a million a year—what is the difference? A mathematician or a wit would give you the wrong answer. The Magi brought valuable gifts, but that was not among them. This dark assertion will be illuminated later on.

The Present, 1845 (oil on canvas) 49 x 42 cm. © Harris Museum and Art Gallery, Preston, Lancashire, UK/Bridgeman Art Library

B LITERARY ANALYSIS

What do you think might be in the package?

_____

_____

_____

_____

C QUICK CHECK

Circle what Jim has bought for Della.

Jim drew a package from his overcoat pocket and threw it upon the table.

"Don't make any mistake, Dell," he said, "about me. I don't think there's anything in the way of a haircut or a shave or a
160 shampoo that could make me like my girl any less. But if you'll unwrap that package, you may see why you had me going awhile at first." **B**

White fingers and nimble tore at the string and paper. And then an ecstatic scream of joy; and then, alas! a quick feminine change to hysterical tears and wails, necessitating the immediate employment of all the comforting powers of the lord of the flat.

For there lay The Combs—the set of combs, side and back, that Della had worshiped for long in a Broadway window. **C** Beautiful combs, pure tortoise shell, with jeweled rims—just
170 the shade to wear in the beautiful vanished hair. They were

LITERARY FOCUS

Situational irony occurs when an event is the *opposite* of what you expected or of what would be appropriate. How does Jim's gift to Della create **situational irony**?

_____

_____

_____

_____

B **VOCABULARY**

Selection Vocabulary

The word *coveted* comes from the Latin word *cupidus*, meaning "desirous." Knowing this, what do you think *coveted* means?

_____

_____

_____

_____

C **LITERARY FOCUS**

Describe the **situational irony** you find in this paragraph.

_____

_____

_____

_____

_____

expensive combs, she knew, and her heart had simply craved and yearned over them without the least hope of possession. And now, they were hers, but the tresses that should have adorned the coveted adornments were gone. **A** **B**

But she hugged them to her bosom, and at length she was able to look up with dim eyes and a smile and say: "My hair grows so fast, Jim!"

And then Della leaped up like a little singed cat and cried, "Oh, oh!"

180 Jim had not yet seen his beautiful present. She held it out to him eagerly upon her open palm. The dull precious metal seemed to flash with a reflection of her bright and ardent spirit.

"Isn't it a dandy, Jim? I hunted all over town to find it. You'll have to look at the time a hundred times a day now. Give me your watch. I want to see how it looks on it."

Instead of obeying, Jim tumbled down on the couch and put his hands under the back of his head and smiled.

"Dell," said he, "let's put our Christmas presents away and keep 'em a while. They're too nice to use just at present. I sold 190 the watch to get the money to buy your combs. And now suppose you put the chops on." **C**

The Magi, as you know, were wise men—wonderfully wise men—who brought gifts to the Babe in the manger. They invented the art of giving Christmas presents. Being wise, their gifts were no doubt wise ones, possibly bearing the privilege of exchange in case of duplication. And here I have lamely related to you the uneventful chronicle of two foolish children in a flat who most unwisely sacrificed for each other the greatest treasures of their house. But in a last word to the 200 wise of these days, let it be said that of all who give gifts, these two were the wisest. Of all who give and receive gifts, such as they are wisest. Everywhere they are wisest. They are the Magi.

© Andrew Sadler/Alamy

Applying Your Skills

The Gift of the Magi

VOCABULARY DEVELOPMENT

DIRECTIONS: Write vocabulary words from the Word Box on the correct blanks to complete the paragraph. Not all words will be used.

Word Box

agile

prudence

scrutiny

coveted

ardent

To avoid (1) _____, Della wore a hat in public to hide her short haircut. She was (2) _____ about getting Jim a Christmas present, so she did what she had to. After the haircut, running her (3) _____ fingers through her hair was just not the same anymore. She still couldn't believe Jim had sold his (4) _____ watch.

LITERARY FOCUS: SITUATIONAL IRONY

DIRECTIONS: Fill in the chart below to understand the story's **situational irony**.

What Della Sells:	What Jim Sells:
1.	2.
What Della Buys:	**What Jim Buys:**
3.	4.
Why Della Buys It:	**Why Jim Buys It:**
5.	6.
What Della Receives:	**What Jim Receives:**
7.	8.
Situational Irony/Why the Gift is Useless:	**Situational Irony/Why the Gift is Useless:**
9.	10.

READING FOCUS: ANALYZING DETAILS

DIRECTIONS: Details enrich stories by bringing characters, settings, and events to life. Review the story and underline or highlight details that provide important information about the characters' lives. Discuss with a partner how this information makes the characters more interesting.

SKILLS FOCUS

Literary Skills
Understand situational irony in a story.

Reading Skills
Analyze details of what an author is *showing*, rather than *telling*.

Three Readings by Albert Einstein

INFORMATIONAL TEXT FOCUS: SYNTHESIZING SOURCES—WORKS BY ONE AUTHOR

As you read the following three primary sources written by Albert Einstein, do the following:

- **Paraphrase** (restate in your own words) the ideas you read.

- **Analyze** the sources by **comparing** and **contrasting** them. Does the author express different opinions in different sources? What is the author's **purpose** in writing each source? Who is the **audience**?

- **Relate** the ideas you read with things you have already learned about the author and his or her topic.

- **Synthesize** the sources by thinking about them as a group. What have you learned about the author's opinions?

SELECTION VOCABULARY

eradicate (IH RAD UH KAYT) *v.:* eliminate completely; get rid of.
 Einstein would like to eradicate some of humanity's worst traits.

phenomenon (FUH NAHM UH NAHN) *n.:* extraordinary thing or occurrence.
 Einstein learned of a new science phenomenon unlike any other.

conceivable (KUHN SEE VUH BUHL) *adj.:* capable of being imagined or understood.
 Einstein thought new ideas could make a new technology conceivable.

radical (RAD UH KUHL) *adj.:* extreme; thorough.
 A ban on war is Einstein's radical solution.

WORD STUDY

DIRECTIONS: Match the vocabulary words in the left column with their synonyms from the right column.

_____ 1. conceivable   **a.** destroy

_____ 2. eradicate   **b.** imaginable

_____ 3. phenomenon   **c.** wonder

_____ 4. radical   **d.** revolutionary

SKILLS FOCUS

Informational Text Skills
Synthesize multiple sources by the same author.

WEAPONS OF THE SPIRIT

by Albert Einstein

from an interview with George Sylvester Viereck

from *Einstein on Peace*

> **BACKGROUND**
> Albert Einstein (1879–1955) is considered one of the most important scientists of all time. Born and raised in Germany, Einstein studied physics, the science of matter and energy. Einstein, who was Jewish, escaped from Nazi Germany in 1933, and settled in the United States. Einstein was a pacifist who strongly opposed war.

It may not be possible in one generation to eradicate the combative instinct.[1] It is not even desirable to eradicate it entirely. Men should continue to fight, but they should fight for things worthwhile, not for imaginary geographical lines, racial prejudices, and private greed draped in the colors of patriotism. Their arms should be weapons of the spirit, not shrapnel[2] and tanks. **A**

Think of what a world we could build if the power unleashed in war were applied to constructive tasks! One tenth of the energy that the various belligerents[3] spent in the World War, a fraction of the money they exploded in hand grenades and poison gas, would suffice to raise the standard of living in every country and avert the economic catastrophe of worldwide unemployment. **B**

---

1. **combative instinct**: Einstein views the tendency of human beings to fight with one another as an inborn trait.
2. **shrapnel** (SHRAP NUHL): in this case, shells that explode, releasing many small metal balls. Shrapnel more often describes the fragments, or pieces, from an exploded bomb, mine, or similar weapon.
3. **belligerents** (BUH LIHJ UHR UHNTS): persons engaged in fighting one another.

From "Einstein's interview with George Sylvester Viereck" from *Einstein on Peace*, edited by Otto Nathan and Heinz Norden. Copyright © 1960 by Otto Nathan. Reproduced by permission of **The Albert Einstein Archives, the Hebrew University Of Jerusalem, Israel.**

A **QUICK CHECK**

According to Einstein, there are good and bad reasons to fight. What reasons do you think he might have considered worthwhile?

_____

_____

_____

B **READING FOCUS**

In the second paragraph, Einstein explains what could be done with the money spent on war. Briefly **paraphrase** that idea.

_____

_____

_____

We must be prepared to make the same heroic sacrifices for
the cause of peace that we make ungrudgingly for the cause of
war. **A** There is no task that is more important or closer to my
heart.

Nothing that I can do or say will change the structure of the
20 universe. But maybe, by raising my voice, I can help the greatest
of all causes—goodwill among men and peace on earth. **B**

—1931

© Popperfoto/Alamy

LETTER TO PRESIDENT ROOSEVELT

by Albert Einstein

BACKGROUND
Although Einstein was a pacifist, he was concerned about Germany's work on an atomic bomb during World War II. Scientists persuaded Einstein to sign a letter addressed to the President of the United States that urged the U.S. to move ahead with a nuclear weapons program.

Old Grove Rd.

Nassau Point

Peconic, Long Island

August 2nd, 1939

F. D. Roosevelt,

President of the United States,

White House

Washington, D.C.

Sir:

Some recent work by E. Fermi and L. Szilard, which has been communicated to me in manuscript, leads me to expect that the element uranium may be turned into a new and important source of energy in the immediate future. Certain aspects of the situation which has arisen seem to call for watchfulness and, if necessary, quick action on the part of the Administration. **C**

I believe therefore that it is my duty to bring to your attention the following facts and recommendations:

C LITERARY ANALYSIS

At the time this letter was written, scientists in the United States and Europe were attempting to create a nuclear chain reaction that would release a huge amount of energy. This reaction could be used to create powerful bombs. Based on what you have read so far, how would you expect Einstein to feel about this?

_____

_____

_____

_____

_____

"Letter to President Roosevelt" from *Dr. Einstein's Warning to President Roosevelt* by Albert Einstein. Copyright © 1939 by Albert Einstein. Reproduced by permission of **The Albert Einstein Archives, the Hebrew University Of Jerusalem, Israel.**

The word *conceivable* means "capable of being imagined or understood." Use the word in a sentence of your own.

_____

_____

_____

_____

_____

B ⟨ QUICK CHECK ⟩

What is Einstein suggesting President Roosevelt should do in this paragraph?

_____

_____

_____

_____

_____

10   In the course of the last four months it has been made probable—through the work of Joliot in France as well as Fermi and Szilard in America—that it may become possible to set up a nuclear chain reaction in a large mass of uranium, by which vast amounts of power and large quantities of new radium-like elements would be generated. Now it appears almost certain that this could be achieved in the immediate future.

      This new phenomenon would also lead to the construction of bombs, and it is conceivable—though much less certain— that extremely powerful bombs of a new type may thus be
20 constructed. **A** A single bomb of this type, carried by boat and exploded in a port, might very well destroy the whole port together with some of the surrounding territory. However, such bombs might very well prove to be too heavy for transportation by air.

      The United States has only very poor ores of uranium in moderate quantities. There is some good ore in Canada and the former Czechoslovakia while the most important source of uranium is Belgian Congo.

      In view of this situation you may think it desirable to have
30 some permanent contact maintained between the Administration and the group of physicists working on chain reactions in America. One possible way of achieving this might be for you to entrust with this task a person who has your confidence and who could perhaps serve in an inofficial capacity. **B** His task might comprise the following:

      a) to approach Government Departments, keep them informed of the further development, and put forward recommendations for Government action giving particular attention to the problem of securing a supply of uranium ore for
40 the United States;

      b) to speed up the experimental work, which is at present being carried on within the limits of the budgets of University laboratories, by providing funds, if such funds be required, through his contacts with private persons who are willing to make contributions for this cause, and perhaps also by obtaining the co-operation of industrial laboratories which have the necessary equipment. **C**

I understand that Germany has actually stopped the sale of uranium from the Czechoslovakian mines which she has taken
50 over. That she should have taken such early action might perhaps be understood on the ground that the son of the German Under-Secretary of State, von Weizsäcker, is attached to the Kaiser-Wilhelm-Institut in Berlin where some of the American work on uranium is now being repeated.

Yours very truly,

A. Einstein

(Albert Einstein) **D**

C READING FOCUS

Einstein is advising President Roosevelt to create a plan for the development of a nuclear weapon. **Compare** and **contrast** the ideas Einstein expresses here with his opinion in "Weapons of the Spirit."

_____

_____

_____

_____

_____

D READING FOCUS

Einstein's **audience** for this letter is the President of the United States. Would the advice contained in these paragraphs be appropriate for any other person? Why or why not?

_____

_____

_____

_____

ON THE ABOLITION OF THE THREAT OF WAR

by Albert Einstein, from the magazine *Ideas and Opinions*

My part in producing the atomic bomb consisted in a single act: I signed a letter to President Roosevelt, pressing the need for experiments on a large scale in order to explore the possibilities for the production of an atomic bomb.

I was fully aware of the terrible danger to mankind in case this attempt succeeded. But the likelihood that the Germans were working on the same problem with a chance of succeeding forced me to this step. I could do nothing else although I have always been a convinced pacifist. To my mind, to kill in war is not a whit better than to commit ordinary murder. **A**

As long, however, as the nations are not resolved to abolish[1] war through common actions and to solve their conflicts and protect their interests by peaceful decisions on a legal basis, they feel compelled to prepare for war. They feel obliged to prepare all possible means, even the most detestable ones, so as not to be left behind in the general armament race.[2] This road necessarily leads to war, a war which under the present conditions means universal destruction.

Under these circumstances the fight against *means* has no chance of success. **B** Only the radical abolition of wars and of the threat of war can help. This is what one has to work for. One has to be resolved not to let himself be forced to actions that run counter to this goal. This is a severe demand on an individual who is conscious[3] of his dependence on society. But it is not an impossible demand.

---

1. **abolish** (UH BAHL IHSH): put an end to. *Abolition* is the noun form of this word, meaning "the ending."
2. **armament race:** rivalry between hostile nations to build up larger and larger stores of weapons.
3. **conscious** (KAHN SHUHS): aware.

Gandhi,[4] the greatest political genius of our time, has pointed the way. He has shown of what sacrifices people are capable once they have found the right way. His work for the liberation of India is a living testimony[5] to the fact that a will governed by firm conviction is stronger than a seemingly invincible material power.[6]

—1952

4. **Ghandi** (GAHN DEE): Mohandas Gandhi (1869–1948) led the struggle for India's independence from Britain. He practiced the use of nonviolent protest to achieve political goals.
5. **testimony** (TEHS TUH MOH NEE): evidence; proof.
6. **invincible material power:** here, an undefeatable nation.

© Corbis

In this paragraph, Einstein holds up Mohandas Gandhi, a man who led a movement of nonviolent protest, as a role model. Why does he choose to use Gandhi instead of someone else?

_____

_____

_____

_____

_____

_____

Three Readings by Albert Einstein

USE A TABLE

DIRECTIONS: Fill in the following table to help deepen your understanding of these three texts. Write who you think the intended audience is for each selection, and write the main idea of each selection.

	Genre	Intended Audience	Main Idea
Weapons of the Spirit	Interview		
Letter to President Roosevelt	Letter		
On the Abolition of the Threat of War	Magazine Article		

Applying Your Skills

Three Readings by Albert Einstein

VOCABULARY DEVELOPMENT

DIRECTIONS: Write the vocabulary words from the Word Box on the correct blanks to complete the paragraph. One word will not be used.

Word Box

eradicate

phenomenon

conceivable

radical

Albert Einstein was an important scientist who understood that the (1) _____ of a nuclear chain reaction could be used to create an incredibly powerful bomb. He was a pacifist who hoped that people would be able to (2) _____ the threat of war. He knew that it was (3) _____ that Nazi Germany would be the first to develop nuclear weapons.

INFORMATIONAL TEXT FOCUS: SYNTHESIZING SOURCES

DIRECTIONS: Answer the following questions about the selections to help you **synthesize sources**.

1. If you read only the "Letter to President Roosevelt," what would you think was Einstein's opinion of war? _____
_____

2. If you read only "Weapons of the Spirit" and "On the Abolition of the Threat of War," what would you think was Einstein's opinion of war?
_____
_____

3. What did you learn in "On the Abolition of the Threat of War" that helped you to understand Einstein's reasons for writing the "Letter to President Roosevelt"? _____
_____

4. How did reading these three passages together deepen your understanding of Einstein's views on war? _____
_____
_____

Informational Text Skills
Synthesize multiple sources by the same author.

Skills Review

Collection 4

VOCABULARY REVIEW

DIRECTIONS: Read the sentences below and write the correct vocabulary word from the Word Box in the blank. Some words will not be used.

Word Box

agile

ardent

associate

conceivable

coveted

eradicate

imminent

imply

infallibility

iridescent

literal

mar

phenomenon

prudence

radical

scrutiny

symbolic

1. From the first time I saw it, I _____ her gorgeous new dress.

2. In the movie, darkness is _____ of fear.

3. Then, he thought long and hard about the possible interpretations of each object to help him figure out the paragraph's _____ meaning.

4. She was a careful person, and very good at managing her money, so she was always known for her _____.

5. She has an _____ love for her boyfriend.

6. The little boy had always believed in his mother's _____, so he was shocked the first time he saw her make a mistake.

7. I would like to _____ ants from my apartment.

8. As I watched her jump from stone to stone, I was impressed by how _____ she was.

9. The smell of fresh pizza from the kitchen told us that dinner was _____.

10. She stared at me for a long time, and I was embarrassed by the careful _____.

Skills Review

Collection 4

LANGUAGE COACH

DIRECTIONS: *Beautifully* is a **word derivation** of *beautiful*; the part of speech and the meaning of the word *beautiful* change when the *–ly* ending is added, but the words are still related. Each of the words listed below is related to one of this collection's vocabulary words, found in the Word Box on the previous page. For each word below, write which vocabulary word it is most like. Then, use your knowledge of that word to guess the definition of the new word. Write your definition and use a dictionary to check your answer. Some of the words in the word box will be not used.

1. agility (n.) _____

2. scrutinize (v.) _____

3. phenomenal (adj.) _____

4. covetous (adj.) _____

5. prudent (adj.) _____

6. association (n.) _____

7. implication (n.) _____

8. infallible (adj.) _____

9. iridescence (n.) _____

10. inconceivable (adj.) _____

ORAL LANGUAGE ACTIVITY

DIRECTIONS: Look back at the three readings by Albert Einstein. Take turns with a partner interviewing each other about the three selections. Each partner should ask three or four questions drawn from the selections. Here are some sample questions you can use, but feel free to make up your own:

- Do you agree with Einstein's views on war? Why or why not?

- Do you think Einstein was right to go against his own beliefs and encourage President Roosevelt to develop the nuclear bomb?

- Do you think Einstein's goal of eradication of the threat of war is possible?

Collection

5

Form and Style

View on the Mississippi River by Ferdinand Reichardt, 1857
© Minnesota Historical Society/Corbis

Literary and Academic Vocabulary for Collection 5

establish (EHS TAB LIHSH) *v.:* to set up; create.

The author used his childhood memories to help establish the plot.

attitude (AT UH TOOD) *n.:* a way of thinking or feeling; outlook.

She has a good attitude about her education; she is always trying to learn more.

implied (IHM PLYD) *adj.:* understood without being formally expressed; indirect.

Throughout the story, there is an implied sense of regret.

appeal (UH PEEL) *v.:* to be attractive, pleasing, interesting, or enjoyable.

She chose a variety of images to appeal to different senses.

diction (DIHK SHUN) *n.:* word choice.

Much of a writer's style is revealed through his or her diction.

mood (MOOHD) *n.:* emotional attitude of a story.

The mood of the horror story was dark and threatening.

imagery (IH MUHJ REE) *n.:* words or phrases that appeal to one or more of our senses.

The story is full of vivid imagery describing the look and smell of the garden.

Cub Pilot on the Mississippi

by Mark Twain

LITERARY FOCUS: STYLE AND TONE

Mark Twain's writing **style**, or way of using language, is unusual and fun. His **diction**, or word choice, is an important part of this style. The words are simple and direct, and are often playful or sarcastic. Twain's writing is full of striking (and often funny) images. Through his use of language, Twain creates a distinctive **tone**, or attitude about a subject. Think about what the following Twain quote tells you about his style:

> "I never write 'metropolis' for seven cents, because I can get the same money for 'city.' I never write 'policeman' because I can get the same price for 'cop.'"

READING FOCUS: READING ALOUD AND PARAPHRASING

To understand and appreciate a writer's style and tone, try the following:

1. **Read aloud** a passage to "hear" the writer's voice. Listen for the author's word choices, and how they affect the tone.

2. **Paraphrase** the passage, or retell it in your own words, to figure out the meaning. Then, compare your paraphrase with the original text. Look for ways in which the style or tone has changed in your translation.

Use the Skill   Read aloud and paraphrase the following passages from "Cub Pilot on the Mississippi":

> "The figure that comes before me oftenest, out of the shadows of that vanished time, is that of Brown. . . whose memory was so good and tiresome. He was a middle-aged, long, slim, bony, smooth-shaven, horse-faced, ignorant, stingy, malicious, snarling, fault hunting, mote-magnifying tyrant."

> "There was silence for ten minutes; then my new boss turned and inspected me deliberately and painstakingly from head to heel for about—as it seemed to me—a quarter of an hour."

SKILLS FOCUS

Literary Skills
Understand style, diction, and tone.

Reading Skills
Read aloud and paraphrase a text.

Vocabulary Development

Cub Pilot on the Mississippi

SELECTION VOCABULARY

transient (TRAN SHUHNT) *adj.*: quickly passing; fleeting.

   Twain's wish to join the circus was transient, lasting just a few months.

judicious (JOO DIHSH UHS) *adj.*: showing good judgment; wise.

   Twain knew it would be judicious to keep quiet; otherwise, he would make his boss mad.

inoffensive (IHN UH FEHN SIHV) *adj.*: harmless; not objectionable in any way.

   Henry was so completely inoffensive that he seemed unable to be rude or angry.

indulgent (IHN DUHL JUHNT) *adj.*: giving in to someone else's wishes; permissive.

   The indulgent captain put up with minor mistakes and never punished the cubs for them.

confronted (KUHN FRUHNT IHD) *n.*: came face to face with someone; challenged.

   After a serious mistake, the captain confronted Twain.

WORD STUDY

DIRECTIONS: Match the vocabulary words in the left-hand column with the people they describe in the right-hand column.

_____ indulgent	**a.** someone who quietly sits in the corner and doesn't bother anyone
_____ inoffensive	**b.** a student who studies hard for a test she knows will be difficult
_____ judicious	**c.** a father who gives his daughter everything she asks for

CUB PILOT ON THE MISSISSIPPI

By Mark Twain

> ### BACKGROUND
> In the 1800s (when this story was written), paddle wheel steamboats carried cargo and passengers up and down the Mississippi River. Steamboat pilots had to know the river well because boats could be damaged by going in shallow water. When Mark Twain was 22 he got a job as an assistant, or cub pilot, on a steamboat. In this selection from his book *Life on the Mississippi*, Twain writes about his early days on a steamboat.

A VOCABULARY

Selection Vocabulary
The adjective *transient* means "quickly passing; fleeting." *Transient* can also be used as a noun, meaning "someone who passes through a place with only a short stay." Use the noun *transient* in a sentence.

_____

_____

_____

_____

B LITERARY FOCUS

What is the **tone** so far?

_____

_____

_____

When I was a boy, there was but one permanent ambition among my comrades in our village on the west bank of the Mississippi River. That was, to be a steamboatman. We had transient ambitions of other sorts, but they were only transient. **A** When a circus came and went, it left us all burning to become clowns; the first minstrel show that came to our section left us all suffering to try that kind of life; now and then we had a hope that if we lived and were good, God would permit us to be pirates. These ambitions faded out, each in its turn; but the ambition to be a steamboatman always remained.

I first wanted to be a cabin-boy, so that I could come out with a white apron on and shake a tablecloth over the side, where all my old comrades could see me; later I thought I would rather be the deckhand who stood on the end of the stage-plank with the coil of rope in his hand, because he was particularly conspicuous. **B**

Boy after boy managed to get on the river. The minister's son became an engineer. The doctor's and the post-master's sons became "mud clerks";[1] the wholesale liquor dealer's son became

---

1. **mud clerks**: the lowest of several clerks who assisted the financial officer.

20 a barkeeper on a boat; four sons of the chief merchant, and two sons of the county judge, became pilots. Pilot was the grandest position of all. The pilot, even in those days of trivial wages, had a princely salary—from a hundred and fifty to two hundred and fifty dollars a month, and no board to pay. Two months of his wages would pay a preacher's salary for a year. Now some of us were left disconsolate. We could not get on the river—at least our parents would not let us.

So by and by I ran away. I said I never would come home again till I was a pilot and could come in glory.

30 During the two or two and a half years of my apprenticeship, I served under many pilots, and had experience of many kinds of steamboatmen and many varieties of steamboats. I am to this day profiting somewhat by that experience; for in that brief, sharp schooling, I got personally and familiarly acquainted with about all the different types of human nature that are to be found in fiction, biography, or history. **C**

The figure that comes before me oftenest, out of the shadows of that vanished time, is that of Brown, of the steamer "Pennsylvania"—the man referred to in a former chapter, whose

© Mary Evans Picture Library/Alamy

C READING FOCUS

Paraphrase this paragraph. How is your version different from Twain's? Is it more or less formal?

_____
_____
_____
_____
_____
_____
_____
_____
_____
_____
_____
_____
_____
_____
_____
_____
_____
_____
_____
_____
_____
_____

A LITERARY FOCUS

This sentence is a good example of Twain's **style**. What is the effect of the string of adjectives used to describe Brown?

_____

_____

_____

B VOCABULARY

Academic Vocabulary

Attitude is a feeling with regard to a person or thing. Based on this paragraph, what is Twain's attitude toward Brown?

_____

_____

_____

_____

C LITERARY FOCUS

Part of Twain's **style** is that he often suggests an incorrect reason for an event. Do you think that Brown actually forgot Twain's name? Why else might he not have called Twain by his name?

_____

_____

_____

_____

40 memory was so good and tiresome. He was a middle-aged, long, slim, bony, smooth-shaven, horse-faced, ignorant, stingy, malicious, snarling, fault hunting, mote-magnifying tyrant. **A** I early got the habit of coming on watch with dread at my heart. No matter how good a time I might have been having with the off-watch below, and no matter how high my spirits might be when I started aloft, my soul became lead in my body the moment I approached the pilot-house. **B**

I still remember the first time I ever entered the presence of that man. The boat had backed out from St. Louis and was

50 executive family of so fast and famous a boat. Brown was at the wheel. I paused in the middle of the room, all fixed to make my bow, but Brown did not look around. I thought he took a furtive glance at me out of the corner of his eye, but as not even this notice was repeated, I judged I had been mistaken. By this time he was picking his way among some dangerous "breaks" abreast the woodyards; therefore it would not be proper to interrupt him; so I stepped softly to the high bench and took a seat.

There was silence for ten minutes; then my new boss turned and inspected me deliberately and painstakingly from

60 head to heel for about—as it seemed to me—a quarter of an hour. After which he removed his countenance[2] and I saw it no more for some seconds; then it came around once more, and this question greeted me—

"Are you Horace Bixby's[3] cub?"

"Yes, sir."

After this there was a pause and another inspection. Then—

"What's your name?"

I told him. He repeated it after me. It was probably the

70 only thing he ever forgot; for although I was with him many months he never addressed himself to me in any other way than "Here!" and then his command followed. **C**

---

2. **countenance**: face.
3. **Horace Bixby**: Twain met steamboat pilot Horace Bixby in 1857. When Bixby agreed to take him on as an apprentice, Twain happily quit his job writing comic letters for a local newspaper.

"Where was you born?"

"In Florida, Missouri."

A pause. Then—

"Dern sight better staid there!"

By means of a dozen or so of pretty direct questions, he pumped my family history out of me.

The leads[4] were going now, in the first crossing. **D** This interrupted the inquest.

It must have been all of fifteen minutes—fifteen minutes of dull, homesick silence—before that long horse-face swung round upon me again—and then, what a change! It was as red as fire, and every muscle in it was working. Now came this shriek—

"Here!—You going to set there all day?"

I lit in the middle of the floor, shot there by the electric suddenness of the surprise. As soon as I could get my voice I said, apologetically:—"I have had no orders, sir."

"You've had no ORDERS! My, what a fine bird we are! We must have ORDERS! Our father was a GENTLEMAN— owned slaves—and we've been to SCHOOL. Yes, WE are a gentleman, TOO, and got to have ORDERS! ORDERS, is it? ORDERS is what you want! Dod dern my skin, I'LL learn you to swell yourself up and blow around here about your dod-derned ORDERS! G'way from the wheel! (I had approached it without knowing it.) **E** **F**

I moved back a step or two, and stood as in a dream, all my senses stupefied by this frantic assault.

"What you standing there for? Take that ice-pitcher down to the texas-tender![5] Come, move along, and don't you be all day about it!"

The moment I got back to the pilot-house, Brown said—

"Here! What was you doing down there all this time?"

"I couldn't find the texas-tender; I had to go all the way to the pantry."

---

4. **leads** (LEHDZ): weights lowered to test the depth of the river.
5. **texas tender**: a tray in the officer's quarters. The rooms on Mississippi steamboats were named after states. Since the officer's area was the largest, it was named after Texas, the largest state at the time.

D (LANGUAGE COACH)

Leads is an example of **jargon**, specialized vocabulary used in specific jobs, interests, or areas of study, such as piloting, computers, or psychology. Often, jargon uses words that have a different definition than what is normally used by most people. Write *leads* and at least three other examples of jargon in this story on the lines below.

_____

_____

_____

E (READING FOCUS)

Read aloud this paragraph. What impact does the use of capital letters create?

_____

_____

_____

F (LITERARY ANALYSIS)

Throughout the story, Brown's dialogue is written in non-standard English. What effect does this have on your understanding of his character?

_____

_____

_____

A **READING FOCUS**

Paraphrase lines 118 through 127. What does this humorous situation tell you about Twain's time with Brown?

_____

_____

_____

_____

_____

_____

_____

_____

_____

_____

_____

"Derned likely story! Fill up the stove."

I proceeded to do so. He watched me like a cat. Presently he shouted—

"Put down that shovel? Deadest numskull I ever saw—

110 ain't even got sense enough to load up a stove.

All through the watch this sort of thing went on. Yes, and the subsequent watches were much like it, during a stretch of months. As I have said, I soon got the habit of coming on duty with dread. The moment I was in the presence, even in the darkest night, I could feel those yellow eyes upon me, and knew their owner was watching for a pretext to spit out some venom on me. Preliminarily he would say—

"Here! Take the wheel."

Two minutes later—

120 "WHERE in the nation you going to? Pull her down! pull her down!"

After another moment—

"Say! You going to hold her all day? Let her go—meet her! meet her!"

Then he would jump from the bench, snatch the wheel from me, and meet her himself, pouring out wrath upon me all the time. A

George Ritchie was the other pilot's cub. He was having good times now; for his boss, George Ealer, was as kindhearted

130 as Brown wasn't. Ritchie had steeled for Brown the season before; consequently he knew exactly how to entertain himself and plague me, all by the one operation. Whenever I took the wheel for a moment on Ealer's watch, Ritchie would sit back on the bench and play Brown, with continual ejaculations of "Snatch her! snatch her! Derndest mud-cat I ever saw!" "Here! Where you going NOW? Going to run over that snag?" "Pull her DOWN! Don't you hear me? Pull her DOWN!" "There she goes! JUST as I expected! I TOLD you not to cramp that reef! G'way from the wheel!" B

140 So I always had a rough time of it, no matter whose watch it was; and sometimes it seemed to me that Ritchie's good-natured

badgering was pretty nearly as aggravating as Brown's dead-earnest nagging.

I often wanted to kill Brown, but this would not answer. A cub had to take everything his boss gave, in the way of vigorous comment and criticism; and we all believed that there was a United States law making it a penitentiary offense[6] to strike or threaten a pilot who was on duty.

150 Two trips later, I got into serious trouble. Brown was steering; I was "pulling down." My younger brother appeared on the hurricane deck, and shouted to Brown to stop at some landing or other a mile or so below. Brown gave no intimation that he had heard anything. But that was his way: he never condescended to take notice of an under clerk. The wind was blowing; Brown was deaf (although he always pretended he wasn't), and I very much doubted if he had heard the order. If I had two heads, I would have spoken; but as I had only one, it seemed judicious to take care of it; so I kept still. **C**

Presently, sure enough, we went sailing by that
160 plantation. Captain Klinefelter appeared on the deck, and said—

"Let her come around, sir, let her come around. Didn't Henry tell you to land here?"

"NO, sir!"

"I sent him up to do, it."

"He did come up; and that's all the good it done, the dod-derned fool. He never said anything."

"Didn't YOU hear him?" asked the captain of me.

Of course I didn't want to be mixed up in this business, but there was no way to avoid it; so I said—
170 "Yes, sir."

I knew what Brown's next remark would be, before he uttered it; it was—

"Shut your mouth! you never heard anything of the kind."

I closed my mouth according to instructions. An hour later, Henry entered the pilot-house, unaware of what had been

---

6. **penitentiary offense**: an action for which one would be sent to jail.

C **LITERARY FOCUS**

This sentence contains an example of Twain's unusual **diction**. Once again, the reason Twain gives for an action is not the literal truth. What is the real reason he didn't tell Brown of the request for a stop?

_____

_____

_____

_____

_____

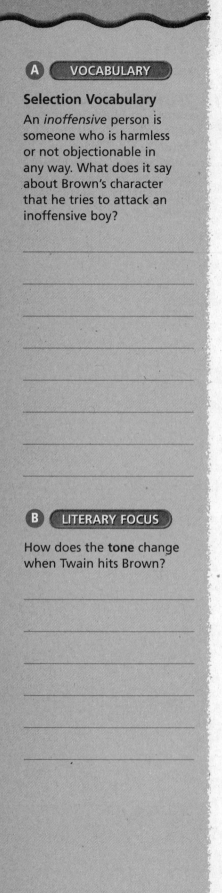

going on. He was a thoroughly inoffensive boy, and I was sorry to see him come, for I knew Brown would have no pity on him. Brown began, straightway—

"Here! why didn't you tell me we'd got to land at that
180   plantation?"

"I did tell you, Mr. Brown."

"It's a lie!"

I said—

"You lie, yourself. He did tell you."

Brown glared at me in unaffected surprise; and for as much as a moment he was entirely speechless; then he shouted to me—

"I'll attend to your case in half a minute!" then to Henry, "And you leave the pilot-house; out with you!"

It was pilot law, and must be obeyed. The boy started out,
190   and even had his foot on the upper step outside the door, when Brown, with a sudden access of fury, picked up a ten-pound lump of coal and sprang after him; but I was between, with a heavy stool, and I hit Brown a good honest blow which stretched-him out. **A**

I had committed the crime of crimes—I had lifted my hand against a pilot on duty! **B** I supposed I was booked for the penitentiary sure, and couldn't be booked any surer if I went on and squared my long account with this person while I had the chance; consequently I stuck to him and pounded him with my
200   fists a considerable time—I do not know how long, the pleasure of it probably made it seem longer than it really was;—but in the end he struggled free and jumped up and sprang to the wheel: a very natural solicitude, for, all this time, here was this steamboat tearing down the river at the rate of fifteen miles an hour and nobody at the helm! However, Eagle Bend was two miles wide at this bank-full stage, and correspondingly long and deep; and the boat was steering herself straight down the middle and taking no chances. Still, that was only luck—a body MIGHT have found her charging into the woods.

210   Perceiving, at a glance, that the "Pennsylvania" was in no danger, Brown gathered up the big spy-glass, war-club fashion,

© Index Stock/Alamy

Paraphrase this sentence. What is Twain doing here? How does Brown respond?

_____

_____

_____

_____

_____

_____

_____

_____

_____

and ordered me out of the pilot-house with more than bluster. But I was not afraid of him now; so, instead of going, I tarried, and criticized his grammar; I reformed his ferocious speeches for him, and put them into good English, calling his attention to the advantage of pure English over the dialect of the Pennsylvanian collieries[7] whence he was extracted. He could have done his part to admiration in a cross-fire of mere vituperation,[8] of course; but he was not equipped for this species of controversy; so he

220 presently laid aside his glass and took the wheel, muttering and shaking his head; and I retired to the bench. **C** The racket had brought everybody to the hurricane deck, and I trembled when I saw the old captain looking up from the midst of the crowd. I said to myself, "Now I AM done for!"—For although, as a rule, he was so fatherly and indulgent toward the boat's family, and so patient of minor shortcomings, he could be stern enough when the fault was worth it. **D**

D VOCABULARY

Selection Vocabulary

Indulgent means "giving in to someone else's wishes; permissive." Describe how you think an indulgent parent would behave. How about an indulgent boss?

_____

_____

_____

_____

_____

_____

---

7. **collieries** (KAHL YUHR EEZ): coal mines.
8. **vituperation** (VY TOO PUH RAY SHUHN): abusive language.

I tried to imagine what he WOULD do to a cub pilot who had been guilty of such a crime as mine, committed on a boat guard-deep[9] with costly freight and alive with passengers. Our watch was nearly ended. I thought I would go and hide somewhere till I got a chance to slide ashore. So I slipped out of the pilot-house, and down the steps, and around to the texas door—and was in the act of gliding within, when the captain confronted me! **A** I dropped my head, and he stood over me in silence a moment or two, then said impressively—

"Follow me."

I dropped into his wake; he led the way to his parlor in the forward end of the texas. We were alone, now. He closed the after door; then moved slowly to the forward one and closed that. He sat down; I stood before him. He looked at me some little time, then said—

"So you have been fighting Mr. Brown?

I answered meekly—

"Yes, sir."

"Do you know that that is a very serious matter?"

"Yes, sir."

"Are you aware that this boat was plowing down the river fully five minutes with no one at the wheel?"

"Yes, sir."

"Did you strike him first?"

"Yes, sir."

"What with?"

"A stool, sir."

"Hard?"

"Middling, sir."

"Did it knock him down?"

"He—he fell, sir."

"Did you follow it up? Did you do anything further?"

"Yes, sir."

"What did you do?"

"Pounded him, sir."

---

9. **guard-deep:** loaded to the guard, an extension of the deck.

182   Cub Pilot on the Mississippi

"Pounded him?"

"Yes, sir."

"Did you pound him much?—that is, severely?"

"One might call it that, sir, maybe." **B**

"I'm deuced glad of it! Hark ye, never mention that I
said that. You have been guilty of a great crime; and don't
you ever be guilty of it again, on this boat. BUT—lay for him
270 ashore! Give him a good sound thrashing, do you hear? I'll
pay the expenses. Now go—and mind you, not a word of this
to anybody. Clear out with you!—you've been guilty of a great
crime, you whelp!"[10] **C**

I slid out, happy with the sense of a close shave and a
mighty deliverance; and I heard him laughing to himself and
slapping his fat thighs after I had closed his door.

When Brown came off watch he went straight to the
captain, who was talking with some passengers on the boiler
deck, and demanded that I be put ashore in New Orleans—and
280 added—

"I'll never turn a wheel on this boat again while that cub
stays."

The captain said—

"But he needn't come round when you are on watch,
Mr. Brown."

"I won't even stay on the same boat with him. One of us has
got to go ashore."

"Very well," said the captain, "let it be yourself"; and
resumed his talk with the passengers.

B (LITERARY FOCUS)

How do Twain's short
responses to the captain
affect the story's humorous
tone?

_____

_____

_____

_____

_____

_____

_____

C (LITERARY FOCUS)

How does the difference
between a normal
expectation of the captain's
reaction and his actual
reaction have an impact on
the story's **tone**?

_____

_____

_____

_____

_____

10. **whelp**: a puppy or cub; here, a disrespectful young man.

Skills Practice

Cub Pilot on the Mississippi

USE A CHART

DIRECTIONS: Choose three passages from "Cub Pilot on the Mississippi." Write them in the first column of boxes (choose passages short enough to write in the boxes). Then, write a sentence paraphrasing each passage in the boxes in the second column.

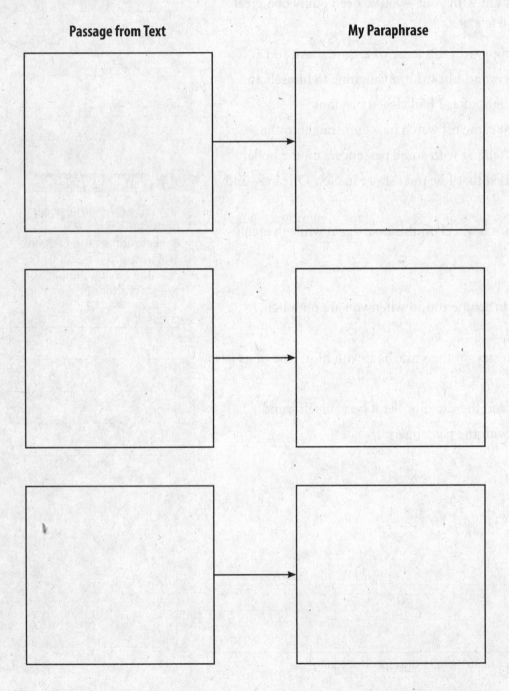

Passage from Text   **My Paraphrase**

Applying Your Skills

Cub Pilot on the Mississippi

VOCABULARY DEVELOPMENT

DIRECTIONS: Write vocabulary words from the Word Box on the correct blanks to complete the paragraph. Not all words will be used.

Word Box

transient

judicious

inoffensive

indulgent

confronted

While working as a cub pilot on a steamboat, Twain (1) _____ his boss, Brown, and struck him. Luckily for Twain, the ship's captain was an (2) _____ man. The captain made the (3) _____ decision to allow Mr. Brown to resign.

LITERARY FOCUS: STYLE AND TONE

DIRECTIONS: Read the following passage from the story. As you read, underline examples of Twain's unusual **diction**. Then, answer the question below.

"I had committed the crime of crimes—I had lifted my hand against a pilot on duty! I supposed I was booked for the penitentiary sure, and couldn't be booked any surer if I went on and squared my long account with this person while I had the chance; consequently I stuck to him and pounded him with my fists a considerable time—I do not know how long, the pleasure of it probably made it seem longer than it really was. . . ."

1. Based on this passage, how would you describe Twain's **style**?

_____

_____

READING FOCUS: READING ALOUD AND PARAPHRASING

DIRECTIONS: Choose two **paragraphs** from "Cub Pilot on the Mississippi and **read** them **aloud** to a partner. Then, **paraphrase** the paragraphs to help your partner better understand what they mean.

_____

_____

_____

_____

_____

_____

SKILLS FOCUS

Literary Skills
Analyze a passage to understand its style, diction, and tone.

Reading Skills
Paraphrase passages in the story to improve comprehension.

The Grandfather

by Gary Soto

LITERARY FOCUS: STYLE AND IMAGERY

This piece is a personal essay. Personal essays are written in the first person, using "I" as a narrator. They tell us what the writer thinks and feels about things that happen to him or her.

The writer's use of **style** and **imagery** can help us to understand the feelings and ideas in the essay. Style is the way that writers use language. The words a writer chooses or the way he or she forms sentences creates a mood. Imagery is words or phrases that paint a picture for one or more of our senses (taste, touch, smell, hearing, or sight).

See It   Choose a section of the passage that appeals to your sense of sight. Draw a picture of the scene that the passage describes.

READING FOCUS: MAKING GENERALIZATIONS

A **generalization** is a statement that uses specific evidence or details to support an idea that applies to a wider group. People often make generalizations, such as, "it's lonely at the top." We can also make generalizations about literature, such as "Stories teach us about ourselves." To make generalizations about literature, you:

• Examine details in the text

• Think about the effect those details create

• Make a broad statement

Use the Skill   As you read, gather details about Soto's writing style using a chart similar to the one below. After you finish the story, make generalizations about Soto's writing style.

Literary Skills
Understand and analyze elements of style; understand imagery.

Reading Skills
Make generalizations.

Style	Details from the Essay
Type of language (formal or informal; everyday or poetic)	
Use of imagery	
Sentence structure (short or long; simple or complex)	

Vocabulary Development

The Grandfather

SELECTION VOCABULARY

gurgle (GUR GUHL) *v.:* to flow or run with a bubbling sound.

I watched the water gurgle out of the hose and onto the rosebush.

hovered (HUHV UHRD) *v.:* stayed suspended over something.

The lemon tree hovered over the clothesline.

sulked (SUHLKT) *v.:* showed resentment and ill-humor.

Grandfather sulked about the high amount of pollution in Fresno as compared to Mexico.

meager (MEE GUHR) *adj.:* thin; small; inadequate.

The meager tree provided little shade.

WORD STUDY

DIRECTIONS: Write a synonym (word with a similar meaning) for each of the vocabulary words below.

1. gurgle _____

2. hovered _____

3. sulked _____

4. meager _____

THE GRANDFATHER

By Gary Soto

> **BACKGROUND**
>
> Gary Soto grew up in a Mexican American family in California. Much of his award-winning fiction and poetry is inspired by his childhood memories. This essay is about Soto's grandfather, who immigrated from Mexico to the United States. Like many immigrants, his grandfather worked hard and earned little money. The fruit he grew in his backyard helped him to save money.

A READING FOCUS

Based on what you have read so far, make a **generalization** about Grandfather's attitude toward money.

_____

_____

_____

B LANGUAGE COACH

An **onomatopoeia** (AHN NAH MAH TUH PEE YAH) is a word whose sound imitates or suggests its meaning. Circle the word in this sentence that is an onomatopoeia.

C LITERARY ANALYSIS

Why do you think the avocado tree is Grandfather's favorite?

_____

_____

Grandfather believed a well-rooted tree was the color of money. His money he kept hidden behind portraits of sons and daughters or taped behind the calendar of an Aztec[1] warrior. He tucked it into the sofa, his shoes and slippers, and into the tight-lipped pockets of his suits. He kept it in his soft brown wallet that was machine tooled with "MEXICO" and a campesino[2] and donkey climbing a hill. He had climbed, too, out of Mexico, settled in Fresno[3] and worked thirty years at Sun Maid Raisin, first as a packer and later, when he was old, as a watchman with a large clock on his belt. **A**

After work, he sat in the backyard under the arbor,[4] watching the water gurgle in the rosebushes that ran along the fence. **B** A lemon tree hovered over the clothesline. Two orange trees stood near the alley. His favorite tree, the avocado, which had started in a jam jar from a seed and three toothpicks lanced in its sides, rarely bore fruit. **C** He said it was the wind's fault, and the mayor's, who allowed office buildings so high that the haze of pollen from the countryside could never find its way into

---

1. **Aztec:** of the Aztecs, a culture existing in Mexico before the Spanish conquest of the early 1500s.
2. **campesino** (KAHM PEH SEE NOH): Spanish for "peasant" or "farmworker."
3. **Fresno:** city in central California.
4. **arbor:** shelter made of branches or covered with vines.

"The Grandfather" from *A Summer Life* by Gary Soto (Dell 1991). Copyright © 1990 by University Press of New England. Reproduced by permission of **University Press of New England** and electronic format by permission of **Gary Soto**.

the city. He sulked about this. He said that in Mexico buildings
20   only grew so tall. You could see the moon at night, and the stars
were clear points all the way to the horizon. And wind reached
all the way from the sea, which was blue and clean, unlike the
oily water sloshing against a San Francisco pier. **D**

During its early years, I could leap over that tree, kick my
bicycling legs over the top branch and scream my fool head off
because I thought for sure I was flying. I ate fruit to keep my
strength up, fuzzy peaches and branch-scuffed plums cooled in
the refrigerator. From the kitchen chair he brought out in the
evening, Grandpa would scold, "Hijo,[5] what's the matta with you?
30   You gonna break it."

By the third year, the tree was as tall as I, its branches
casting a meager shadow on the ground. **E** I sat beneath the
shade, scratching words in the hard dirt with a stick. I had
learned "Nile"[6] in summer school and a dirty word from my
brother who wore granny sunglasses. The red ants tumbled into
my letters, and I buried them, knowing that they would dig
themselves back into fresh air.

A tree was money. If a lemon cost seven cents at Hanoian's
Market, then Grandfather saved fistfuls of change and more
40   because in winter the branches of his lemon tree hung heavy
yellow fruit. **F** And winter brought oranges, juicy and large as
softballs. Apricots he got by the bagfuls from a son, who himself
was wise for planting young. Peaches he got from a neighbor, who
worked the night shift at Sun Maid Raisin. The chile plants, which
also saved him from giving up his hot, sweaty quarters, were
propped up with sticks to support an abundance of red fruit. **G**

But his favorite tree was the avocado because it offered hope
and the promise of more years. After work, Grandpa sat in the
backyard, shirtless, tired of flagging trucks loaded with crates of
50   raisins, and sipped glasses of ice water. His yard was neat: five
trees, seven rosebushes, whose fruit were the red and white flowers

---

5. **Hijo** (EE HOH): Spanish for "child" or "son."
6. **Nile**: very long river in Africa, flowing through Egypt into the
    Mediterranean Sea.

D **LITERARY FOCUS**

How would you describe
Soto's **style** and his word
choice?

_____

_____

_____

E **VOCABULARY**

Selection Vocabulary
Meager means "thin; small;
inadequate." What does this
meager shadow say about
the tree?

_____

_____

_____

F **VOCABULARY**

Academic Vocabulary
Sometimes authors *imply*,
or suggest without formally
expressing, the personality
traits of their characters.
What do these sentences
imply about Grandfather?

_____

_____

_____

G **LITERARY FOCUS**

What feeling does the
imagery in this sentence
create?

_____

_____

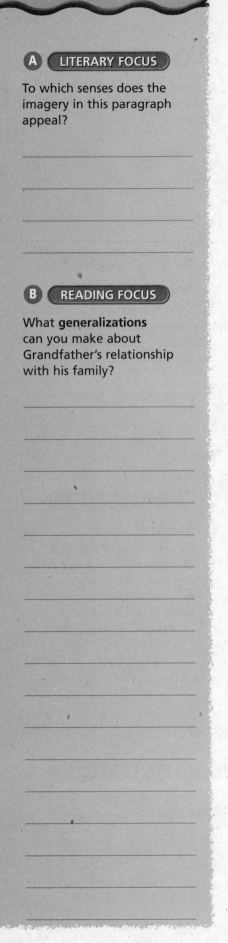

A LITERARY FOCUS

To which senses does the imagery in this paragraph appeal?

_____

_____

_____

B READING FOCUS

What **generalizations** can you make about Grandfather's relationship with his family?

_____

_____

_____

_____

_____

_____

_____

_____

_____

_____

_____

_____

he floated in bowls, and a statue of St. Francis that stood in a circle of crushed rocks, arms spread out to welcome hungry sparrows.

After ten years, the first avocado hung on a branch, but the meat was flecked with black, an omen, Grandfather thought, a warning to keep an eye on the living. Five years later, another avocado hung on a branch, larger than the first and edible when crushed with a fork into a heated tortilla. Grandfather sprinkled it with salt and laced it with a river of chile.

60   "It's good," he said, and let me taste.

I took a big bite, waved a hand over my tongue, and ran for the garden hose gurgling in the rosebushes. I drank long and deep, and later ate the smile from an ice cold watermelon. **A**

Birds nested in the tree, quarreling jays with liquid eyes and cool, pulsating throats. Wasps wove a horn-shaped hive one year, but we smoked them away with swords of rolled up newspapers lit with matches. By then, the tree was tall enough for me to climb to look into the neighbor's yard. But by then I was too old for that kind of thing and went about with my brother, hair

70   slicked back and our shades dark as oil.

After twenty years, the tree began to bear. Although Grandfather complained about how much he lost because pollen never reached the poor part of town, because at the market he had to haggle over the price of avocados, he loved that tree. It grew, as did his family, and when he died, all his sons standing on each other's shoulders, oldest to youngest, could not reach the highest branches. The wind could move the branches, but the trunk, thicker than any waist, hugged the ground. **B**

Applying Your Skills

The Grandfather

VOCABULARY DEVELOPMENT

DIRECTIONS: Write vocabulary words from the Word Box on the correct blanks to complete the paragraph. One word will not be used.

Word Box

gurgle

hovered

sulked

meager

In Soto's memories of his grandfather's garden, a big tree
(1) _____ over the clothesline. He remembers the
rose bushes along the fence, and a constant (2) _____
of water from a hose. Soto's grandfather stretched his
(3) _____ income by growing fruit in the backyard.

LITERARY FOCUS: STYLE AND IMAGERY

DIRECTIONS: This essay is full of **imagery**. Go back through the essay and find one or two images that appeal to each sense. List them in the spaces below.

Sense	Example
sight	
sound	
touch	
taste	
smell	

READING FOCUS: MAKING GENERALIZATIONS

DIRECTIONS: Below, write what you think are the most important details about Grandfather.

1. _____

2. _____

3. _____

Based on these details, make a **generalization** about Grandfather's personality.

_____

Literary Skills
Analyze style and imagery.

Reading Skills
Use details from the story to make generalizations.

About StoryCorps

INFORMATIONAL TEXT FOCUS: STRUCTURE AND FORMAT OF FUNCTIONAL DOCUMENTS

At school, work, and other areas of your life you will read many **functional documents**—a set of instructions, a memo, or other texts that give you information or teach you how to do something. Usually the **structure** (the organization a writer uses) is designed to give information in a simple way. Many documents are divided into sections. Each section may have a heading which tells you what information will be included.

The document's **format**, or design, can also help you to find the key words, sections, and important ideas. The design features can include:

- **Formatting elements** such as **bold** and *italic* type, margin widths, indentations, and line spacing.
- **Graphic elements** such as drawings, photos, charts, or other artwork.
- **Design elements** such as placement of the words and pictures on the page, use of white space, and choice of colors.

SELECTION VOCABULARY

facilitator (FUH SIHL UH TAY TUHR) *n.:* a person who assists.

If you need help recording your interview for StoryCorps, a facilitator will assist you.

collective (KUH LEHK TIHV) *adj.:* of or as a group.

StoryCorps' mission is to make a record of our nation's collective identity.

WORD STUDY

DIRECTIONS: The word *facilitator* is related to the adjective *facile,* which means "easy." The same type of relationship exists for other words. Look at the following word pairs. Based on the definitions below, write down what you think the definition of the related word might be:

1. aviation: the operation of airplanes	aviator:
2. spectacle: an unusual public display	spectator:

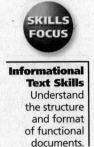

SKILLS FOCUS

Informational Text Skills
Understand the structure and format of functional documents.

ABOUT STORYCORPS

> **BACKGROUND**
> The following document is the StoryCorps mission statement—a summary of an organization's plans and values. StoryCorps is modeled on the Works Project Administration (WPA), which was created by President Franklin D. Roosevelt in 1935. The WPA was created to give work to the unemployed during the Great Depression. Many arts projects were created by the WPA, giving work to authors, actors, and artists around the country.

© AP Images/Manuel Balce Ceneta

STORYCORPS

StoryCorps is a national project to instruct and inspire people to record each others' stories in sound.

We're here to help you interview your grandmother, your uncle, the lady who's worked at the luncheonette down the block for as long as you can remember—anyone whose story you want to hear and preserve. **A**

To start, we're building soundproof recording studios across the country, called StoryBooths. You can use these StoryBooths to record broadcast-quality interviews with the help of a trained

10 facilitator. **B** Our first StoryBooth opened in New York City's Grand Central Terminal on October 23, 2003. StoryCorps

Slightly adapted from "About StoryCorps" from *StoryCorps*. Reproduced by permission of **Sound Portraits Productions, Inc.**

opened its second StoryBooth in New York City in Lower Manhattan on July 12, 2005. We also have two traveling recording studios, called MobileBooths, which embarked on cross-country tours on May 19, 2005.

We've tried to make the experience as simple as possible: We help you figure out what questions to ask. We handle all the technical aspects of the recording. At the end of the hour-long session, you get a copy of your interview on CD.

20   Since we want to make sure your story lives on for generations to come, we'll also add your interview to the StoryCorps Archive, housed at the American Folklife Center at the Library of Congress, which we hope will become nothing less than an oral history of America.

OUR VISION A

We've modeled StoryCorps—in spirit and in scope—after the Works Progress Administration (WPA) of the 1930s, through which oral-history interviews with everyday Americans across the country were recorded. These recordings remain the single most important collection of American voices gathered to date. 30   We hope that StoryCorps will build and expand on that work, becoming a WPA for the 21st Century.

© Andrew Holbrooke/Corbis

To us, StoryCorps celebrates our shared humanity and collective identity. **B** It captures and defines the stories that bond us. We've found that the process of interviewing a friend, neighbor, or family member can have a profound impact on both the interviewer and interviewee. We've seen people change, friendships grow, families walk away feeling closer, understanding each other better. Listening, after all, is an act of love. **C**

40   A StoryCorps interview is an opportunity to ask the questions that never get asked because the occasion never arises. *How did you come to this country? How did you and mom meet? How did Uncle Harry get the nickname "Twinkles?"* **D**

B VOCABULARY

Selection Vocabulary
Collective means "of or as a group." What do you think is meant by the phrase "collective identity"?

_____

_____

C LANGUAGE COACH

Interviewer and interviewee are **derivations** of *interview*. Derivations are words that are made from other related words. Circle the word in this paragraph that is a derivation of *friend*.

_____

_____

_____

D READING FOCUS

Italic type is a **formatting element**. Why do you think italic type is used here?

_____

_____

_____

Skills Practice

About StoryCorps

USE A CHART

DIRECTIONS: In the chart below, describe the structure and format of the functional document "About StoryCorps." Also, explain where you found these elements in the document.

	Description	Examples
Formatting elements		
Graphic elements		
Design elements		

Applying Your Skills

About StoryCorps

VOCABULARY DEVELOPMENT

DIRECTIONS: Write the vocabulary words from the Word Box on the correct blanks to complete the paragraph.

> **Word Box**
>
> facilitator
> collective

The founders of StoryCorps hope to help preserve our (1) _____ history and identity. Recording a StoryCorps interview is easy to do at a StoryCorps booth. When you visit a booth, you will have the help of a trained (2) _____. Recording a StoryCorps interview is a wonderful way to preserve family memories and to become even closer with someone important to you.

INFORMATIONAL TEXT FOCUS: STRUCTURE AND FORMAT OF FUNCTIONAL DOCUMENTS

DIRECTIONS: Answer the following questions about the **functional document**: About StoryCorps.

1. If you were going to improve the format of the selection, what might you do? _____
   _____
   _____

2. What does the heading "Our Vision" tell you about the text that follows it? _____
   _____
   _____

3. What information is the document trying to explain? _____
   _____
   _____

4. Do you think the document is effective at teaching that information? Why or why not? _____
   _____
   _____

SKILLS FOCUS

Informational Text Skills
Understand the format and structure of functional documents.

Collection 5

VOCABULARY REVIEW

DIRECTIONS: Use the context clues to help you figure out the meaning of the boldfaced word. Circle the letter of the correct meaning.

1. She was so angry that she turned her back on him and **sulked** all day.

    a. smiled

    b. delighted

    c. showed resentment

    d. yelled

2. She had a negative **attitude** about her writing abilities.

    a. outlook

    b. tone

    c. symbol

    d. positive

3. He studied every word carefully to better understand the author's **diction**.

    a. intelligence

    b. interest

    c. disinterest

    d. word choice

4. He is an **indulgent** father and never says "no" to his daughter.

    a. kind

    b. cautious

    c. permissive

    d. strict

5. I had a **transient** wish to become a chef, but I ended up becoming an engineer.

    a. fleeting

    b. strong

    c. slight

    d. long-lasting

Skills Review

Collection 5

LANGUAGE COACH

DIRECTIONS: *Onomatopoeia* is a word whose sound imitates or suggests its meaning. "Moo," for example, describes the sound a cow makes. Look at the chart below. Put a checkmark in the right-hand column for each correct example of onomatopoeia.

Word	Onomatopoeia?
1. meow	
2. oink	
3. quiet	
4. hum	
5. noisy	
6. gurgle	
7. buzz	
8. soft	
9. music	
10. click	

WRITING ACTIVITY

Both "Cub Pilot on the Mississippi" and "The Grandfather" paint vivid pictures of a character through the use of imagery. Mark Twain carefully and humorously describes both the looks and personality of the unpleasant Mr. Brown. Gary Soto uses images from his grandfather's garden to paint a picture of his grandfather's life.

DIRECTIONS: Write a short personal essay (one or two paragraphs) about someone who is important you. As you describe him or her, include imagery that appeals to each of the five senses.

Collection
6

Persuasion

© Adam Jones/Getty Images

Literary and Academic Vocabulary for Collection 6

influence (IHN FLOO UHNS) *v.:* to persuade or affect someone.

A powerful speech can influence people to take action.

counter (KOWN TUHR) *v.:* to say something that opposes another statement.

Her writings effectively counter the argument that women should stay out of the workplace.

valid (VAL IHD) *adj.:* supported by facts; true.

I know the statement is valid because it is based on the facts.

verify (VEHR UH FY) *v.:* to prove something to be true.

You can verify that fact by looking it up in an encyclopedia.

argument (AHR GYU MIHNT) *n.:* a writer's main point of view.

The writer's argument is that unintentional plagiarism is impossible.

tone (TOHN) *n.:* a writer's attitude toward a subject, a character, or the audience.

The argument is made in a passionate tone.

structure (STRUK CHER) *n.:* the organization a writer uses to make a point.

The clear structure of the article makes it easy to understand.

Cinderella's Stepsisters

by Toni Morrison

LITERARY FOCUS: ARGUMENT—INTENT AND TONE

A writer's **intent**, or purpose for writing, affects both the **argument** and the **tone** (attitude toward the subject or the audience) of a piece of writing. In this speech, Morrison's tone is shown by the analogy she uses to make her argument. An **analogy** is a comparison that explains something complicated by relating it to something simple and familiar. These two sentences below make the same argument but with a different tone. What do you think the tone of each sentence is?

1. I think you should reconsider setting an early curfew because it's unfair.

2. I will be so miserable if you give me an early curfew.

READING FOCUS: QUESTIONING

When you read any sort of persuasive writing (writing that tries to convince the reader of something), challenge the writer by **questioning** him or her as you read. Such questioning will help you to evaluate the author's argument.

Use the Skill Read these passages from "Cinderella's Stepsisters." Ask at least one question about each passage. As you read the speech, attempt to answer your own questions.

SKILLS FOCUS

Literary Skills
Understand an author's argument, intent, analogies, and tone.

Reading Skills
Ask questions to evaluate an author's argument.

Passage	Question
"I am alarmed by the violence that women do to each other: professional violence, competitive violence, emotional violence. I am alarmed by the willingness of women to enslave other women."	
"You are moving toward self-fulfillment, and the consequences of that fulfillment should be to discover that there is something just as important as you are and that just-as-important thing may be Cinderella—or your stepsister."	

Vocabulary Development

Cinderella's Stepsisters

SELECTION VOCABULARY

deflect (DIH FLEHKT) *v.:* turn aside.

The stepsisters do not take action to deflect their mother's abuse of Cinderella.

expendable (EHK SPEHN DUH BUHL) *adj.:* can be sacrificed; not worth saving; unnecessary.

In pursuing our goals, we should not view other people's needs as expendable.

indispensable (IHN DIHS PEHN SUH BUHL) *adj.:* absolutely necessary; essential.

While trying to pursue her goals, she found that the support from her family was indispensible.

sensibilities (SEHN SUH BIHL UH TEES) *n.:* sensitive feelings; ability to respond emotionally.

We should not let our ambition overwhelm our better sensibilities.

diminish (DUH MIHN IHSH) *v.:* lessen; reduce.

I find that studying helps to diminish my fears about a test.

WORD STUDY

An analogy is a word problem that is made up of one complete word pair and one incomplete pair:

GRACEFUL : CLUMSY :: early : _____

In an analogy, you need to find a word that correctly completes the second pair. The words in the first pair have the same relationship to each other as the two words in the second pair. Read the analogy above like this: "Graceful is to clumsy as early is to _____." *Graceful* and *clumsy* are words with opposite meanings (antonyms). The opposite of *early* is *late*.

DIRECTIONS: Complete the following analogies.

1. INDISPENSABLE : EXPENDABLE :: heavy : _____

2. DIMINISH : REDUCE :: tired : _____

3. DEFLECT : ATTRACT :: stop : _____

CINDERELLA'S STEPSISTERS

by Toni Morrison

BACKGROUND

Toni Morrison was the first African American to win the Nobel Prize for literature. She grew up during the Great Depression, facing both segregation and racism. This selection is a speech which Morrison delivered at Barnard College's 1979 graduation, during the women's rights movement. Barnard is an all-women's college in New York City.

A **READING FOCUS**

As you read persuasive writing, **ask questions** to challenge the writer's argument. What questions do you have at this point in the text?

_____

_____

_____

_____

B **LITERARY FOCUS**

Based on what the author has written so far, what do you think the **tone** of this speech will be?

_____

_____

_____

Let me begin by taking you back a little. Back before the days at college. To nursery school, probably, to a once-upon-a-time when you first heard, or read, or, I suspect, even saw "Cinderella." Because it is Cinderella that I want to talk to you about; because it is Cinderella who causes me a feeling of urgency. What is unsettling about that fairy tale is that it is essentially the story of a household—a world, if you please—of women gathered together and held together in order to abuse another woman. There is, of course, a rather vague absent

10 father and a nick-of-time prince with a foot fetish.[1] But neither has much personality. And there are the surrogate "mothers" of course (god- and step-) who contribute both to Cinderella's grief and to her release and happiness. But it is her stepsisters who interest me. How crippling it must have been for those young girls to grow up with a mother, to watch and imitate that mother, enslaving another girl. **A** **B**

I am curious about their fortunes after the story ends. For contrary to recent adaptations, the stepsisters were not ugly, clumsy, stupid girls with outsize feet. The Grimm collection[2]

---

1. **fetish** (FEHT IHSH): irrational devotion.
2. **Grimm Collection**: reference to the famous collection of fairy tales compiled by Jacob and Wilhelm Grimm in the early nineteenth century.

---

20 describes them as "beautiful and fair in appearance." When
we are introduced to them they are beautiful, elegant, women
of status, and clearly women of power. Having watched and
participated in the violent dominion[3] of another woman, will
they be any less cruel when it comes their turn to enslave other
children, or even when they are required to take care of their
own mother? **C**

It is not a wholly medieval[4] problem. It is quite a
contemporary one: feminine power when directed at other
women has historically been wielded in what has been described
30 as a "masculine" manner. Soon you will be in a position to
do the very same thing. Whatever your background—rich or
poor—whatever the history of education in your family—five
generations or one—you have taken advantage of what has been
available to you at Barnard and you will therefore have both the
economic and social status of the stepsisters *and* you will have
their power. **D**

I want not to *ask* you but to *tell* you not to participate in the
oppression of your sisters. Mothers who abuse their children are
women, and another woman, not an agency, has to be willing
40 to stay their hands. Mothers who set fire to school buses are
women, and another woman, not an agency, has to tell them
to stay their hands. Women who stop the promotion of other
women in careers are women, and another woman must come
to the victim's aid. Social and welfare workers who humiliate
their clients may be women, and other women colleagues have to
deflect their anger. **E**

I am alarmed by the violence that women do to each other:
professional violence, competitive violence, emotional violence.
I am alarmed by the willingness of women to enslave other
50 women. I am alarmed by a growing absence of decency on the
killing floor of professional women's worlds. You are the women
who will take your place in the world where *you* can decide who

---

Academic Vocabulary
How is Morrison trying to *influence,* or affect, your opinion of the Cinderella story?

_____

_____

_____

_____

D QUICK CHECK

Why does Morrison think that the story of Cinderella's stepsisters is important to the Barnard graduates?

_____

_____

_____

_____

E LITERARY ANALYSIS

Underline the repeated words in this paragraph. How can repetition be an effective writing technique?

_____

_____

_____

_____

---

3. **dominion** (DUH MIHN YUHN): rule; control.
4. **medieval** (MEHD EE VUHL): relating to the Middle Ages, a period in Western European history from the fifth through the fifteenth centuries.

shall flourish and who shall wither; you will make distinctions between the deserving poor and the undeserving poor; where you can yourself determine which life is expendable and which is indispensable. **A** Since you will have the power to do it, you may also be persuaded that you have the right to do it. As educated women the distinction between the two is first-order business.

60   I am suggesting that we pay as much attention to our nurturing[5] sensibilities as to our ambition. **B** You are moving in the direction of freedom and the function of freedom is to free somebody else. You are moving toward self-fulfillment, and the consequences of that fulfillment should be to discover that there is something just as important as you are and that just-as-important thing may be Cinderella—or your stepsister.

In your rainbow journey toward the realization of personal goals don't make choices based only on your security and your safety. Nothing is safe. That is not to say that anything ever was, or that anything worth achieving ever should be. Things of value

70   seldom are. It is not safe to have a child. It is not safe to challenge

---

5.   nurturing (NUR CHUHR IHNG): promoting growth or development.

A LANGUAGE COACH

The words *deserving* and *undeserving* are **antonyms,** or words with opposite meanings. Underline two other words in this sentence that are antonyms.

_____

_____

B VOCABULARY

Selection Vocabulary

Sensibilities are "sensitive feelings" or "the ability to respond emotionally." Why does Morrison think that nurturing sensibilities is so important?

_____

_____

_____

_____

_____

_____

_____

_____

_____

the status quo.[6] It is not safe to choose work that has not been done before. Or to do old work in a new way. There will always be someone there to stop you. But in pursuing your highest ambitions, don't let your personal safety diminish the safety of your stepsister. **C** In wielding the power that is deservedly yours, don't permit it to enslave your stepsisters. Let your might and your power emanate[7] from that place in you that is nurturing and caring.

80   Women's rights is not only an abstraction, a cause; it is also a personal affair. It is not only about "us"; it is also about me and you. Just the two of us. **D**

---

6.   **status quo** (STAT UHS KWOH): existing state of affairs.
7.   **emanate** (EHM UH NAYT): come from.

C   VOCABULARY

Selection Vocabulary
To *diminish* is to lessen or reduce. Use the word in a sentence of your own.

_____

_____

_____

_____

_____

_____

D   LITERARY FOCUS

What is the **tone** of this paragraph? Explain whether you think this paragraph is an effective ending for the speech.

_____

_____

_____

_____

_____

_____

_____

_____

_____

_____

_____

Skills Practice

Cinderella's Stepsisters

USE A CHART

DIRECTIONS: Complete the chart below by listing several different questions you can use to evaluate Toni Morrison's argument, and write the answers to those questions. Review the speech for ideas. The first question has been provided.

Questions	Answers
1. Why is Morrison beginning a college graduation speech by talking about "Cinderella"?	**1.**
2.	**2.**
3.	**3.**
4.	**4.**
5.	**5.**
6.	**6.**

Applying Your Skills

Cinderella's Stepsisters

VOCABULARY DEVELOPMENT

DIRECTIONS: Circle the letter of the synonym (word with a similar meaning) listed for each vocabulary word.

1. deflect
   a. give
   b. take
   c. repel

2. expendable
   a. indispensable
   b. unimportant
   c. necessary

3. diminish
   a. decrease
   b. increase
   c. change

4. indispensable
   a. heroic
   b. crucial
   c. expendable

5. sensibilities
   a. change
   b. insensitivities
   c. feelings

LITERARY FOCUS: ARGUMENT—INTENT AND TONE

DIRECTIONS: Complete the chart below by describing Morrison's **intent** and **tone** in "Cinderella's Stepsisters" in the boxes on the right.

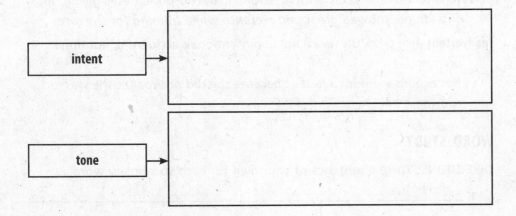

intent →

tone →

READING FOCUS: QUESTIONING

DIRECTIONS: Answer the following questions about "Cinderella's Stepsisters."

1. What is Morrison's overall argument? _____

_____

2. Is the argument persuasive? Why or why not? _____

_____

_____

SKILLS FOCUS

Literary Skills
Describe the intent and tone of a piece of writing.

Reading Skills
Question an author's argument.

Kaavya Viswanathan: Unconscious Copycat or Plagiarist? *and* Kaavya Syndrome

INFORMATIONAL TEXT FOCUS: EVALUATING ARGUMENTS

When you read opposing views, you will need to read carefully to **evaluate arguments**. A **pro argument** is in support of an issue, and a **con argument** is opposed to an issue. As you read, use these steps to evaluate arguments:

1. Decide what argument the author is trying to make. Look for the facts, statistics, examples, and expert quotations used to support a claim.

2. Check whether the reasons make sense and are logical.

3. Decide if the writer gives enough strong evidence to support generalizations.

SELECTION VOCABULARY

internalized (IHN TUR NUH LYZD) *v.:* adopted as one's own.
Kaavya internalized the writer's words and made them her own.

perseverance (PUR SUH VEER UHNS) *n.:* sticking to a purpose, never giving up.
The athlete showed great perseverance while training for the race.

inadvertent (IHN UHD VUR TUHNT) *adj.:* unintentional, accidental; not done on purpose.
Her actions were inadvertent because she did not realize she was copying.

WORD STUDY

DIRECTIONS: Write a sentence of your own for each vocabulary word.

1. _____

2. _____

3. _____

4. _____

SKILLS FOCUS

Informational Text Skills
Evaluate pro and con arguments.

KAAVYA VISWANATHAN: UNCONSCIOUS COPYCAT OR PLAGIARIST?

by Sandhya Nankani

> **BACKGROUND**
> Read the following pro and con arguments and decide whether Kaavya Viswanathan intentionally plagiarized another writer's work. The first selection is from the literary blog WORD, an online journal, by the writer Sandhya Nankani. The second selection is an online article from Slate magazine by Joshua Foer, a freelance writer who often writes about science.

Friday, April 28, 2006

Plagiarism is no laughing matter. If you are found guilty of doing it, you can fail a class or be expelled from school. **A** In the real world, the penalties are much stiffer. In 2003, a 27-year-old *New York Times* reporter, Jayson Blair, lost his job after he admitted to copying other journalists' writing and faking reports. **B**

In 2006, the person in the spotlight was Kaavya Viswanathan.

© Jodi Hilton/The New York Times/ Redux

A ⬤ **QUICK CHECK**

What claim about plagiarism does the writer make? What facts and examples does she give to support her claim?

_____

_____

_____

_____

_____

_____

B ⬤ **READING FOCUS**

It is important to look at facts when trying to **evaluate arguments**. Underline the specific example the writer gives to support her claim about plagiarism.

Slightly adapted from "Kaavya Viswanathan: Unconscious Copycat or Plagiarist?" by Sandhya Nankani from *WORD: Official Blog of Read and Writing magazines*, Friday, April 28, 2006. Reproduced by permission of **Weekly Reader Corporation**.

10

A **LITERARY ANALYSIS**

Why do you think the writer tells us her first impression of Viswanathan?

_____

_____

_____

_____

_____

B **VOCABULARY**

Selection Vocabulary

Underline the context clues in this paragraph that help explain the meaning of the word *internalized*.

20 The Harvard student was given a $500,000 advance by the publishing giant Little, Brown to write a novel about an overachieving high school senior's attempts to get popular and gain admission to Harvard University. The book: *How Opal Mehta Got Kissed, Got Wild, and Got a Life.*

In February, I read an advance copy of the book with much interest. It's not every day that a new "young literary genius" is discovered and publicized by a major publishing company. Kaavya was 17 when she got her book deal; she was the youngest author signed by Little, Brown in decades.

My friend and colleague Pooja read *How Opal Mehta . . .* too. The following week, we got together for lunch and talked

30 about it, dissecting it bit by bit. Literary tastes aside (there were a few things about the book that bothered us), we decided that any 19-year-old who could write a 250+-page novel deserved to be credited for her accomplishments. After reaching this conclusion, we sat back and waited for the book to come out—we were curious to know what others would think, whether our concerns would be mirrored by critics and readers, and whether the book would be as big a hit as the publisher had hoped for. **A**

On April 1, Kaavya Viswanathan's much-anticipated book came to life in bookstores. A flurry of reviews followed in all

40 major newspapers and literary outfits. Then, things took an unexpected turn. The downward spiral began.

Neither Pooja nor I had expected this.

Last Sunday, *The Harvard Crimson* newspaper published a story alleging that Kaavya had plagiarized over 40 sections from two young adult novels by Megan McCafferty, *Sloppy Firsts* and *Second Helpings.*

In an email she sent on Monday, Kaavya said that she had "internalized" McCafferty's work without realizing. That is, she had been such a fan of McCafferty's books since high

50 school and had read them 3 or 4 times and had copied her style without realizing. "Any phrasing similarities between her works and mine," Kaavya wrote, "were completely unintentional and unconscious." **B**

Many were not convinced. . . .

I read one document at *Publisher's Weekly* that cited 49 different examples. Some seemed a stretch and others were pretty compelling. . . .

The plot thickens.

Tuesday: Kaavya's publisher issued a statement saying that
60   they would reprint the book with revisions and an acknowledgment to McCafferty.

Wednesday: Kaavya appeared on NBC's *Today Show.* "When I was writing, I genuinely believed each word was my own," she said.

Later Wednesday: At an interview at her publisher's office, she also added that some of the plagiarism may have happened because she "had a photographic memory." She also admitted that she had help developing the plot from 17th Street Media Productions, a "book packager."

70   Thursday: Publisher Little, Brown essentially pulled the book off the shelves. They "sent a notice to retail and wholesale accounts asking them to stop selling copies of the book and to return unsold inventory to the publisher for full credit," said Michael Pietsch, senior vice president and publisher of Little, Brown. **C**

Is this the end of Kaavya's story? Has she had her 15 minutes of fame, and will everyone forget about her by next Friday at this time? I'm not sure.

This controversy does not seem so black and white to me.
80   Is Kaavya an intentional plagiarist or an unconscious copycat? What role did her editor(s) and the marketing company play in this story? And if she did sit down and cut and paste the alleged 49 sections, did she think it was OK because she was paraphrasing—i.e., rewriting another writer's words in her own words and changing the nouns, names, places, and things around?

As writers—whether we are writing for fun, for school, or for money—we all bear a mighty responsibility to our readers and to ourselves. That responsibility is to select each word we

C   VOCABULARY

Academic Vocabulary
To *verify* is "to prove something to be true." What evidence does the author give to verify the claim that Viswanathan plagiarized another writer's work? Underline each piece of evidence in lines 45–65.

A LITERARY ANALYSIS

In this sentence, the writer uses an informal voice. Why do you think she chose to do so? Does it have any effect on her argument?

_____

_____

_____

_____

B READING FOCUS

What new idea does the writer introduce in this paragraph? Is this argument a **pro** or **con argument**?

_____

_____

_____

C LITERARY ANALYSIS

What final idea does the writer present?

_____

_____

_____

D READING FOCUS

What is the overall **argument** of this selection? Do you think the argument is logical? Explain.

_____

_____

_____

90 use with precision and to do our utmost best to offer original thoughts and words to the world.

That task is not always easy—and in this respect, I empathize with Kaavya. There have been many occasions when I have written something and thought, "Hmmm, that sounds familiar. Did someone else say that?" **A** As a writer, I need to be responsible for looking it up, investigating, poking around to see whether that is the case. If I find that yes, my words do sound a great deal like someone else's, I need to go back and delete and rewrite. **B**

Of course, there are some things that there just aren't too

100 many ways of saying:

> Her name was Lucy. She lived in a house
>
> She was named Lucy. In a house she lived.
>
> Lucy was her name. She resided in a house.

If you rewrite something like that or state a fact that's widely known—"There are 12 months in a year"—that's not plagiarism. Plagiarism is copying someone else's writing without noting the source. That's very different from being inspired by another writer and learning from his or her style.

You see why this is so complicated? I'm still trying to wrap

110 my brain around it. What I think we should take away from this is not a sense of glee ("Aha! Kaavya got caught. Serves her right!" I've been hearing a lot of that out there.) Rather, we should step away from this situation and use Kaavya's experience to remind us of the importance of consciously choosing our words. We should use it to remind ourselves that when it comes to writing, there's nothing better than writing in our own voices. **C**

At the end of the day, when Kaavya's book has disappeared from bookshelves and her life has returned to a sense of normalcy, I hope that she will pick up a pen again and ask

120 herself: What is my original writing voice? I wish her good luck in finding it. From what I've seen so far, it is a voice that glimmers with wit. **D**

KAAVYA SYNDROME

by Joshua Foer

April 27, 2006

Kaavya Viswanathan has an excuse. In this morning's *New York Times*, the author of *How Opal Mehta Got Kissed, Got Wild, and Got a Life* explained how she "unintentionally and unconsciously" plagiarized upward of 29 passages from the books of another young-adult novelist, Megan McCafferty. Viswanathan said she has a photographic memory. "I never take notes."

130   This seems like as good an opportunity as any to clear up the greatest enduring myth about human memory. Lots of people claim to have a photographic memory, but nobody actually does. Nobody. **E**

Well, maybe one person.

In 1970, a Harvard vision scientist named Charles Stromeyer III published a landmark paper in *Nature* about a Harvard student named Elizabeth, who could perform an astonishing feat. Stromeyer showed Elizabeth's right eye a pattern of 10,000 random dots, and a day later, he showed her left eye

140   another dot pattern. She mentally fused the two images to form a random-dot stereogram and then saw a three-dimensional image floating above the surface. Elizabeth seemed to offer the first conclusive proof that photographic memory is possible. But then in a soap-opera twist, Stromeyer married her, and she was never tested again. **F**

In 1979, a researcher named John Merritt published the results of a photographic memory test he had placed in magazines and newspapers around the country. Merritt hoped someone might come forward with abilities similar to Elizabeth's, and he

150   figures that roughly 1 million people tried their hand at the test. Of that number, 30 wrote in with the right answer, and he visited 15 of them at their homes. However, with the scientist looking

E QUICK CHECK

What claim does the author make in this passage?

_____

_____

_____

_____

F READING FOCUS

Underline any evidence in this paragraph that might **argue** against claims that Elizabeth had a photographic memory.

A READING FOCUS

What effect does the use of the word "trick" to describe Elizabeth's accomplishments have? Is the writer's argument **pro** or **con**?

_____

_____

B READING FOCUS

Now you decide. Are you **pro** or **con** on this argument? Do you think that Elizabeth had photographic memory? Why or why not?

_____

_____

_____

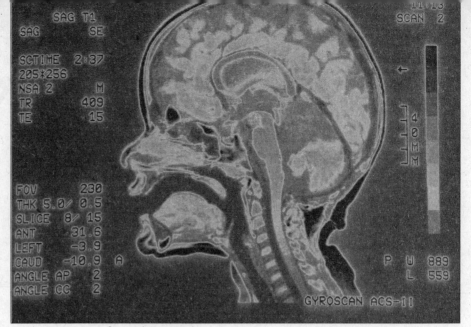

MRI brain scan. © age fotostock/SuperStock

over their shoulders, not one of them could pull off Elizabeth's trick. **A**

There are so many unlikely circumstances surrounding the Elizabeth case—the marriage between subject and scientist, the lack of further testing, the inability to find anyone else with her abilities—that some psychologists have concluded that there's something fishy about Stromeyer's findings. He denies it. "We don't have any doubt about our data," he told me recently. Still, his one-woman study, he says, "is not strong evidence for other people having photographic memory." **B**

That's not to say there aren't people with extraordinarily good memories—there are. They just can't take mental snapshots and recall them with perfect fidelity. Kim Peek, the 53-year-old savant[1] who was the basis for Dustin Hoffman's character in *Rain Man,* is said to have memorized every page of the 9,000-plus books he has read at 8 to 12 seconds per page (each eye reads its own page independently), though that claim has never been rigorously tested. Another savant, Stephen Wiltshire, has been called the "human camera" for his ability to create sketches of a scene after looking at it for just a few seconds. But even he doesn't have a truly photographic memory. His mind doesn't work like a Xerox. He takes liberties. . . .

_____

1. **savant** (SUH VAHNT): person with a mental disability who displays exceptional skill in a specialized field.

In every case except Elizabeth's where someone has claimed to possess a photographic memory, there has always been another explanation. A group of Talmudic scholars[2] known as the Shass Pollaks supposedly stored mental snapshots of all 5,422 pages of the Babylonian Talmud. According to a paper published in 1917 in the journal *Psychological Review*, psychologist George Stratton tested the Shass Pollaks by sticking a pin through various tractates of the Talmud. They responded by telling him exactly which words the pin passed through on every page. In fact, the Shass Pollaks probably didn't possess photographic memory so much as heroic perseverance. If the average person decided he was going to dedicate his entire life to memorizing 5,422 pages of text, he'd probably also be pretty good at it. It's an impressive feat of single-mindedness, not of memory. **C**

Truman Capote famously claimed to have nearly absolute recall of dialogue and used his prodigious memory as an excuse never to take notes or use a tape recorder, but I suspect his memory claims were just a useful cover to invent dialogue whole cloth. Not even S, the Russian journalist and professional mnemonist[3] who was studied for three decades by psychologist A.R. Luria, had a photographic memory. Rather, he seemed to have implicitly mastered a set of mnemonic[4] techniques that allowed him to memorize certain kinds of information. **D**

Viswanathan is hardly the first plagiarist to claim unconscious influence from memory's depths. George Harrison said he never intended to rip off the melody of the Chiffons' "He's So Fine" when he wrote "My Sweet Lord." He had just forgotten he'd ever heard it. And when a young Helen Keller cribbed from Margaret Canby's "The Frost Fairies" in her story "The Frost King," Canby herself said, "Under the circumstances, I do not see how any one can be so unkind as to call it a plagiarism; it is a wonderful feat of memory." Keller claimed she was forever after

180

190

200

---

2. **Talmudic** (TAHL MOOD IHK) **scholars:** The Talmud is a collection of writings on Jewish civil and religious law.
3. **mnemonist** (NEE MAHN IHST): someone who is able to recall large amounts of information.
4. **mnemonic** (NEE MAHN IHK): aiding or intended to aid the memory.

C **VOCABULARY**

Selection Vocabulary

Perseverance means "sticking to a purpose, never giving up." Why do you think the author describes the Shass Pollaks' memorization of 5,422 pages as "heroic perseverance"?

_____

_____

_____

_____

_____

D **READING FOCUS**

Underline each explanation in this paragraph that the author gives to refute (deny) **arguments** that photographic memory is possible.

The word *inadvertent* includes the prefix *in-*, which generally means either "not" or "absence of." Can you think of at least one other word that includes the **word part** *in-*? Write its definition below.

_____

_____

_____

B READING FOCUS

Based on the evidence presented in this paragraph, do you think cryptomnesia could present an **argument** to explain Viswanathan's plagiarism?

_____

_____

_____

C READING FOCUS

What is the overall **argument** of this selection? Do you think the argument is logical? Explain.

_____

_____

_____

_____

_____

terrified. "I have ever since been tortured by the fear that what I write is not my own. For a long time, when I wrote a letter, even to my mother, I was seized with a sudden feeling, and I would spell the sentences over and over, to make sure that I had not read them in a book," she wrote. "It is certain that I cannot always distinguish my own thoughts from those I read, because what I read becomes the very substance and texture of my mind."

Psychologists label this kind of inadvertent appropriation cryptomnesia, and have captured the phenomenon in the laboratory. **A** In one study, researchers had subjects play Boggle against a computer and then afterward try to recreate a list of the words they themselves found. Far more often then expected, the researchers found that their subjects would claim words found by the computer opponent as their own. Even if cryptomnesia is a real memory glitch that happens to all of us from time to time, however, it's hard to figure how it could lead to the involuntary swiping of 29 different passages. **B**

Then again, who knows, maybe Viswanathan really does have a photographic memory. She could be the first (or second). Earlier this year, a group of memory researchers at the University of California-Irvine published an astonishing article about a woman called AJ who can apparently remember every day of her life since childhood. Such people weren't supposed to exist. Her case totally upends everything we thought we knew about the limits of human memory. The scientists even had to coin a new name for her disorder, hyperthymestic syndrome. If Viswanathan really wants to stick to her story, I know a few scientists who'd probably like to meet her. She might even be able to get a syndrome named after her. **C**

Applying Your Skills

Kaavya Viswanathan: Unconscious Copycat or Plagiarist? *and* Kaavya Syndrome

VOCABULARY DEVELOPMENT

DIRECTIONS: Circle the letter of the word that is the best antonym (word with an opposite meaning) of each vocabulary word.

1. internalized
   a. ate
   b. adopted
   c. rejected

2. inadvertent
   a. intentional
   b. unplanned
   c. careless

3. perseverance
   a. nervousness
   b. laziness
   c. persistence

INFORMATIONAL TEXT FOCUS: EVALUATING ARGUMENTS

Evaluate the **arguments** made by the authors of "Kaavya Viswanathan: Unconscious Copycat or Plagiarist?" and "Kaavya Syndrome." Do you agree with the authors? Do they give logical reasons and support for their arguments? Write your evaluation on the lines below, giving as much detail as possible.

_____

_____

_____

_____

_____

_____

_____

_____

**Informational
Text Skills**
Evaluate
pro and con
arguments.

Skills Review

Collection 6

VOCABULARY REVIEW

DIRECTIONS: Circle the letter of the correct antonym, or word with the opposite meaning, of the vocabulary words listed below.

1. expendable
   a. useful
   b. essential
   c. unnecessary
   d. good

2. indispensable
   a. necessary
   b. unnecessary
   c. emotional
   d. attractive

3. verify
   a. assist
   b. deny
   c. accept
   d. confirm

4. counter
   a. agree
   b. oppose
   c. number
   d. true

5. valid
   a. false
   b. true
   c. known
   d. accepted

Collection 6

LANGUAGE COACH

DIRECTIONS: Adding a prefix to a word often changes the word's meaning. These four common prefixes all mean "not": *a-*, *in-*, *non-*, and *un-*. Guess the definition of each of the following words, and then use each word in a sentence.

1. amoral _____

_____

2. insincere _____

_____

3. nonbinding _____

_____

4. untidy _____

_____

5. incomplete _____

_____

6. unnecessary _____

_____

7. nonexistent _____

_____

8. informal _____

_____

9. uncovered _____

_____

10. inseparable _____

_____

ORAL LANGUAGE ACTIVITY

DIRECTIONS: All of the selections in this collection present arguments and try to persuade their readers of something. Suppose that you are a candidate for class president. Prepare a short oral presentation that tries to persuade your classmates to vote for you. Be sure to present a clear argument in your favor, and to back up your argument with concrete evidence.

Collection

7

Poetry

Literary and Academic Vocabulary for Collection 7

nuances (NOO AHNS IHZ) *n.:* shades of meaning or feeling.
The meaning of the poem is obvious, but the nuances make it special.

associate (UH SOH SHEE AYT) *v.:* connect in thought.
Some poets associate the moon with love.

evoke (IH VOHK) *v.:* bring a memory or feeling to mind.
Pine trees might evoke memories of winter.

elaborate (IH LAB UH RAYT) *v.:* to go into greater detail about something.
Her novel will elaborate on the ideas of the opening chapter.

speaker (SPEE KUHR) *n.:* the voice that speaks to us from a poem.
The poem's speaker is a young woman.

ballad (BAL UHD) *n.:* a song that tells a story; a poem with a steady rhythm, strong rhymes, and repetition.
"Ballad of Birmingham" is a poem that describes a historical event.

image (IHM IHJ) *n.:* a word or phrase that appeals to one or more of the five senses.
The poem's most powerful image describes the smell of the father's kitchen.

simile (SIHM UH LEE) *n.:* a comparison of two dissimilar things using a word such as *like, as,* or *than.*
When she said that the tree was like a cloud, she was using a simile.

metaphor (MEHT UH FAWR) *n.:* a comparison of two dissimilar things without the use of a word such as *like, as,* or *than.*
The phrase "you're a gazelle" is a metaphor.

rhyme (RYM) *n.:* the repetition of the end sound of words.
Find is a rhyme for mind and kind.

meter (MEE TUHR) *n.:* a regular pattern of stressed and unstressed syllables in a poem.
The poem has a simple, sing-song meter.

A Blessing

by James Wright

LITERARY FOCUS: IMAGERY AND THEME

Poets help us share their experiences by using **imagery**—language that appeals to one or more of the five senses: sight, hearing, touch, smell, and taste. The images in "A Blessing" appeal mostly to two senses, sight and touch. As you read, think about how these images help you share the speaker's experience. All of the images in a poem help create its **theme**, or the central idea.

READING FOCUS: ANALYZING DETAILS

Poets can pack a lot of meaning into short poems. One way to fully understand a poem is by **analyzing details**—looking closely at the text to really understand what the author is saying. For example, sometimes a poet will use words whose denotations (dictionary definitions) differ from their connotations (the feelings they evoke). One example of analyzing details by looking at denotations and connotations is provided below. Write your own denotation and connotation for *darken*.

SKILLS FOCUS

Literary Skills
Understand imagery and theme.

Reading Skills
Analyze details in a poem.

Word from poem	Denotation	Connotation
bounds	leaps forward	Positive; moving with youthful energy
darken		

Vocabulary Development

A Blessing

SELECTION VOCABULARY

twilight (TWY LYT) *n.:* soft light just after sunset; period between sunset and night.

The ponies grazed at twilight.

bounds (BOWNDZ) *v.:* leaps or springs forward.

As night falls, the growing darkness bounds over the pasture.

nuzzled (NUHZ UHLD) *v.:* rubbed gently with the nose.

The affectionate pony nuzzled the speaker.

caress (KUH REHS) *v.:* touch gently in an affectionate manner.

The speaker wants to caress the pony's ear.

WORD STUDY

DIRECTIONS: Pair each vocabulary word in the left column with the phrase it best matches in the right column.

_____ **1.** twilight   **a.** touch gently

_____ **2.** bounds   **b.** jumps ahead

_____ **3.** nuzzled   **c.** late afternoon

_____ **4.** caress   **d.** rubbed softly

A BLESSING

by James Wright

Just off the highway to Rochester, Minnesota,
Twilight bounds softly forth on the grass,
And the eyes of those two Indian ponies
Darken with kindness. **A** **B**

5   They have come gladly out of the willows
To welcome my friend and me.
We step over the barbed wire into the pasture
Where they have been grazing all day, alone.
They ripple tensely, they can hardly contain their happiness

10 That we have come.
They bow shyly as wet swans. They love each other.
There is no loneliness like theirs.
At home once more,
They begin munching the young tufts of spring in the
        darkness.

15 I would like to hold the slenderer one in my arms,
For she has walked over to me
And nuzzled my left hand.
She is black and white,
Her mane falls wild on her forehead,

20 And the light breeze moves me to caress her long ear
That is delicate as the skin over a girl's wrist.
Suddenly I realize
That if I stepped out of my body I would break
Into blossom. **C**

A **READING FOCUS**

What can you learn from **analyzing details** in the opening lines?

_____

_____

_____

_____

B **VOCABULARY**

Selection Vocabulary

Why do you think the author uses the word *bounds* here?

_____

_____

_____

_____

C **LITERARY FOCUS**

The speaker uses surprising **imagery** here. To what is he comparing himself?

_____

_____

"A Blessing" from *Collected Poems* by James Wright. Copyright © 1963, 1971 by James Wright. Reproduced by permission of **Wesleyan University Press**, www.wesleyan.edu/wespress.

226   **A Blessing**

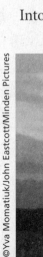

©Yva Momatiuk/John Eastcott/Minden Pictures

Applying Your Skills

A Blessing

VOCABULARY DEVELOPMENT

DIRECTIONS: Write the vocabulary words from the Word Box on the correct blanks to complete the paragraph. One word will not be used.

Word Box

twilight

bounds

nuzzled

caress

I wanted to (1) _____ the ponies, because they looked so soft running through the field. They paused, and one (2) _____ the other behind the ear. I stood there amazed, but as (3) _____ arrived, they faded into the darkness.

LITERARY FOCUS: IMAGERY AND THEME

DIRECTIONS: Complete the exercise below by deciding which sense or senses each example of **imagery** appeals to. The first one has been done for you.

1. "Twilight bounds softly on the grass": sight

2. "They bow shyly as wet swans": _____

3. "They begin munching on tufts of spring": _____

4. "And the light breeze moves me to caress her long ear": _____

READING FOCUS: ANALYZING DETAILS

DIRECTIONS: Analyze the **details** in the lines from the poem provided below and write what you feel the author is trying to say with those details in the correct boxes.

Details from Poem	My Analysis
"They bow shyly as wet swans. They love each other. / There is no loneliness like theirs."	1.
"Her mane falls wild on her forehead, / And the light breeze moves me to caress her long ear."	2.

SKILLS FOCUS

Literary Skills
Recognize imagery.

Reading Skills
Analyze details.

Women

by Alice Walker

LITERARY FOCUS: SPEAKER AND TONE

The voice that talks to us in a poem is called the **speaker**. Sometimes the speaker is the poet, and sometimes they are not the same. The speaker can be anything—a child, a woman, a man, an animal, or even an object.

Tone is a writer's or speaker's attitude toward a subject or the audience. To create a tone, a poet chooses words and details carefully. The tone of a story or poem may be serious, happy, or fearful, for example.

Use the Skill   Read the following sentences, and write down as much information as you can about each speaker.

1. I held my baby for nearly four hours last night to protect her from the cold.

   _____

   _____

2. I have been studying for that test for weeks.

   _____

   _____

3. During my cross-country trip, my car broke down and I had to walk to the nearest gas station.

   _____

   _____

4. Growing up on a farm helped me in my career as an adult.

   _____

   _____

SKILLS FOCUS

Literary Skills
Understand speaker and tone.

Preparing to Read

Women

READING FOCUS: ANALYZING DETAILS

Poets choose their words carefully. When they describe a person, for example, they might use words that are short and blunt or they might create complicated phrases that are imaginative or playful.

Use the Skill Read the following phrases from the poem "Women." As you read the poem, **analyze details** to help you explain what these phrases tell you about the women being described.

Phrases from poem	How women are being described
My mama's generation	
they led armies	
Without knowing a page / Of it / Themselves	

SKILLS FOCUS

Reading Skills
Analyze details.

WOMEN

by Alice Walker

BACKGROUND
Alice Walker is a poet, novelist, short story writer, and essayist. She was born in 1944 in a small town in Georgia. Her father was a sharecropper and her mother was a maid. Walker has said that the poem "Women" was written for her mother. Other important people to her were teachers: "I also had terrific teachers. . . Right on through grammar school and high school and college, there was one—sometimes even two—teachers who saved me from feeling alone. . ."

They were women then

My mama's generation

Husky of voice—stout of

Step

5 With fists as well as

Hands

How they battered down

Doors

And ironed

10 Starched white

Shirts

How they led

Armies

Headragged generals **A**

15 Across mined

Fields

Booby-trapped

Ditches

To discover books

20 Desks

A place for us **B**

© Frances Benjamin Johnston Collection, Prints & Photographs Division, Library of Congress

How they knew what we

Must know

Without knowing a page

25   Of it

Themselves.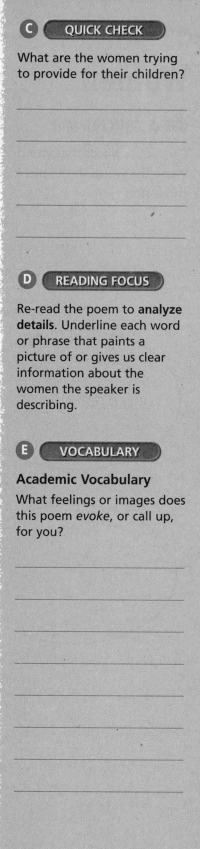

C QUICK CHECK

What are the women trying to provide for their children?

_____

_____

_____

_____

D READING FOCUS

Re-read the poem to **analyze details**. Underline each word or phrase that paints a picture of or gives us clear information about the women the speaker is describing.

E VOCABULARY

Academic Vocabulary

What feelings or images does this poem *evoke*, or call up, for you?

_____

_____

_____

_____

_____

_____

_____

Women

USE A CONCEPT MAP

Choose six words that you think describe the tone of the poem "Women."
Write the words in the blank ovals below. Then, in each oval, explain why you
chose that word.

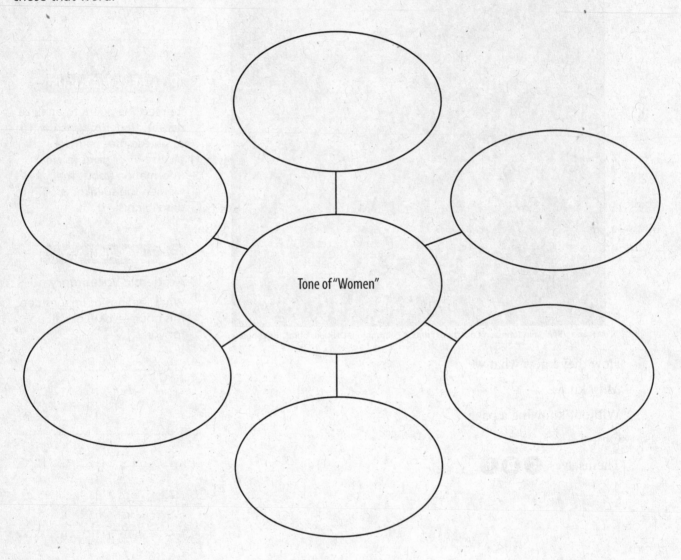

Tone of "Women"

Applying Your Skills

Women

LITERARY FOCUS: SPEAKER AND TONE

DIRECTIONS: Circle the letter of the best answer for each question.

1. How would you describe the speaker of "Women"?

    a. The speaker is a small child.

    b. The speaker is a woman.

    c. The speaker is an animal.

2. How would you describe the tone of the poem?

    a. bored and tired

    b. angry and resentful

    c. respectful and admiring

READING FOCUS: ANALYZING DETAILS

DIRECTIONS: In the left column of the chart below, create a list of **details** from the poem. In the right column, **analyze** what those details tell you about the people the poem describes.

Detail from poem	What it tells me
1.	2.
3.	4.
5.	6.
7.	8.

Literary Skills
Analyze the speaker and tone.

Reading Skills
Analyze details.

Preparing to Read

I Wandered Lonely as a Cloud

by William Wordsworth

LITERARY FOCUS: RHYTHM AND METER

Rhythm is the repetition of sound patterns. It is what gives poems a musical quality. William Wordsworth creates rhythm by arranging his words so that the lines repeat a regular pattern of stressed and unstressed syllables. This pattern is called **meter**. When you look over a poem to find its meter, mark the stressed syllables with the symbol ´ and unstressed syllables with the symbol ˘.

Read this nursery rhyme to yourself, and pay careful attention to the symbols in the first two lines. Then, fill in the symbols for the remainder of the poem.

´ ˘ ˘ ´ ˘ ˘ ´
Hickory Dickory Dock,

˘ ´ ˘ ´ ˘ ´
The mouse ran up the clock.

The clock struck one,

The mouse ran down!

Hickory Dickory Dock.

SKILLS FOCUS

Literary Skills Understand rhythm and meter.

Reading Skills Read aloud.

READING FOCUS: READING ALOUD

Reading aloud can help you to understand a poem's basic meaning and analyze its rhythm and meter.

Use the Skill Read aloud "I Wandered Lonely as a Cloud," and pay attention to the poem's meaning. At the same time, listen to your own voice so that you can hear which syllables are stressed and which are not.

Vocabulary Development

I Wandered Lonely as a Cloud

SELECTION VOCABULARY

sprightly (SPRYT LEE) *adj.*: lively, full of spirit.

The speaker of the poem remembers the daffodils' sprightly movements in the breeze.

glee (GLEE) *n.*: great delight; merriment.

The poem's speaker thinks that if the daffodils could feel, they would be filled with glee.

pensive (PEHN SIHV) *adj.*: thoughtful in a serious manner; reflective.

When the speaker is in a pensive mood, he likes to lie down on his couch.

solitude (SAHL UH TOOD) *n.*: being alone; isolation.

In solitude, the speaker likes to think back on the field of daffodils that he once saw.

WORD STUDY

DIRECTIONS: Write "Yes" after each sentence if the boldfaced vocabulary word is being used correctly. Write "No" if it is being used incorrectly. If you write "No," rewrite the sentence so that the vocabulary word is used correctly.

1. He lived in **solitude** so he could be around a lot of people. _____

_____

2. Since both my legs were in casts, I could run around in a **sprightly** manner. _____

_____

3. I was in a **pensive** mood, so I decided to be by myself so I could think. _____

_____

4. I hadn't studied at all, so I felt much **glee** and anxiety just before the big test. _____

_____

I WANDERED LONELY AS A CLOUD

by William Wordsworth

BACKGROUND

William Wordsworth was an English poet who lived from 1770–1850. He believed that poetry can occur when people get in touch with a memory and relive the experience long after it has occurred. Wordsworth also believed that nature is the best teacher. This poem describes a special moment in nature.

A **QUICK CHECK**

What happens in the first stanza, or section, of the poem?

_____

_____

_____

_____

B **VOCABULARY**

Selection Vocabulary

Glee means "great delight." Use *glee* in a sentence.

_____

_____

_____

I wandered lonely as a cloud
That floats on high o'er vales[1] and hills,
When all at once I saw a crowd,
A host, of golden daffodils,
5   Beside the lake, beneath the trees,
Fluttering and dancing in the breeze. **A**

Continuous as the stars that shine
And twinkle on the Milky Way,
They stretched in never-ending line
10   Along the margin of a bay;
Ten thousand saw I at a glance,
Tossing their heads in sprightly dance.

The waves beside them danced, but they
Outdid the sparkling waves in glee; **B**
15   A poet could not but be gay,
In such a jocund[2] company;

---

1. **vales** (VAYLZ): valleys.
2. **jocund** (JAHK UHND): merry.

© A. Curtis/Alamy

I gazed—and gazed—but little thought

What wealth the show to me had brought: **C**

For oft,[3] when on my couch I lie

20　In vacant or in pensive mood,

They flash upon that inward eye

Which is the bliss of solitude; **D**

And then my heart with pleasure fills,

And dances with the daffodils. **E** **F**

---

3. **oft** (AWFT): shortened form of often.

C (LITERARY ANALYSIS)

When the poet says the sight of the daffodils brought him wealth, what sort of wealth do you think he means?

_____

_____

_____

D (LANGUAGE COACH)

A word's **connotations** are the feelings associated with the word. Both *pensive* and *solitude* have quiet, thoughtful, slightly sad connotations. Use a thesaurus to find a synonym for each word that has similar connotations.

_____

_____

E (READING FOCUS)

Read the last stanza aloud. How does **reading aloud** help you figure out its meaning?

_____

_____

_____

_____

F (LITERARY FOCUS)

Write stressed (´) and unstressed (˘) symbols above the lines of the last stanza to show the **meter**.

Skills Practice

I Wandered Lonely as a Cloud

USE A CHARACTERIZATION CONCEPT MAP

The language that William Wordsworth uses in "I Wandered Lonely as a Cloud" can be hard to understand. It helps to restate text in your own words to figure out its meaning. In the boxes on the left, rewrite the stanza exactly as Wordsworth wrote it. In the boxes on the right, rewrite each stanza in your own words.

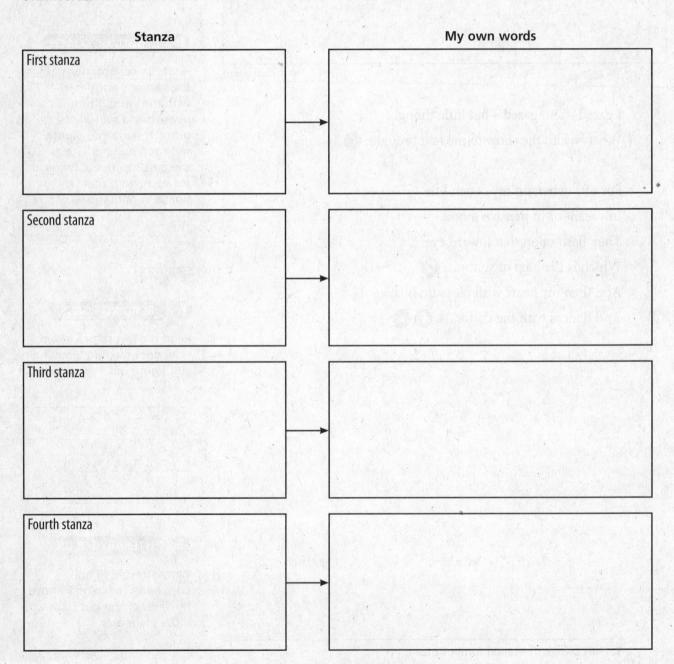

Stanza	My own words
First stanza	
Second stanza	
Third stanza	
Fourth stanza	

Applying Your Skills

I Wandered Lonely as a Cloud

VOCABULARY DEVELOPMENT

DIRECTIONS: Write a synonym for each vocabulary word listed below. A synonym is a word with a meaning that is the same or almost the same. Use a dictionary or thesaurus if you need help.

1. sprightly: _____

2. glee: _____

3. pensive: _____

4. solitude: _____

LITERARY FOCUS: RHYTHM AND METER

DIRECTIONS: Read the following lines from "I Wandered Lonely as a Cloud." Write symbols on top of each line to show which parts are stressed (´) and unstressed (˘).

I wandered lonely as a cloud

That floats on high o'er vales and hills,

When all at once I saw a crowd,

A host of golden daffodils,

Beside the lake, beneath the trees,

Fluttering and dancing in the breeze.

READING FOCUS: READING ALOUD

DIRECTIONS: With a partner, **read aloud** "I Wandered Lonely as a Cloud"; take turns so that you each read the poem aloud once. After you are both done, write a paragraph describing the differences in the two readings. Did the different readings change the meaning, rhythm, or meter of the poem?

SKILLS FOCUS

Literary Skills
Understand rhythm and meter.

Reading Skills
Read aloud.

Preparing to Read

Legal Alien/Extranjera Legal

by Pat Mora

LITERARY FOCUS: SPEAKER, WORD PLAY, AND PARALLEL STRUCTURES

Poets can imagine anyone or anything as their **speaker**, the voice that talks to us in the poem. The speaker is often the poet—but not always. The poet may use a **persona**, or mask, and speak as someone other than him- or herself.

Poems convey ideas through language. As they craft their poems, poets choose each word carefully, playing with meaning and sound, and pairing unlikely words. Poets can also use **parallel structure**, or phrases that have similar grammar and words or phrases that repeat.

Read these lines from "Legal Alien." Circle the lines that have parallel structure.

> viewed by Anglos as perhaps exotic,
>
> perhaps inferior, definitely different,
>
> viewed by Mexicans as alien
>
> (their eyes say, "You may speak
>
> Spanish but you're not like me"),

Why do these lines have a parallel structure?

_____

_____

_____

SKILLS FOCUS

Literary Skills
Understand speaker, word play, and parallel structures.

Preparing to Read

Legal Alien/Extranjera Legal

READING FOCUS: ANALYZING DETAILS

To fully appreciate a poem, you should read it several times: for enjoyment, for comprehension, and for analysis. As you **analyze details** you look for deeper meaning and try to figure out how the poet constructed the poem.

Re-read the lines from "Legal Alien" that appear on the previous page, and answer the questions below.

1. Comprehension: What is the poet trying to say in this segment of the poem?

   _____

   _____

2. Analysis: Why do you think the poet chose to use parallel structure here? Does it reinforce the meaning of the passage? Why or why not?

   _____

   _____

SKILLS FOCUS

Reading Skills
Analyze details.

Use the Skill Read "Legal Alien/Extranjera Legal" at least three times. After each reading, fill in a chart like this one with descriptions of what you took away from the poem.

First Reading (enjoyment)	Second Reading (comprehension)	Third Reading (analysis)

LEGAL ALIEN

by Pat Mora

> ### BACKGROUND
>
> Pat Mora was born on the border of El Paso, Texas and Mexico. Raised in a Mexican American household, she grew up speaking and reading both English and Spanish. Her poetry blends Hispanic culture into American society. This poem is from her first book of poetry. A legal alien is an immigrant who enters a country legally.

Bi-lingual, Bi-cultural, **A**
able to slip from "How's life?"
to *"Me'stan volviendo loca,"*[1] **B**
able to sit in a paneled office
5 drafting memos in smooth English,

---

1. *Me'stan . . . loca* (MEH STAHN VOHL VEE EHN DOH LOH KAH): Spanish for "They're driving me crazy."

© Jason Horowitz/zefa/Corbis

able to order in fluent Spanish
at a Mexican restaurant,
American but hyphenated,
viewed by Anglos as perhaps exotic,
5   perhaps inferior, definitely different,
viewed by Mexicans as alien
(their eyes say, "You may speak
Spanish but you're not like me"),
an American to Mexicans
10 a Mexican to Americans
a handy token
sliding back and forth
between the fringes of both worlds **C**
by smiling
15 by masking the discomfort
of being pre-judged
Bi-laterally.[2] **D**

C VOCABULARY

Word Study

Fringes means "the outer *edges*." What synonym (word with a similar meaning) for *fringes* could Mora have used here?

_____

D READING FOCUS

Re-read this poem **to analyze details**. What did you learn in the second reading that you didn't learn in the first?

_____
_____
_____
_____
_____
_____
_____
_____
_____
_____
_____
_____

---

2. **Bi-laterally** (BY LAT UHR UHL LEE): by both sides. (Mora has added a hyphen to this word.)

EXTRANJERA LEGAL

by Pat Mora

Bi-lingüe, bi-cultural,
capaz de deslizarse de "*How's life?*"
a "Me'stan volviendo loca,"
capaz de ocupar un despacho bien apuntado,
5 redactando memorandums en inglés liso,
capaz de ordenar la cena en español fluido
en restaurante mexicano,
americana pero con guión,
vista por los anglos como exótica,
10 quizás inferior, obviamente distinta,
vista por mexicanos como extranjera
(sus ojos dicen "Hablas español
pero no eres como yo"),
americana para mexicanos
15 mexicana para americanos
una ficha servible
pasando de un lado al otro
de los márgenes de dos mundos
sonriéndome
20 disfrazando la incomodidad
del pre-juicio
bi-lateralmente. **A**

Applying Your Skills

Legal Alien/Extanjera legal

LITERARY FOCUS: SPEAKER, WORD PLAY, AND PARALLEL STRUCTURES

DIRECTIONS: Copy the chart below onto a separate sheet of paper. Find three lines with **parallel structure** in either version of the poem and write each line into one of the lower ovals. Then, in the top oval, write down each characteristic that the lines have in common.

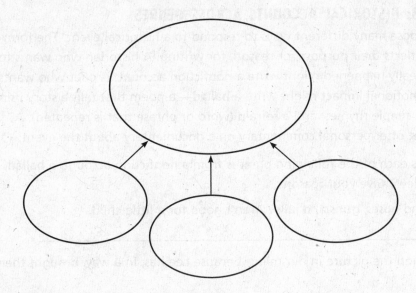

READING FOCUS: ANALYZING DETAILS

DIRECTIONS: Analyze details to answer these questions about "Legal Alien":

1. Do you think the poem's title has multiple meanings? Why or why not?

   _____

   _____

2. Who do you think is the speaker of "Legal Alien"? How do you know?

   _____

   _____

3. Why does the speaker not quite fit into either of the two worlds?

   _____

   _____

Literary Skills
Understand speaker, word play, and parallel structure.

Reading Skills
Analyze details.

The History Behind the Ballad, Ballad of Birmingham, *and* 4 Little Girls

by Taylor Branch, Dudley Randall, and Roger Ebert (respectively)

LITERARY FOCUS: HISTORICAL ACCOUNTS ACROSS GENRES

Writers can choose many different ways to respond to a historical event. The form they choose reflects their purpose, or reason, for writing. A historian who wants to explain what really happened might write a nonfiction account. A poet who wants to show the emotional impact might write a **ballad**— a poem that tells a story using steady rhythm, simple rhymes, and a refrain (word or phrase that is repeated). A film critic might offer personal commentary on a documentary about the event.

Use the Skill   Is each of the following phrases from a nonfiction account, a ballad, or a movie review? Give your reasons.

1. And clubs and hoses, guns and jails / Aren't good for a little child.

_____

2. We can fashion the picture in our minds because Lee has, in a way, brought them back to life . . .

_____

3. They stumbled through the gathering noise of moans and sirens . . .

_____

READING FOCUS: COMPARING MESSAGES IN DIFFERENT FORMS

To **compare messages** in different works inspired by the same historical event, ask yourself, "Why did the writer choose this form?" Think about how the choice of form influenced the writer's description of the event.

Use the Skill   Use a chart like this one to compare these three selections:

SKILLS FOCUS

Literary Skills
Understand historical accounts and different genres.

Reading Skills
Compare and contrast messages in different forms.

Title	Form	Effect of using this form
"Ballad of Birmingham"		
"The History Behind the Ballad"		
"4 Little Girls"		

Vocabulary Development

The History Behind the Ballad, Ballad of Birmingham, *and* 4 Little Girls

SELECTION VOCABULARY

literally (LIHT UHR UH LEE) *adv.:* taking words at their exact meaning.

We were shocked to see that after the bomb blast, the stairs had literally disappeared.

infamous (IHN FUH MUHS) *adj.:* having a bad reputation; notorious.

The infamous crime took the lives of four innocent children.

charisma (KUH RIHZ MUH) *n.:* personal charm.

Successful politicians often have a great deal of charisma.

rationalizations (RASH UH NUH LUH ZAY SHUHNZ) *n.:* excuses made for behavior.

No matter how many rationalizations you give, cheating is wrong.

WORD STUDY

DIRECTIONS: Fill in each blank with the correct vocabulary word.

1. Her _____ makes her very popular at school.

2. I found it _____ impossible to put the broken pieces of the vase back together.

3. After the scandal became known, he was saddened to find that his actions had made him _____.

4. They made many _____ for the crime, but none of them was acceptable.

THE HISTORY BEHIND THE BALLAD

by Taylor Branch

BACKGROUND

On September 15, 1963, in the midst of the struggle for civil rights for African Americans, a bomb exploded in a church in Birmingham, Alabama, killing four girls. "The History Behind the Ballad" is taken from a book that won the Pulitzer Prize for History. "The Ballad of Birmingham" is a poem about this tragic event. "4 Little Girls" is a review of a documentary about the bombing.

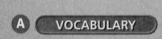

A   VOCABULARY

Word Study

Engaged can mean "involved; took part in." Look up another meaning for the word and use it in a sentence.

_____

_____

_____

B   VOCABULARY

Selection Vocabulary

Literally means "taking words at their exact meaning." If the stairs had "literally vanished," what had happened to them?

_____

_____

That Sunday was the annual Youth Day at the Sixteenth Street Baptist Church. Mamie H. Grier, superintendent of the Sunday school, stopped in at the basement ladies' room to find four young girls who had left Bible classes early and were talking excitedly about the beginning of the school year. All four were dressed in white from head to toe, as this was their day to run the main service for the adults at eleven o'clock. Grier urged them to hurry along and then went upstairs to sit in on her own women's Sunday-school class. They were engaged in a lively

10   debate on the lesson topic, "The Love That Forgives," when a loud earthquake shook the entire church and showered the classroom with plaster and debris. **A** Grier's first thought was that it was like a ticker-tape parade. Maxine McNair, a school teacher next to her, reflexively went stiff and was the one to speak. "Oh my goodness!" she said. She escaped, with Grier, but the stairs down to the basement were blocked and large stone staircase on the outside literally had vanished. **B** They stumbled through the gathering noise of moans and sirens. A

Excerpt [retitled "The History Behind the Ballad"] from *Parting the Waters: America in the King Years, 1956-63* by Taylor Branch. Copyright © 1988 by Taylor Branch. Reproduced by permission of **Simon & Schuster Adult Publishing Group**.

Courtesy of The Birmingham Public Library Archives, Neg. [85.1.20]

20 hysterical church member shouted to Grier that her husband had already gone to the hospital in the first ambulance. McNair searched desperately for her only child until finally she came upon a sobbing old man and screamed, "Daddy, I can't find Denise!" The man helplessly replied, "She's dead, baby. I've got one of her shoes." He held a girl's white dress shoe, and the look on his daughter's face made him scream out, "I'd like to blow the whole town up!" **C** **D**

C LITERARY FOCUS

What do you think is the author's purpose for writing this **historical account**?

_____

_____

_____

_____

D READING FOCUS

How might the **message** of this account be different if the author had written fiction instead?

_____

_____

_____

_____

BALLAD OF BIRMINGHAM

(On the bombing of a church in Birmingham, Alabama, 1963)
by Dudley Randall

A VOCABULARY

Word Study

Fire, as a verb, has multiple meanings. Here it means "to shoot." Look up another meaning of the verb *fire* and use it in a sentence.

_____

_____

_____

_____

_____

_____

A VOCABULARY

Word Study

Fire, as a verb, has multiple meanings. Here it means "to shoot." Look up another meaning of the verb *fire* and use it in a sentence.

_____

_____

_____

_____

_____

_____

B VOCABULARY

Academic Vocabulary

What feelings and images does this poem *evoke,* or bring to mind?

_____

_____

_____

_____

_____

_____

_____

_____

"Mother dear, may I go downtown
Instead of out to play,
And march the streets of Birmingham
In a Freedom March today?"

5 "No, baby, no, you may not go,
For the dogs are fierce and wild,
And clubs and hoses, guns and jails
Aren't good for a little child."

"But, mother, I won't be alone.
10 Other children will go with me,
And march the streets of Birmingham
To make our country free."

"No, baby, no, you may not go,
For I fear those guns will fire. **A**
15 But you may go to church instead
And sing in the children's choir."

She has combed and brushed her night-dark hair,
And bathed rose-petal sweet,
And drawn white gloves on her small brown hands,
20 And white shoes on her feet. **B**

The mother smiled to know her child
Was in the sacred place,
But that smile was the last smile
To come upon her face.

25 For when she heard the explosion,
    Her eyes grew wet and wild.
    She raced through the streets of Birmingham
    Calling for her child.

    She clawed through bits of glass and brick,
30 Then lifted out a shoe.
    "O, here's the shoe my baby wore,
    But, baby, where are you?" Ⓓ Ⓔ

Ⓒ LITERARY FOCUS

Why is this poem considered
a **ballad**?

_____

_____

_____

Ⓓ LITERARY FOCUS

After reading the poem, why
do you think Randall chose
to write a **ballad** about the
bombing instead of a
nonfiction account? What do
you think was his purpose
for writing?

_____

_____

_____

_____

Ⓔ READING FOCUS

How is the **message** in this
poem different from the
message in "The History
Behind the Ballad"?

_____

_____

_____

_____

4 LITTLE GIRLS

by Roger Ebert

B **READING FOCUS**

Compare messages here. How is the opening paragraph of this film review similar to the information in "The History Behind the Ballad"?

_____

_____

_____

_____

_____

Roger Ebert's review of *4 Little Girls* by Spike Lee, from *Chicago Sun Times*, October 24, 1997. Copyright © 1997 by Roger Ebert. Reproduced by permission of **Andrews McMeel Publishing**.

Spike Lee. © Michael Schmelling/AP Images

Spike Lee's "4 Little Girls" tells the story of the infamous Birmingham, Ala., church bombing of Sept. 15, 1963, when the lives of an 11-year-old and three 14-year-olds, members of the choir, were ended by an explosion. A More than any other event, that was the catalyst for the civil rights movement, the moment when all of America could look away no longer from the face of racism. "It was the awakening," says Walter Cronkite[1] in the film. The little girls had gone to church early for choir practice, and we can imagine them, dressed in their Sunday

10 best, meeting their friends in the room destroyed by the bomb. We can fashion the picture in our minds because Lee has, in a way, brought them back to life, through photographs, through old home movies and especially through the memories of their families and friends. B

---

1. **Walter Cronkite** (1916–   ) is a well-known broadcast reporter and journalist. His familiar voice became a trusted source of news on both radio and television.

By coincidence, I was listening to the radio not long after seeing "4 Little Girls," and I heard a report from Charlayne Hunter-Gault. In 1961, when she was 19, she was the first black woman to desegregate the University of Georgia. Today she is an NPR correspondent. That is what happened to her. In 1963, Carole Robertson was 14, and her Girl Scout sash was covered with merit badges. Because she was killed that day, we will never know what would have happened in her life. **C**

That thought keeps returning: The four little girls never got to grow up. Not only were their lives stolen, but so were their contributions to ours. I have a hunch that Denise McNair, who was 11 when she died, would have made her mark. In home movies, she comes across as poised and observant, filled with charisma. **D** Among the many participants in the film, two of the most striking are her parents, Chris and Maxine McNair, who remember a special child.

Chris McNair talks of a day when he took Denise to downtown Birmingham, and the smell of onions frying at a store's lunch counter made her hungry. "That night I knew I had to tell her she couldn't have that sandwich because she was black," he recalls. "That couldn't have been any less painful than seeing her with a rock smashed into her head."

Lee's film re-creates the day of the bombing through newsreel footage, photographs and eyewitness reports. He places it within a larger context of the Southern civil rights movement, and sit-ins and the arrests, the marches, the songs and the killings.

Birmingham was a tough case. Police commissioner Bull Connor is seen directing the resistance to marchers and traveling in an armored vehicle—painted white, of course. Gov. George Wallace makes his famous vow to stand in the schoolhouse door and personally bar any black students from entering. Though they could not know it, their resistance was futile after Sept. 15, 1963, because the hatred exposed by the bomb pulled all of their rhetoric and rationalizations out from under them. **E**

Spike Lee says he has wanted to make this film since 1983, when he read a *New York Times Magazine* article by Howell

C **QUICK CHECK**

What is Ebert comparing in this paragraph?

_____

_____

_____

_____

D **VOCABULARY**

Selection Vocabulary
Charisma is "personal charm." List two or three public figures or people you know who have charisma.

_____

_____

_____

E **VOCABULARY**

Selection Vocabulary
Rationalizations are "excuses made for behavior." What were the rationalizations mentioned here being made for?

_____

_____

_____

_____

How does the **message** in this selection compare to the messages in the previous two selections?

_____

_____

_____

_____

B LITERARY FOCUS

How does Ebert's final judgement on the film also reflect his personal message?

_____

_____

_____

_____

_____

_____

Raines about the bombing. "He wrote me asking permission back then," Chris McNair told me in an interview. "That was before he had made any of his films." It is perhaps good that Lee waited, because he is more of a filmmaker now, and events have supplied him a denouement in the conviction of a man named Robert Chambliss ("Dynamite Bob") as the bomber. He was, said Raines, who met quite a few, "the most pathological racist I've ever encountered." The other victims were Addle Mae Collins and Cynthia Wesley, both 14. In shots that are almost unbearable, 60 we see the victims' bodies in the morgue. Why does Lee show them? To look full into the face of what was done, I think. To show racism its handiwork. There is a memory in the film of a burly white Birmingham policeman who after the bombing tells a black minister, "I really didn't believe they would go this far." The man was a Klansman, the movie says, but in using the word "they" he unconsciously separates himself from his fellows. He wants to disassociate himself from the crime. So did others. Before long even Wallace was apologizing for his behavior and trying to define himself in a different light. There is a scene 70 in the film where the former governor, now old and infirm, describes his black personal assistant, Eddie Holcey, as his best friend. "I couldn't live without him," Wallace says, dragging Holcey in front of the camera, insensitive to the feelings of the man he is tugging over for display.

Why is that scene there? It's sort of associated with the morgue photos, I think. There is mostly sadness and regret at the surface in "4 Little Girls," but there is anger in the depths, as there should be. **A** **B**

Applying Your Skills

The History Behind the Ballad, Ballad of Birmingham, *and* 4 Little Girls

VOCABULARY DEVELOPMENT

DIRECTIONS: Each sentence below uses the boldfaced vocabulary word incorrectly. Re-write each sentence in the space provided so that the word is used correctly.

1. Because everyone loved her so much, she was **infamous**.

   _____

2. From the instant I met her, her **charisma** made me hate her.

   _____

3. The **rationalizations** Fred included in his essay proved without a doubt that the chicken came before the egg.

   _____

   _____

4. Ginger watched a movie that **literally** transported her to ancient China.

   _____

LITERARY FOCUS: HISTORICAL ACCOUNTS ACROSS GENRES

DIRECTIONS: On a separate sheet of paper, describe the author's purpose for each selection. Remember that the form each author chose reflects his purpose.

READING FOCUS: COMPARING MESSAGES IN DIFFERENT FORMS

DIRECTIONS: Choose two of the selections and compare and contrast them in a Venn diagram like the one below. How are the **messages** similar and different?

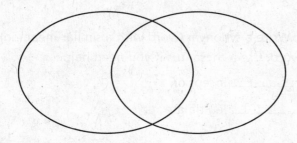

Literary Skills
Understand authors' purposes in historical accounts across genres.

Reading Skills
Compare and contrast messages in different forms.

FBI Art Crime Team *and* Collection Is Found to Contain Stolen Rockwell Art

INFORMATIONAL TEXT FOCUS: GENERATING RESEARCH QUESTIONS

When you research a topic, you work to increase your understanding of a subject from general knowledge to more specific, in-depth knowledge. Often, doing research is a question-and-answer process. You ask yourself questions on the topics you need to know more about and do research to answer those questions.

A good method in **generating research questions** is to ask the **5W-How? questions:** *Who* was involved? *What* happened? *When* and *where* did it happen? *Why* and *how* did it happen? As you read these two selections, ask yourself the 5W-How? questions.

SELECTION VOCABULARY

inception (IHN SEHP SHUHN) *n.:* start of something; beginning.
> *Since the team's inception, it has recovered stolen art worth more than $65 million.*

ceremonial (SEHR UH MOH NEE UHL) *adj.:* having to do with a rite or ceremony.
> *The team found some Native American ceremonial garments.*

legitimate (LUH JIHT UH MIHT) *adj.:* conforming to or abiding by the law.
> *Steven Spielberg was surprised to find out that he had bought a stolen painting from a legitimate art dealer.*

client (KLY UHNT) *n.:* person or group for which a professional person or service works.
> *The client lost the art when the gallery was robbed.*

WORD STUDY

DIRECTIONS: Write a synonym (word with a similar meaning) for each vocabulary word. Use a thesaurus if you need help.

1. _____ inception

2. _____ legitimate

SKILLS FOCUS

Informational Text Skills
Generate research questions.

FBI ART CRIME TEAM

File   Edit   View   Favorites   Tools   Help

Back   Forward   Stop   Refresh   Home   Search   Favorites   History   Mail   Print

Address   http://www.fbi.gov/hq/cid/arttheft/artcrimeteam.htm   Go

Federal Bureau of Investigation

HOME | SITE MAP | FAQs

SEARCH

About Us
Art Theft Program Home

Criminal Investigative Division
America's Criminal Enterprise
Major Theft Unit

Contact Us
Your Local FBI Office
Overseas Offices
Submit a Crime Tip
Report Internet Crime
More Contacts

Learn About Us
Quick Facts
What We Investigate
Natl. Security Branch
Information Technology
Fingerprints & Training
Laboratory Services
Reports & Publications
History
More About Us

Get Our News
Press Room
E-mail Updates
News Feeds

Be Crime Smart
Wanted by the FBI
More Protections

Use Our Resources
For Law Enforcement
For Communities
For Researchers
More Services

Visit Our Kids' Page
Apply for a Job

Art Crime Team

The FBI established a rapid deployment Art Crime Team in 2004. The team is composed of twelve Special Agents, each responsible for addressing art and cultural property crime cases in an assigned geographic region. The Art Crime Team is coordinated through the FBI's Art Theft Program, located at FBI Headquarters in Washington, D.C. Art Crime Team agents receive specialized training in art and cultural property investigations and assist in art-related investigations worldwide in cooperation with foreign law enforcement officials and FBI Legal Attaché offices. The U.S. Department of Justice has assigned three Special Trial Attorneys to the Art Crime Team for prosecutive[1] support.

Since its inception, the Art Crime Team has recovered over 850 items of cultural property with a value exceeding $65 million. These include:

- Approximately 700 pre-Columbian artifacts.[2] The objects recovered in Miami were the result of a sting operation in coordination with the Ecuadorian authorities.

---

1. **prosecutive** (PRAH suh kyoo tihv): relating to legal proceedings in court against someone.
2. **pre-Columbian artifacts**: tools and objects dating from the time period before Columbus arrived in the Americas.

A READING FOCUS

Which of the **5W-How?** questions are answered by this sentence?

_____

_____

_____

B QUICK CHECK

What does the FBI Art Crime Team do?

_____

_____

_____

C VOCABULARY

Selection Vocabulary
Inception means "the start of something; beginning." Look back at the beginning of the article. When was the team's inception?

_____

_____

READING FOCUS

If you wanted to narrow your topic and just focus on this particular art crime, what other questions could you ask to help **generate research questions**?

_____

_____

_____

_____

 B **VOCABULARY**

Selection Vocabulary

Ceremonial means "having to do with a rite or ceremony." Use the word in a sentence of your own.

_____

_____

_____

_____

 C **READING FOCUS**

Were all of the **5W-How?** questions answered by the Web article? Explain.

_____

_____

_____

_____

_____

_____

NORMAN ROCKWELL

"RUSSIAN SCHOOLROOM"

- Three paintings by the German painter Heinrich Buerkel (1802–1869), stolen at the conclusion of World War II and consigned[3] for sale at an auction house near Philadelphia in 2005.

- Rembrandt's *Self Portrait* (1630) in a sting operation in Copenhagen carried out in cooperation with ICE[4] and law enforcement agencies in Sweden and Denmark. The FBI had previously recovered Renoir's *The Young Parisian*. Both paintings had been stolen from the Swedish National Museum in Stockholm in 2000.

- Approximately 100 paintings that had been stolen from a Florida family's art collection in a fine art storage facility. This collection included works by Picasso, Rothko, Matisse, and others that were recovered from Chicago, New York, and Tokyo.

- An extremely rare, experimental Springfield "Trapdoor" rifle to the Armory Museum in Springfield, Massachusetts. It had been stolen from the Armory Museum in the 1970s.

- Native American ceremonial material and eagle feathers belonging to the Taos Pueblo. The items included a war bonnet and a "Butterfly Bustle." With the assistance of the Bureau of Indian Affairs, the items were returned to the Taos Pueblo. **B**

- Four rare books stolen from Transylvania University in Lexington, Kentucky. Among the items recovered were rare pencil sketches by John James Audubon and a first edition of Charles Darwin's *On the Origin of the Species*. **C**

- Eight cylinder seals taken from archaeological sites in Iraq.

_____

3. **consigned** (kuhn SYND): sent or delivered, as goods to be sold.
4. **ICE:** acronym for U.S. Immigration and Customs Enforcement.

 Internet

COLLECTION IS FOUND TO CONTAIN STOLEN ROCKWELL ART

Collection Is Found to Contain Stolen Rockwell Art **D**
from The New York Times, March 4, 2007

Build Background

Norman Rockwell (1894–1978) was a famous American painter who for forty-seven years illustrated covers for the magazine *The Saturday Evening Post*. Rockwell's work is known for its humorous tone and focus on American families and small-town life. The American public had always embraced Rockwell's work, but some art critics were dismissive of his efforts. Despite the critics, President Gerald Ford awarded Rockwell the Presidential Medal of Freedom.

LOS ANGELES, March 3 (AP) — A Norman Rockwell painting stolen from a gallery in Clayton, Mo., more than three decades ago was found in Steven Spielberg's art collection, the F.B.I. said Friday.

Mr. Spielberg bought the painting, *Russian Schoolroom*, in 1989 from a legitimate dealer and did not know it was stolen until his staff spotted its image last week on a Federal Bureau of Investigation Web site listing stolen works of art, the bureau said in a statement. **E**

After Mr. Spielberg's staff brought it to the attention of the authorities, experts inspected the painting at one of Mr. Spielberg's offices and confirmed its authenticity on Friday. Early F.B.I. estimates put the painting's value at $700,000, officials said.

Mr. Spielberg is cooperating and will retain possession of the painting until its "disposition can be determined," the bureau said.

The painting, an oil on canvas, shows children in a classroom with a bust of Lenin.[1] Mary Ellen Shortland, who worked at the Clayton Art Gallery, recalled that someone from Missouri paid $25,000 for the painting after seeing it during a Rockwell exhibition. **F**

The client agreed to keep it on display, she said, but a few nights later someone smashed the gallery's glass door and escaped with the painting. **G**

"That was all they took," Ms. Shortland said. "That's what they wanted, that painting."

There was no sign of the work for years. Then in 1988, it was auctioned in New Orleans.

In 2004, the F.B.I.'s newly formed Art Crime Team initiated an investigation to recover the work after determining it had been advertised for sale at a Rockwell exhibit in New York in 1989.

It was not immediately known whether Mr. Spielberg bought the painting at that New York exhibit.

Russian Schoolroom appeared in *Look* magazine, but Rockwell is best known for more than 300 covers he did for *The Saturday Evening Post*.

---

1. **Lenin:** Vladimir Ilich Lenin (1870–1924), founder of the former Soviet Union, of which Russia was a part.

D READING FOCUS

Which **5W-How**? questions can be answered by this article title?

E LANGUAGE COACH

Legitimate comes from the Latin root *legitimus*, meaning "lawful." Name another word that comes from the Latin root word *leg*, meaning "law."

F VOCABULARY

Word Study

Recall means "remember." Write an antonym, or word with the opposite meaning, for *recall*.

G VOCABULARY

Selection Vocabulary

A *client* is "a person for which a professional service works." Which of these organizations might have a client: a school, amusement park, movie theater, or law practice?

Slightly adapted from "Spielberg Collection Is Found to Contain Stolen Rockwell Art" as it appears in *The New York Times*, March 4, 2007. Copyright © 2007 by **The Associated Press**. Reproduced by permission of the publisher.

Skills Practice

FBI Art Crime Team *and* Collection Is Found to Contain Stolen Rockwell Art

USE A VENN DIAGRAM

When conducting research using multiple sources, Venn Diagrams can help you to keep track of your information. In the left oval, fill in information you found only in "FBI Art Crime Team." In the right oval, fill in information you found only in the article "Collection Is Found to Contain Stolen Rockwell Art." In the area where the ovals overlap, write down information that appears in both selections.

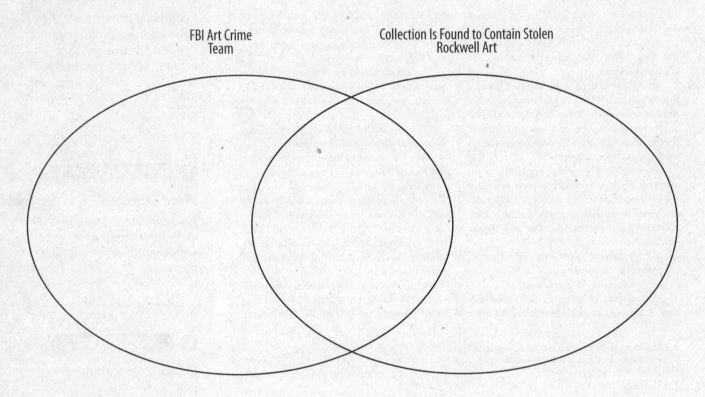

FBI Art Crime Team

Collection Is Found to Contain Stolen Rockwell Art

Applying Your Skills

FBI Art Crime Team *and* Collection Is Found to Contain Stolen Rockwell Art

VOCABULARY DEVELOPMENT

DIRECTIONS: Circle the letter of the correct antonym (word or phrase with the opposite meaning) for each vocabulary word.

1. **inception**

    a. end

    b. beginning

    c. middle

2. **legitimate**

    a. illegal

    b. approved

    c. legal

INFORMATIONAL TEXT FOCUS: GENERATING RESEARCH QUESTIONS

DIRECTIONS: Answer the **5W-How**? questions in the chart below with information from both selections.

Questions	FBI Art Crime Team	Collection Is Found...
Who?		
What?		
When?		
Where?		
Why?		
How?		

SKILLS FOCUS

Informational Text Skills
Answer 5W-How? questions

Skills Review

Collection 7

VOCABULARY REVIEW

Match each vocabulary word in the left column with the best definition from the right column.

1. _____ associate
2. _____ evoke
3. _____ elaborate
4. _____ twilight
5. _____ bounds
6. _____ nuzzled
7. _____ caress
8. _____ glee
9. _____ pensive
10. _____ solitude
11. _____ infamous
12. _____ charisma
13. _____ rationalizations
14. _____ inception
15. _____ legitimate

a. touch affectionately
b. beginning
c. connect
d. describe
e. explanations
f. force of personality
g. thoughtful
h. hops
i. isolation
j. joy
k. before dark
l. legal
m. bring to mind
n. rubbed with the nose
o. notorious

Skills Review

Collection 7

LANGUAGE COACH

A word's **denotation** is its dictionary definition. **Connotations** are the feelings and associations that the word suggests. For example, the word *solitude* has a serious, sad connotation.

DIRECTIONS: Each of the sentences below includes an underlined vocabulary word from one of the selections in this collection. Read the sentence, and in the space below, write down a list of some of the connotations the word has for you.

1. She walked with a <u>sprightly</u> step.

_____

2. He won the election because of his <u>charisma</u>.

_____

3. We had to make sure that the business was <u>legitimate</u>.

_____

4. The <u>infamous</u> crime was shown over and over again on the nightly news.

_____

5. She reacted with <u>glee</u> to the news.

_____

WRITING ACTIVITY

DIRECTIONS: Look back at the use of parallel structure in the poem "Legal Alien." Parallel structure is the use of lines or phrases that have matching grammar, words, or construction. Write a short poem using parallel structure. If you like, you can write about a subject based on one of the poems in this collection.

Drama

Literary and Academic Vocabulary for Collection 8

convention (KUHN VEHN SHUHN) *n.:* a standard technique.

An aside is a theatrical convention—the audience knows the other characters are not supposed to hear it.

embody (EHM BAHD EE) *v.:* give form to something abstract.

The characters Romeo and Juliet embody the ideal of romantic love.

interpretation (IN TUR PRUH TAY SHUHN) *n.:* portrayal that conveys a particular understanding of a work.

From the actor's interpretation, it's clear that he thinks the character is not very smart.

production (PRUH DUHK SHUHN) *n.:* presentation of a play; performance.

The production is updated to take place in Los Angeles.

dialogue (DY UH LAHG) *n.:* conversation between characters in a play.

The audience was swept away by the play's intense dialogue.

monologue (MON UH LAHG) *n.:* a long speech by one character to one or more other characters onstage.

She interrupted his monologue after several minutes.

soliloquy (SUH LIH LUH KWEE) *n.:* a speech by a character alone onstage who is speaking to him- or herself or to the audience.

Shakespeare uses the soliloquy to express the personal thoughts and emotions of his characters.

tragedy (TRA JUH DEE) *n.:* the presentation of serious and important actions, with an unhappy ending.

Romeo and Juliet, *Shakespeare's most famous play, is a tragedy.*

exposition (EK SPUH ZIH SHUHN) *n.:* the telling of the basic situation in a story.

The play has a brief exposition that introduces the main characters and their conflict.

Preparing to Read

The Tragedy of Romeo and Juliet

by William Shakespeare

LITERARY FOCUS: TRAGEDY

A **tragedy** is a story with an unhappy ending. Tragedies are about serious and important events. In some, disaster hits innocent characters; in others, the main characters' actions cause their suffering.

Like most stories, tragedies usually have a five-part **dramatic structure**. First, in the **exposition**, the setting, main characters, and main conflict are introduced. Next, during the **rising action**, the conflict becomes more intense. The **turning point** is when the main characters do something that will decide the story's outcome. The **climax** is the moment of greatest emotional intensity—often the death of a main character. In the **resolution**, the plot's loose ends are tied up.

Use the Skill   Read the following short summary of Romeo and Juliet. Label the exposition, rising action, turning point, climax, and resolution of the story.

The Montague and Capulet families have been fighting for a long time. As the play opens, their servants fight, angering the Prince of Verona, who bans further fighting. Romeo Montague and his friends go in disguise to a party being held by the Capulet family. Romeo and young Juliet Capulet fall in love at first sight, but learn that their families are enemies.

Romeo sneaks into the orchard under Juliet's room, and overhears her talking about her love for him. He declares his feelings for her, and they decide to marry. Friar Laurence marries them the next day.

Romeo fights and kills Tybalt, a Capulet. The Prince banishes Romeo from Verona, threatening death if he returns. Juliet's father, not knowing about her marriage, decides that Juliet must marry someone else. She tries but fails to fight her father's wishes.

Friar Laurence tells Juliet to take a potion that will make her seem dead, so that Romeo can take her away unopposed.

Romeo does not receive Friar Laurence's letter telling him of the plan. Instead he hears of Juliet's death and goes to Verona to visit her tomb. He arrives, takes poison, kisses Juliet, and dies. Juliet now awakens, asking for her Romeo. She sees that he is dead, kisses him, stabs herself, and dies.

Friar Laurence explains what has happened to the Prince, the Capulets, and the Montagues. In their sorrow, the two families finally end their feud.

SKILLS FOCUS

Literary Skills
Understand characteristics of a tragedy.

Preparing to Read

The Tragedy of Romeo and Juliet

READING FOCUS: READING A PLAY

When you read a play, it helps to use a variety of strategies. **Read aloud** dialogue to bring it to life. **Paraphrase**, or restate in your own words, difficult passages to make sure you understand them. **Make inferences**, or guesses based on clues in the text, to figure out why the characters do things. Finally, **analyze causes and effects** to better understand the action and **predict** what might happen next.

Reading Shakespeare can be particularly challenging. This play was written about four hundred years ago. Many of the words Shakespeare used (or their particular meanings) have disappeared from common use. The footnotes in the play will help you with some words that might be unfamiliar to you. When you come across other unfamiliar words or a familiar word that has a strange meaning, it can be confusing at first. Re-read any difficult passages, and look for words that don't seem to make sense. Use context clues to try to figure out the meaning.

Use the Skill   Read this passage from the beginning of the play, first to yourself and then aloud. Then paraphrase it, or re-write it in the kind of English that you would use. Use context clues and a good dictionary for help.

> From forth the fatal loins of these two foes
>
> A pair of star-cross'd lovers take their life,
>
> Whose misadventur'd piteous overthrows
>
> Doth with their death bury their parents' strife.

_____

_____

_____

_____

Reading Skills
Read aloud, paraphrase, make inferences, and analyze cause-and-effect relationships.

THE TRAGEDY OF ROMEO AND JULIET

by William Shakespeare

> **BACKGROUND**
>
> William Shakespeare (1564–1616) is one of the most
> famous writers of all time. *Romeo and Juliet* is one of
> his most popular plays. It is a story about doomed young
> love (Romeo and Juliet are both in their teens). Romeo
> and Juliet's love is hopeless because their families—the
> Montagues and the Capulets—are bitter enemies.

A **LITERARY FOCUS**

A prologue is generally part
of a story's **exposition**. It is
an introduction to the story.
As you read this prologue,
gather as much information
as you can. What does it
tell you?

_____

_____

_____

_____

_____

The Prologue **A**

[*Enter Chorus.*]

CHORUS. Two households both alike in dignity[1]

(In fair Verona where we lay our scene)

From ancient grudge break to new mutiny,

Where civil blood makes civil hands unclean.[2]

---

1. **dignity:** status.
2. **Where. . . unclean:** That is, where civilian's passions ("civil blood")
   make their hands unclean (because they have been used for killing).

From forth the fatal loins of these two foes

A pair of star-cross'd lovers take their life,

Whose misadventur'd piteous overthrows

Doth with their death bury their parents' strife. **B**

10   The fearful passage of their death-mark'd love

And the continuance of their parents' rage

(Which but[3] their children's end naught could remove)

Is now the two hours' traffic[4] of our stage,

The which if you with patient ears attend

What here shall miss our toil shall strive to mend. [*Exit.*]

WHAT HAPPENS NEXT As Act I opens, servants for the Montague and Capulet families meet and argue. A fight breaks out between Benvolio, a Montague, and Tybalt, a Capulet. Romeo, a Montague, tells his friend Benvolio he is in love with a woman who does not love him. To cure Romeo of his heartbreak, Benvolio suggests Romeo go with him to a masked ball at the Capulet home.

    Wearing masks, Romeo and Benvolio go to the home of the Capulets, their family's enemies. As he enters the party, Romeo sees Juliet for the first time and immediately falls in love. Tybalt hears Romeo's voice and, knowing that Romeo is a Montague, draws his sword. The head of the Capulet family tells Tybalt to leave the young man alone. With loving words, Romeo speaks to Juliet for the first time. She speaks to him tenderly and briefly before she is called away.

Act I (continued)

Nurse. Madam, your mother craves a word with you. **C**

Romeo. What is her mother?

Nurse. Marry bachelor,

Her mother is the good lady of the house,

---

3. **but:** except for.
4. **traffic:** business.

B READING FOCUS

Paraphrase, or rewrite in your own words, lines 6–9.

_____

_____

_____

_____

C LANGUAGE COACH

In modern use, the word *craves* means "longs for." In this context, do you think the meaning is the same or different? Why? If you think the meaning is different, what do you think it means?

_____

_____

_____

_____

_____

A **LITERARY FOCUS**

We know from the title that this play is a **tragedy**. How do the lines you have read so far give clues about the trouble that may lie ahead?

_____

_____

_____

_____

_____

B **LANGUAGE COACH**

In modern English, we say that the moon "waxes and wanes," which means that it gets bigger and smaller. What do you think *waxes* means in the context of this line?

_____

_____

C **LITERARY ANALYSIS**

Why do you think Juliet asks Nurse about the identity of two other men before asking about Romeo?

_____

_____

_____

20 And a good lady, and a wise and virtuous.

I nurs'd her daughter that you talk'd withal.[5]

I tell you, he that can lay hold of her

Shall have the chinks.[6]

Romeo. Is she a Capulet?

O dear account! my life is my foe's debt.[7] **A**

Benvolio. Away, be gone, the sport is at the best.

Romeo. Ay, so I fear, the more is my unrest.

Capulet. Nay gentlemen, prepare not to be gone,

We have a trifling foolish banquet towards.[8]

30 (*They whisper in his ear.*)

Is it e'en so? why then I thank you all.

I thank you, honest gentlemen. Good night.

More torches, here! Come on then, let's to bed.

Ah, sirrah, by my fay[9], it waxes late, **B**

I'll to my rest.

{*Exeunt [Capulet and most of the others.*]}

Juliet. Come hither, Nurse. What is yond gentleman?

Nurse. The son and heir of old Tiberio.

Juliet. What's he that now is going out of door?

40 *Nurse.* Marry, that I think be young Petruchio.

Juliet. What's he that follows here that would not dance? **C**

Nurse. I know not.

Juliet. Go ask his name. If he be married

My grave is like to be my wedding bed.

Nurse. His name is Romeo, and a Montague,

The only son of your great enemy.

Juliet. My only love sprung from my only hate!

Too early seen unknown, and known too late!

Prodigious[10] birth of love it is to me

---

5. **withal:** with.
6. **chinks:** money.
7. **My life is my foe's debt:** My foe now owns my life.
8. **towards:** in preparation.
9. **fay:** faith.
10. **Prodigious** (PROH DIHJ UHS): huge and monstrous.

50   That I must love a loathed enemy. **D**

Nurse. What's this? what's this?

Juliet. A rhyme I learn'd e'en now

Of one I danc'd withal.

One calls within, 'Juliet!'

Nurse. Anon, anon!¹¹

Come, let's away, the strangers are all gone.

Act II

[*Enter Chorus.*]

CHORUS. Now old Desire doth in his deathbed lie,

And young Affection gapes to be his heir.

60   That fair¹² for which Love groan'd for and would die,

With tender Juliet match'd, is now not fair.

Now Romeo is belov'd and loves again,

Alike¹³ bewitched by the charm of looks;

But to his foe suppos'd he must complain,¹⁴

And she steal love's sweet bait from fearful hooks.

Being held a foe, he may not have access

To breathe such vows as lovers use to swear;¹⁵

And she, as much in love, her means much less

To meet her new beloved anywhere.

70   But passion lends them pow'r, time means, to meet,

Temp'ring extremities¹⁶ with extreme sweet.¹⁷ **E** [*Exit.*]

WHAT HAPPENS NEXT As Act II begins, Romeo's friends Benvolio and Mercutio have left the party and are outside the Capulet home. They look for Romeo, who has turned back to see Juliet once more. Mercutio jokes that love has made Romeo crazy. Benvolio and Mercutio stop looking for Romeo and start for home. Romeo stands beneath Juliet's balcony.

11. **anon:** at once.
12. **That fair:** Rosaline.
13. **Alike:** both (both Romeo and Juliet).
14. **complain:** Ask Juliet's father, his foe, for her hand in marriage.
15. **use to swear:** are used to promising.
16. **extremities:** difficulties.
17. **extreme sweet:** very sweet delights

D **READING FOCUS**

Paraphrase lines 47–50. How does Juliet feel when she discovers that Romeo is a Montague?

_____

_____

_____

E **LITERARY FOCUS**

Underline any clues in the Chorus lines that tell you that Act II will be part of the play's **rising action**.

Act II (continued)

Romeo. But soft, what light through yonder window breaks?

It is the East and Juliet is the sun.

Arise fair Sun and kill the envious Moon,

Who is already sick and pale with grief

That thou her maid[18] art far more fair than she.

Be not her maid, since she is envious,

Her vestal liv'ry[19] is but sick and green,[20]

And none but fools do wear it, cast it off.

80 [*Enter Juliet at the window.*]

It is my lady! O it is my love!

O that she knew she were!

She speaks yet she says nothing, what of that?

Her eye discourses,[21] I will answer it.

I am too bold, 'tis not to me she speaks.

Two of the fairest stars in all the heaven,

Having some business, do entreat her eyes

To twinkle in their spheres till they return.

What if her eyes were there, they in her head?

90 The brightness of her cheek would shame those stars

As daylight doth a lamp; her eye in heaven

Would through the airy region stream so bright

That birds would sing and think it were not night.

See how she leans her cheek upon her hand!

O that I were a glove upon that hand

That I might touch that cheek. (A)

Juliet. Ay me!

Romeo. She speaks.

O speak again, bright angel, for thou art

100 As glorious to this night, being o'er my head,

As is a winged messenger of Heaven.

---

18. **thou her maid:** Juliet, whom Romeo sees as the servant of the virgin goddess of the moon, Diana in Roman mythology.
19. **vestal livery:** maidenly clothing.
20. **sick and green:** Unmarried girls supposedly had "greensickness," or anemia.
21. **discourses:** speaks.

A READING FOCUS

Paraphrase the last three lines of Romeo's speech. What feeling is he expressing?

_____

_____

_____

_____

_____

Unto the white-upturned wond'ring eyes

Of mortals that fall back to gaze on him

When he bestrides the lazy puffing clouds

And sails upon the bosom of the air. **B**

Juliet. O Romeo, Romeo, wherefore[22] art thou Romeo?

Deny thy father and refuse thy name;

Or if thou wilt not, be but sworn my love

And I'll no longer be a Capulet.

110 *Romeo.* Shall I hear more or shall I speak at this? **C**

Juliet. 'Tis but thy name that is my enemy,

Thou art thyself, though not[23] a Montague.

What's Montague? it is nor hand nor foot

Nor arm nor face, O be some other name

Belonging to a man.

What's in a name? that which we call a rose

By any other word would smell as sweet.

So Romeo would, were he not Romeo call'd,

Retain that dear perfection which he owes[24]

120 Without that title. Romeo, doff thy name,

And for thy name, which is no part of thee,

Take all myself.

Romeo. I take thee at thy word.

Call me but Love and I'll be new baptiz'd,

Henceforth I never will be Romeo.

Juliet. What man art thou that thus bescreen'd in night

So stumblest on my counsel?[25] **D**

Romeo. By a name

I know not how to tell thee who I am.

130 My name, dear saint, is hateful to myself

Because it is an enemy to thee.

Had I it written, I would tear the word.

Juliet. My ears have yet not drunk a hundred words

---

22. **Wherefore:** why. In other words, "Why is your name Romeo?" (It is the name of her enemy.)
23. **though not:** even if you were not.
24. **owes:** owns.
25. **counsel:** private thoughts.

B VOCABULARY

Academic Vocabulary

Romeo and Juliet almost never describe each other with simple, straightforward words. Re-read Romeo's *dialogue* and underline all of the figures of speech and images that Romeo uses to describe Juliet.

C LITERARY ANALYSIS

Juliet is talking to herself, and does not know that Romeo is standing under her balcony. What reasons might Romeo have for not letting her know that he is there?

_____

_____

_____

_____

D READING FOCUS

Paraphrase Juliet's lines. How do you think she feels knowing that she has been overheard?

_____

_____

_____

_____

_____

_____

B READING FOCUS

Based on this scene, it is possible to **make inferences** about Juliet and Romeo's personalities. Juliet seems practical here. What does Romeo's personality seem like?

_____

_____

_____

Of thy tongue's utt'ring, yet I know the sound.

Art thou not Romeo, and a Montague?

Romeo. Neither, fair maid, if either thee dislike.

Juliet. How cam'st thou hither, tell me, and wherefore?

The orchard walls are high and hard to climb,

And the place death, considering who thou art,

140   If any of my kinsmen find thee here. **A**

Romeo. With Love's light wings did I o'erperch[26] these walls.

For stony limits cannot hold Love out,

And what Love can do, that dares Love attempt.

Therefore thy kinsmen are no stop to me.

Juliet. If they do see thee they will murder thee.

Romeo. Alack, there lies more peril in thine eye

Than twenty of their swords, look thou but sweet

And I am proof[27] against their enmity.

Juliet. I would not for the world they saw thee here.

150   *Romeo.* I have night's cloak to hide me from their eyes,

And but[28] thou love me, let me find them here.

My life were better ended by their hate

Than death prorogued,[29] wanting of thy love. **B**

Juliet. By whose direction found'st thou out this place?

Romeo. By Love, that first did prompt me to inquire.

He lent me counsel, and I lent him eyes.

I am no pilot, yet wert thou as far

As that vast shore wash'd with the farthest sea,

I should adventure for such merchandise.

160   *Juliet.* Thou know'st the mask of night is on my face.

Else would a maiden blush bepaint my cheek

For that which thou hast heard me speak tonight.

Fain would I dwell on form—fain, fain deny

What I have spoke. But farewell compliment.[30]

Dost thou love me? I know thou wilt say 'Ay,'

---

26. **o'erperch:** fly over.
27. **proof:** armored.
28. **but:** if only.
29. **prorogued:** postponed.
30. **compliment:** good manners.

And I will take they word. Yet if thou swear'st

Thou mayst prove false—at lovers' perjuries

170 They say Jove laughs. O gentle Romeo,

If thou dost love pro-
nounce it faithfully—

Or if thou think'st I am too quickly won,

I'll frown and be perverse and say thee nay,

So thou wilt woo; but else, not for the world.

In truth, fair Montague, I am too fond.[31]

180 And therefore thou mayst think my havior[32] light,

But trust me, gentleman, I'll prove more true

Than those that have more cunning to be strange.[33]

I should have been more strange, I must confess,

But that thou overheard'st, ere I was ware,

My true-love passion. Therefore pardon me,

And not impute this yielding to light love,

Which the dark night hath so discovered.[34]

Romeo. Lady, by yonder blessed moon I vow,

That tips with silver all these fruit-tree tops—

190 *Juliet.* O swear not by the moon, th' inconstant moon.

That monthly changes in her circl'd orb,

Lest that thy love prove likewise variable. **D**

Romeo. What shall I swear by?

Juliet. Do not swear at all,

Or if thou wilt, swear by thy gracious self,

Which is the god of my idolatry,

And I'll believe thee.

Romeo. If my heart's dear love—

---

31. **fond:** affectionate, tender.
32. **havior:** behavior.
33. **strange:** aloof or cold.
34. **discovered:** revealed.

© 2002 Production of Romeo and Juliet/Photo by Terry Manzo/Courtesy of the Stratford Shakespeare Festival Archives

C VOCABULARY

Word Study

Here, *pronounce* means "to declare something." Write a synonym (word that has a similar meaning) for *pronounce* that you could use here instead. Does the synonym have the same effect in this line?

_____

_____

_____

D QUICK CHECK

Why doesn't Juliet want Romeo to swear his love by the moon?

_____

_____

_____

_____

A **LITERARY ANALYSIS**

Romeo has made many quick vows and promises. Why has Juliet become fearful and cautious?

_____

_____

_____

_____

B **LANGUAGE COACH**

In this sentence, Juliet uses figurative language called a simile (a comparison of two things that uses the words *like, as,* or *than*). What is she comparing?

_____

_____

_____

_____

Juliet. Well, do not swear. Although I joy in thee
200 I have no joy of this contract tonight.
It is too rash, too unadvis'd, too sudden,
Too like the lightning, which doth cease to be
Ere one can say 'It lightens.' Sweet, good night.
This bud of love by Summer's rip'ning breath
May prove a beauteous flow'r when next we meet.
Good night, good night! As sweet repose and rest
Come to they heart as that within my breast. **A**
Romeo. O wilt thou leave me so unsatisfy'd?
Juliet. What satisfaction canst thou have tonight?
210 *Romeo.* Th' exchange of thy love's faithful vow for mine.
Juliet. I gave thee mine before thou didst request it,
And yet I would it were to give again.
Romeo. Wouldst thou withdraw it? for what purpose, love?
Juliet. But to be frank[35] and give it thee again.
And yet I wish but for the thing I have,
My bounty[36] is as boundless as the sea,
My love as deep—the more I give to thee,
The more I have, for both are infinite. **B**
I hear some noise within. Dear love, adieu—
220 [*Nurse calls within.*]
Anon, good Nurse! Sweet Montague, be true.
Stay but a little, I will come again.
Romeo. O blessed blessed night! I am afear'd,
Being in night, all this is but a dream
Too flatt'ring sweet to be substantial.
[*Enter Juliet again.*]
Juliet. Three words, dear Romeo, and good night indeed.
If that thy bent[37] of love be hon'rable,
Thy purpose marriage, send me word tomorrow
230 By one that I'll procure to come to thee
Where and what time thou wilt perform the rite,

---

35. **frank:** generous.
36. **bounty:** capacity for giving.
37. **bent:** intention.

And all my fortunes at thy foot I'll lay

And follow thee my lord throughout the world.

Nurse. [*Within.*] Madam!

Juliet. I come anon. But if thou mean'st not well,

I do beseech thee—

Nurse. [*Within.*] Madam!

Juliet. By and by, I come.

—To cease thy strife[38] and leave me to my grief.

240 Tomorrow will I send.

Romeo. So thrive my soul.

Juliet. A thousand times good night. [*Exit.*]

Romeo. A thousand times the worse to want thy light!

Love goes toward love as schoolboys from their books.

But love from love toward school with heavy looks.

Enter Juliet again.

Juliet. Hist Romeo, hist! O for a falc'ner's voice

To lure this tassel-gentle[39] back again.

Bondage is hoarse[40] and may not speak aloud,

250 Else would I tear the cave where Echo[41] lies

And make her airy tongue more hoarse than mine

With repetition of my Romeo. **D**

Romeo. It is my soul that calls upon my name.

How silver-sweet sound lovers' tongues by night,

Like softest music to attending ears.

Juliet. Romeo—

Romeo. My dear?

Juliet. What o'clock tomorrow

Shall I send to thee?

260 *Romeo.* By the hour of nine.

Juliet. I will not fail, 'tis twenty years till then.

I have forgot why I did call thee back.

---

38. **strife:** efforts to win her.
39. **tassel-gentle:** male falcon.
40. **Bondage is hoarse:** Juliet is in "bondage" to her parents and must whisper.
41. **Echo:** In Greek mythology, a girl who could only repeat others' final words.

C LITERARY ANALYSIS

Why do you think Juliet returns to the balcony?

_____

_____

_____

_____

D READING FOCUS

Shakespeare's language can be quite confusing. **Paraphrase** Juliet's dialogue here (lines 247–252).

_____

_____

_____

_____

_____

_____

_____

_____

_____

_____

_____

Do you think this scene is part of the play's **rising action**? Give your reasons why or why not.

_____

_____

_____

Academic Vocabulary

Suppose that you are seeing a stage *production*, or performance, of *Romeo and Juliet*. How would you expect the balcony scene to look? In other words, what might Romeo and Juliet be doing while they are talking?

_____

_____

_____

_____

_____

_____

Romeo. Let me stand here till thou remember it.

Juliet. I shall forget, to have thee still stand there,

Rememb'ring how I love thy company.

Romeo. And I'll still stay, to have thee still forget,

Forgetting any other home but this.

Juliet. 'Tis almost morning, I would have thee gone,

And yet no farther than a wanton's[42] bird

270 That lets it hop a little from his hand,

Like a poor pris'ner in his twisted gyves,[43]

And with a silken thread plucks 't back again,

So loving-jealous of his liberty.

Romeo. I would I were thy bird.

Juliet. Sweet, so would I,

Yet I should kill thee with much cherishing,

Good night, good night! Parting is such sweet sorrow **A**

That I shall say good night ere it be morrow. [*Exit.*]

Romeo. Sleep dwell upon thine eyes, peace in thy breast—

280 Would I were sleep and peace, so sweet to rest!

Hence will I to my ghostly friar's[44] close cell,

His help to crave and my dear hap[45] to tell. **B** [*Exit.*] **C**

FINAL SUMMARY In the remaining scenes of Act II, Romeo tells Nurse to ask Juliet to meet him that afternoon to marry him. Friar Laurence, a monk, will perform the ceremony. Juliet arrives at Friar Laurence's cell and embraces Romeo.

In Act III, Tybalt and Romeo argue, and Tybalt kills Mercutio. Angry over Mercutio's death, Romeo kills Tybalt. When Prince Escalus, the local ruler, learns what has happened, he says that Romeo must leave Verona or die for his crime. Juliet is very upset and sends Nurse to find Romeo, give him a ring, and ask him to come and say goodbye to Juliet. Friar Laurence tells Romeo to say goodbye to Juliet and then go to Mantua, another city in northern Italy, and

---

42. **wanton's:** careless child's.
43. **gyves** (JYVZ): chains, like the threads that hold the bird captive.
44. **ghostly friar's:** spiritual father's.
45. **hap:** luck.

stay there until the Prince forgives him. Romeo says goodbye to Juliet at her window and tells her he will see her again.

In Act IV Friar Laurence advises Juliet to drink a potion that will cause her to look as if she's dead. Then she will be taken to the family burial vault. There the Friar and Romeo will wait for her to awaken, and she will then go with Romeo to Mantua. Juliet follows Friar Laurence's plan. When Nurse discovers her cold, motionless body, everyone believes Juliet is dead.

In Act V, Romeo learns that Juliet has died and has been laid in her family's vault. Romeo buys poison, intending to kill himself now that his beloved Juliet is dead. Romeo does not know Juliet is really still alive. Paris, who also loved Juliet, places flowers at her burial site. Romeo is there, determined to see his beloved once last time. When Paris sees Romeo open the tomb, he believes Romeo has come to vandalize the tomb in an act of vengeance against the Capulets. Paris and Romeo struggle, and Romeo kills Paris. Romeo dies from the poison he has swallowed. When Juliet awakens in the tomb, she sees them both dead. She kisses her beloved Romeo, hoping some of the poison on his lips will kill her. Then she stabs herself and dies.

At the conclusion of the play, Friar Laurence explains to the Prince, the Capulets, and the Montagues what has happened. The families express deep sadness and remorse. Romeo's family vows to honor Juliet, and Juliet's family vows to honor Romeo. With the losses of their children, the ancient feud between the families has finally come to an end. **D**

© 2002 Production of Romeo and Juliet/Photo by Terry Manzo/ Courtesy of the Stratford Shakespeare Festival Archives

D LITERARY FOCUS

Put a star next to the lines in the final summary that include the story's **turning point**. Put a check mark next to the lines containing the **climax**. Underline the lines that include the **resolution**.

Skills Practice

The Tragedy of Romeo and Juliet

USE A TIME LINE

DIRECTIONS: *Romeo and Juliet* is a complicated play, and there's a lot going on. To keep track of all of the events, it helps to create a time line. On the time line below, list all of the main events from the play in the order that they happen. Try to summarize each main event in one sentence. Use as many marks on the time line as you need. You may add marks if you need more.

Applying Your Skills

The Tragedy of Romeo and Juliet

LITERARY FOCUS: TRAGEDY

DIRECTIONS: Fill in the chart. In the second column, write short summaries that explain when in the play the **exposition**, **rising action**, **turning point**, **climax**, and **resolution** take place. In the third column, write a line from the play that is an example of the part of the **dramatic structure** given in the first column.

Dramatic structure	Summary	Example line from play
Exposition		
Rising action		
Turning point		
Climax		
Resolution		

READING FOCUS: READING A PLAY

DIRECTIONS: Choose one part of the play that most interests you, such as the balcony scene or the death scene at the end. Which strategy helped you most when reading that scene—**read aloud**, **paraphrase**, **make inferences**, or **analyze cause and effect**? Explain.

_____

_____

_____

_____

_____

SKILLS FOCUS

Literary Skills
Describe the elements of a tragedy.

Reading Skills
Read aloud, paraphrase, make inferences, and analyze cause-and-effect relationships.

"Dear Juliet": Seeking Succor from a Veteran of Love *and from* The Juliet Club

INFORMATIONAL TEXT FOCUS: PRIMARY AND SECONDARY SOURCES

When you do research, you use two main kinds of sources: primary sources and secondary sources. A **primary source** is a firsthand account, such as a speech, an autobiography, or a letter. A primary source tells you the thoughts and feelings of its writer, who might be biased or might not know the whole story. A **secondary source** is a secondhand account, often based on more than one point of view. Writers of secondary sources often analyze events in which they did not participate. Encyclopedias, textbooks, biographies, and most newspaper and magazine articles are secondary sources.

SELECTION VOCABULARY

precipice (PREHS UH PIHS) *n.:* rock face that projects out, such as a cliff; the brink of a dangerous or disastrous situation.

Some lovelorn writers feel as if they are hanging over the edge of an emotional precipice.

vital (VY TUHL) *adj.:* very important.

The club members provide a vital service.

missives (MIHS IHVZ) *n.:* written messages, such as letters.

Most of the missives are addressed to Juliet, not Romeo.

collaborate (KUH LAB UH RAYT) *v.:* to work together.

The authors decided to collaborate on a book about the letters.

WORD STUDY

DIRECTIONS: Write the correct vocabulary word on each blank to complete the sentences. Some words will not be used.

1. Learning how to read is _____ to having success in school.

2. After they broke up, she burnt all of the romantic _____ he had mailed to her through the years.

3. When a man entered the bank with a gun, Gene knew he was on the _____ of a dangerous situation.

SKILLS FOCUS

Informational Text Skills
Understand primary and secondary sources.

"Dear Juliet": Seeking Succor[1] from a Veteran of Love

by Dinitia Smith
from The New York Times, March 27, 2006

> **BACKGROUND**
> This newspaper article discusses the Juliet Club
> in Verona, Italy. The club's members have been
> answering letters addressed to Juliet since the 1930s.
> Each year on Valentine's Day, the Juliet Club awards
> the *Dear Juliet* Prize for "the most beautiful letter
> sent to Juliet." In the second selection, you will read
> one of the letters selected to receive the prize.

Courtesy of Club di Giulietta

"Dear Juliet," the letters all begin.

"Dear Juliet . . . You are my last hope. The woman I love
more than anything in the world has left me. . . ."

"Dear Juliet, I live on the third floor. My parents don't allow
my boyfriend to come to my house."

"Dear Juliet, my name is Riccardo. I am 10 years old."
Riccardo is in love with an older woman, 14. He saw her in
Verona the summer before. Does Juliet have news of her? **A**

Every week, hundreds of letters pour into the office of the
Club di Giulietta,[2] in Verona, Italy, the city that is the setting for

---

1. **succor** (SUHK UHR): assistance in a difficult time; relief.
2. **Club di Giulietta** (KLUHB DEE JYOO LEE EHT UH): in Italian, "Juliet's
    Club."

Selection Vocabulary

A *precipice* is "a rock face that projects out, such as a cliff, or the brink of a dangerous or disastrous situation." How would it feel to be "suspended on a precipice"? Do you think the writer of the letter chose a good word to describe her feelings?

_____

_____

_____

B LANGUAGE COACH

Vital comes from the Latin verb *vivere,* which means "to live." Two other words taken from the same root word are *vivid* and *vivacious.* Find both words in the dictionary. What's similar about all three definitions?

_____

_____

_____

_____

_____

Shakespeare's "Romeo and Juliet." Some are addressed simply "To Juliet, Verona," but the postman always knows to deliver them to the club's Via Galilei headquarters. Every letter is answered by the club's group of volunteers, no matter what the language, sometimes with the assistance of outside translators. (In the past, the owner of a local Chinese restaurant helped.)

"Help me! Save me!" wrote an Italian woman whose husband had left her. "I feel suspended on a precipice. I am afraid of going mad." **A**

20   Her answer came from Ettore Sabina who was the custodian of Juliet's tomb for nearly 20 years, beginning in the 1930's.

"Have faith . . .," Mr. Solana added later in the letter. "The day of humiliation will come for the intruder, and your husband will come back to you."

Now two American sisters, Lise and Ceil Friedman, have put some of the letters and a few of the responses into a book, "Letters to Juliet," along with the story of the club and the play's historical background. It is being published in November by Stewart, Tabori & Chang. But on Wednesday, Lise Friedman, an 30   adjunct professor at New York University, will read from it at the university's Bronfman Center for Jewish Student Life.

And what is the real history of the play? The theme of tragic love between two young people from feuding families goes back at least to Ovid. Luigi da Porto, in "Newly Discovered Story of Two Noble Lovers" (1530), set the tale in Verona with rival families, the Montecchis and Cappellettis. There is no evidence that Shakespeare ever visited Italy, and some scholars think he based "Romeo and Juliet" on a poem by Arthur Brooke, published some three decades before. But the myth of Romeo and Juliet— 40   and it is something of a myth—has become vital to the tourism industry in Verona, where Juliet's house and tomb are supposedly located. **B** Giulio Tamassia, president of the Club di Giulietta, has said that the house on Via Cappello has been called "Juliet's" only since the 19th century. And the balcony on its front dates from the first half of the 20th century. (Shakespeare mentions no balcony in the play. For her famous Act II, Scene 2 speech, Juliet comes from "above.") **C**

For years, tourists stuck notes to Juliet on the walls of the house with bubblegum. Last year the gum was removed, and white plasterboard put up for those who feel they must write. There is also a letterbox at the house, and its missives are collected and answered by the club. **D** These days you can even send an e-mail to Juliet at info@julietclub.com. Very few letters, oddly enough, are sent to Romeo.

"There are hundreds of letters from U.S. teenagers," said Elena Marchi, the assistant to Mr. Tamassia, in a telephone interview from Verona. One reason is that "Romeo and Juliet" is part of many American high school curriculums.

"It's easier to talk to someone you don't know," said Ms. Marchi, a professional translator when she is not answering letters. "There are things you wouldn't say to your mother." **E**

Ms. Marchi goes to the club every day, she said. "Once you start," she said, "you never give up, it's so interesting."

At least since the turn of the last century, messages have been left at Juliet's tomb in a former monastery on the Via del Pontiere, about a 15-minute walk from Juliet's house. But the letters really began flowing in 1937, the year after George Cukor's film "Romeo and Juliet" was released. That same year, Mr. Solimani was hired as the custodian of the tomb, which was probably originally an animal trough. (There are no bones there. Although the two lovers are supposedly buried together, over the years Romeo seems to have vanished from the picture, and it is now usually called just Juliet's tomb.)

Mr. Solimani planted rose bushes and a willow tree, trained two dozen turtledoves to fly around the cloister and to land on the shoulders of female visitors, and took it upon himself to answer the letters.

In the late 1980's, the club began to answer them. It receives money from the city for stationery and postage, but is otherwise run by volunteers.

C READING FOCUS

What source (or sources) might the author have used to find the information in this paragraph? Are the sources you list **primary** or **secondary sources**?

_____

_____

_____

D LANGUAGE COACH

Forward comes from the Latin word *mittere*, meaning "to send." How are the definitions of *forward* and *mittere* related?

_____

_____

_____

E VOCABULARY

Academic Vocabulary

What is your *interpretation*, or explanation of the meaning, of this paragraph? What does Ms. Marchi mean?

_____

_____

_____

_____

VOCABULARY

Selection Vocabulary

To *collaborate* is to "work together." List some common situations in which you might have to collaborate with someone.

_____

_____

_____

_____

_____

B **READING FOCUS**

Re-read lines 92–103, and underline each passage that comes from a **primary source**.

 READING FOCUS

What **primary source** does the writer use in the last two paragraphs?

_____

_____

About two years ago, when the Friedman sisters who, according to Lise, "tend to finish each other's sentences" were looking for a project on which to collaborate, Ceil was given some of the letters to translate. **A** She sent copies to her sister, who immediately thought they might make a book.

The club has about 50,000 letters stored in boxes. The Friedman sisters went through about 5,000, choosing representative examples from different times: A few choice letters were remembered by the volunteers. The Friedmans have
90 included about 75 in their book, changing the writers' names to protect their privacy.

The sisters found that during the nearly 70 years the letters have been arriving, they have become a reflection of the changing times. In 1970, a girl from Montana wrote, "Five years ago I met a Negro boy, William, at Bible camp." They had fallen in love, she explained, but added: "My parents and friends are against us getting married. William and I have separated many times, trying to get over each other."

In 1967 a Louisiana woman wrote that her husband was in
100 Vietnam, and that she had fallen in love with his best friend. And in 1972, a soldier wrote from Vietnam itself: "I am in a bunker. Outside I hear missiles exploding, bullets being fired. I am 22 years old and I'm scared." **B**

And then there are those who have yet to find love, who write to Juliet the way children write to Santa Claus, hoping he can bring them the gift they most desire. A woman from Ukraine asks: "I have a daughter, 27, who has never been married, but is looking for a fiancé." Can Juliet help?

"It's about suspending disbelief," Lise Friedman said,
110 trying to explain why so many people would write to Juliet, unseen, perhaps only a chimera.[3] "It's about having a life of the imagination."

"It's one of those ineffable[4] things." **C**

---

3. **chimera** (KUH MIHR UH): in Greek mythology, a grotesque creature formed from a lion, goat, and serpent; here, a strange product of the imagination.
4. **ineffable** (IHN EHF UHB BUHL): indescribable.

from THE JULIET CLUB

Courtesy of Club di Giulietta

Dear Juliet,

My dear friend, I dream of being on your balcony, which guarded your secret love, under which Romeo declared his passion, on which you proved to him that same dangerous passion. **D**

As I write you this letter, I'm not desperate, just a little melancholy and romantic, but still fascinated by the great power of love.

Yes, Juliet, you are the hurricane and the calm, salt and sugar, tenderness and strength. But wherever did you get this strength?

10   I, too, listen to the song of the nightingale and the lark. I look for the dawn's light and await the tender night.

My thoughts are both timid and bold, sensible and foolish or imaginary because we are the stuff that dreams are made of.

"Letter to Juliet" by Charlotte Scheir from *The Juliet Club*. Copyright © 1994 by **Club de Giulietta**. Reproduced by permission of the author.

D (VOCABULARY)

Word Study

The word *dream* can be used as a noun, a verb, or an adjective. How is it being used in this sentence? Write a sentence using *dream* in one of its other forms.

_____

_____

_____

_____

from The Juliet Club   **287**

Reading Focus

Is this letter an example of a **primary** or **secondary source**? How do you know?

_____

_____

_____

_____

_____

But must we really believe that our destiny is rarely to be with our beloved?

Yes, I dream of being part of this tragedy, if only for a moment, of entering the legend of love.

Charlotte Schein
Hondschoote, France **A**

Applying Your Skills

"Dear Juliet": Seeking Succor from a Veteran of Love *and* *from* The Juliet Club

VOCABULARY DEVELOPMENT

DIRECTIONS: The sentences in the table below include some boldfaced vocabulary words. Make a checkmark in the second column if the word is used correctly. If a word is used incorrectly, write a new sentence using the vocabulary word correctly.

	Correct	New Sentence
I called out to warn him that he was nearing the **precipice**.		
We enjoyed the **vital** afternoon.		
The two enemies **collaborate** all the time.		
She agreed to read **missives** I sent to her.		

INFORMATIONAL TEXT FOCUS: PRIMARY AND SECONDARY SOURCES

DIRECTIONS: Fill in the chart below with examples of primary and secondary sources found in "'Dear Juliet': Seeking Succor from a Veteran of Love."

Primary sources in the text	Secondary sources in the text

SKILLS FOCUS

Informational Text Skills
Understand primary and secondary sources.

Skills Review

Collection 8

VOCABULARY REVIEW

DIRECTIONS: The Word Box includes vocabulary words from this collection. Read the sentences below and write the vocabulary word that best completes the sentence in the blank. Some words will not be used.

Word Box

collaborate
convention
dialogue
embody
exposition
interpretation
missives
monologue
precipice
production
soliloquy
tragedy
vital

1. The _____ between Romeo and Juliet in the play showed that they were very much in love.

2. I was not impressed by the actor's _____ of Romeo; he didn't seem to understand Romeo's true motivation.

3. Juliet felt as if she were standing at a _____, alone and in great danger.

4. The two friends decided that they would like to _____ on a project.

5. He kept all of the sweet _____ she wrote to him.

6. The fire department provides a _____ service.

7. Although many people love his comedies, Shakespeare's most popular play is a _____.

8. The other characters on stage listened eagerly to his long _____.

9. The play's _____ was too long; it seemed to take forever before the action started.

10. The actor stood alone at the center of the stage and delivered a touching _____ to the audience.

Skills Review

Collection 8

LANGUAGE COACH

DIRECTIONS: Each of the following passages from *Romeo and Juliet* contains an underlined word whose intended meaning is slightly different from (but related to) its modern English meaning. Use a dictionary to look up the common meaning, and then use the context clues and the modern definition to guess at the word's meaning in the line. Write the intended meaning on the line.

1. As glorious to this night, being o'er my head,
   As is a winged messenger of Heaven.
   Unto the white-upturned wond'ring eyes
   Of mortals that fall back to gaze on him
   When he <u>bestrides</u> the lazy puffing clouds

   _____

   _____

2. Call me but Love and I'll be new <u>baptiz'd</u>, [short for *baptized*]
   Henceforth I never will be Romeo.

   _____

   _____

3. I am no pilot, yet wert thou as far
   As that vast shore wash'd with the farthest sea,
   I should <u>adventure</u> for such merchandise.

   _____

   _____

ORAL LANGUAGE ACTIVITY

DIRECTIONS: Imagine that Juliet's father has just found out about her secret marriage to Romeo. How do you think he would react? What do you think Juliet would say to try to make him accept her marriage? Team up with a classmate to develop this scene between Juliet and her father. One person should play Juliet, the other should play her father. First, write the dialogue you and your partner will have. Then, act it out for your classmates. You may use modern English for your dialogue.

Collection 9

Epic and Myth

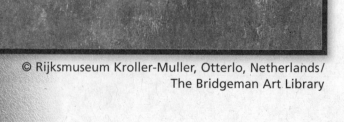

© Rijksmuseum Kroller-Muller, Otterlo, Netherlands/
The Bridgeman Art Library

Literary and Academic Vocabulary for Collection 9

portrayed (PAWR TRAYD) *v.:* showed.

The story portrayed Odysseus as a great hero.

destiny (DEHS TIH NEE) *n.:* unavoidable future; fate.

Some myths describe how their characters fulfill their destiny.

mutual (MYOO CHU UHL) *adj.:* done, said, or felt by each toward the other.

Romeo and Juliet had a mutual attraction.

express (EHK SPREHS) *v.:* put into words; show feeling or emotion.

Odysseus' wife, Penelope, chose to express her joy at Odysseus' return
by hosting a feast.

conflicts (KAHN FLIKTS) *n.:* obstacles.

The characters experience many conflicts as the story progresses.

external conflicts (EHK STUR NUHL) *n.:* obstacles created by forces of nature.

The characters experienced external conflicts that slowed their journey.

myths (MIHTHS) *n.:* stories that are usually in some sense religious; legendary
narratives that tell part of the beliefs of a culture or explain a practice
or natural phenomenon.

She spent part of her summer reading ancient Greek myths and
learning about ancient Greek culture and religion.

Preparing to Read

from the Odyssey

by Homer, translated by Robert Fitzgerald

LITERARY FOCUS: EPIC HEROES AND CONFLICT

An "ordinary" hero saves children from a roaring river or rescues people from a burning building. An **epic hero** is a larger than life character, usually with uncommon strength, great knowledge, cunning, courage, and daring. An epic hero often goes on a dangerous journey or quest of discovery. On his journey, the hero faces **conflicts**, or obstacles. The conflict may be a battle against nature, gods, or other people.

READING FOCUS: READING AN EPIC

When you read an excerpt from a long work, it helps to use many strategies. If you don't understand a passage, try **paraphrasing**, or restating it in your own words. To be sure you understand what happened, **summarize**, or briefly note each event in the order it occurred. You can also **ask questions** to make sure you understand what you read.

Use the Skill   In the space provided, paraphrase the following passage from the "Odyssey."

> I drew it from the coals and my four fellows
>
> gave me a hand, lugging it near the Cyclops
>
> as more than natural force nerved them; straight
>
> forward they sprinted, lifted it, and rammed it
>
> deep in his crater eye, and I leaned on it
>
> turning it as a shipwright turns a drill
>
> in planking, having men below to swing
>
> the two-handled strap that spins it in the groove.

_____

_____

_____

5W-How?   As you read, use the _5W-How?_ questions (**Who? What? Where and When? Why? How?**) to make sure you understand the epic.

SKILLS FOCUS

Literary Skills
Understand epic heroes and conflict.

Reading Skills
Paraphrase and summarize a text. Ask questions to understand what you read.

Vocabulary Development

from the *Odyssey*

SELECTION VOCABULARY

profusion (PRUH FYOO zhuhn) *n.:* large supply; abundance.

> *Odysseus hid the weapon under a profusion of dung piles.*

adversary (AD vuhr SEHR ee) *n.:* enemy; opponent.

> *The Cyclops was a terrifying adversary.*

WORD STUDY

DIRECTIONS: Use each of the selection vocabulary words in a sentence of your own.

1. _____

2. _____

DIRECTIONS: Come up with an antonym for each of the vocabulary words.
An antonym is a word that has the opposite meaning.

1. profusion _____

2. adversary _____

from the ODYSSEY

by Homer
translated by Robert Fitzgerald

BACKGROUND

No one knows for sure who Homer was. The later Greeks believed he was a blind minstrel, or singer who went from town to town. He is known for the epic poems the *Iliad* (the story of the Trojan War) and the *Odyssey*. The *Odyssey* tells of the many adventures of the hero Odysseus on his ten-year journey home from the war. As this passage begins, curiosity has led Odysseus and his men to wait in the cave of the Cyclops.

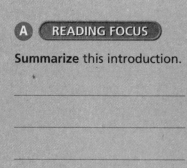

A (**READING FOCUS**)

Summarize this introduction.

_____

_____

_____

_____

THE CYCLOPS

In this adventure, Odysseus describes his encounter with the Cyclops named Polyphemus, Poseidon's one-eyed monster son. Polyphemus may represent the brute forces that any hero must overcome before he can reach home. Now Odysseus must rely on the special intelligence associated with his name. Odysseus is the cleverest of the Greek heroes because he is guided by the goddess of wisdom, Athena.

It is Odysseus' famed curiosity that leads him to the Cyclops' cave and that makes him insist on waiting for the barbaric giant.

In this passage Odysseus is telling his story to the court of King Alcinous. **A**

"We lit a fire, burnt an offering,
and took some cheese to eat; then sat in silence
around the embers, waiting. When he came
he had a load of dry boughs on his shoulder
5   to stoke his fire at suppertime. He dumped it
with a great crash into that hollow cave,

From "Book 9: New Coasts and Poseidon's Son" from *The Odyssey* by Homer, translated by Robert Fitzgerald. Copyright © 1961, 1963 by Robert Fitzgerald; copyright renewed © 1989 by Benedict R. C. Fitzgerald, on behalf of the Fitzgerald children. Reproduced by permission of **Benedict R.C. Fitzgerald.**

© Erich Lessing/Art Resource, NY

B (LITERARY FOCUS)

Epic heroes must face **conflict** with mighty opponents in order to show their strength and resourcefulness. How does Homer show that the Cyclops is a fierce opponent?

_____

_____

_____

_____

and we all scattered fast to the far wall.

Then over the broad cavern floor he ushered

the ewes he meant to milk. He left his rams

10 and he-goats in the yard outside, and swung

high overhead a slab of solid rock

to close the cave. Two dozen four-wheeled wagons,

with heaving wagon teams, could not have stirred

the tonnage of that rock from where he wedged it

15 over the doorsill. Next he took his seat **B**

and milked his bleating ewes. A practiced job

he made of it, giving each ewe her suckling;

thickened his milk, then, into curds and whey,

sieved out the curds to drip in withy[1] baskets,

20 and poured the whey to stand in bowls

cooling until he drank it for his supper.

When all these chores were done, he poked the fire,

heaping on brushwood. In the glare he saw us.

1. **withy:** made from willow twigs.

'Strangers,' he said, 'who are you? And where from?

25   What brings you here by seaways—a fair traffic?

Or are you wandering rogues, who cast your lives

like dice, and ravage other folk by sea?'

We felt a pressure on our hearts, in dread

of that deep rumble and that mighty man. **A**

30   But all the same I spoke up in reply:

'We are from Troy, Achaeans, blown off course

by shifting gales on the Great South Sea;

homeward bound, but taking routes and ways

uncommon; so the will of Zeus would have it.

35   We served under Agamemnon,[2] son of Atreus[3]—

the whole world knows what city

he laid waste, what armies he destroyed.

It was our luck to come here; here we stand, **B**

beholden for your help, or any gifts

40   you give—as custom is to honor strangers.

We would entreat you, great Sir, have a care

for the gods' courtesy; Zeus will avenge

the unoffending guest.'

He answered this

45   from his brute chest, unmoved:

'You are a ninny,

or else you come from the other end of nowhere,

telling me, mind the gods! We Cyclopes

care not a whistle for your thundering Zeus

50   or all the gods in bliss; we have more force by far.

I would not let you go for fear of Zeus—

you or your friends—unless I had a whim to.

Tell me, where was it, now, you left your ship—

around the point, or down the shore, I wonder?'

---

2. **Agamemnon** (AG UH MEHM NAHN).
3. **Atreus** (AY TREE UHS).

55   He thought he'd find out, but I saw through this,

    and answered with a ready lie: **C**

    'My ship?

    Poseidon Lord, who sets the earth atremble,

    broke it up on the rocks at your land's end.

60   A wind from seaward served him, drove us there.

    We are survivors, these good men and I.'

    Neither reply nor pity came from him,

    but in one stride he clutched at my companions

    and caught two in his hands like squirming puppies

65   to beat their brains out, spattering the floor.

    Then he dismembered them and made his meal,

    gaping and crunching like a mountain lion—

    everything: innards, flesh, and marrow bones.

    We cried aloud, lifting our hands to Zeus,

70   powerless, looking on at this, appalled;

    but Cyclops went on filling up his belly

    with manflesh and great gulps of whey,

    then lay down like a mast among his sheep.

    My heart beat high now at the chance of action,

75   and drawing the sharp sword from my hip I went

    along his flank to stab him where the midriff

    holds the liver. I had touched the spot

    when sudden fear stayed me: if I killed him

    we perished there as well, for we could never

80   move his ponderous doorway slab aside.

    So we were left to groan and wait for morning. **D**

    When the young Dawn with fingertips of rose **E**

    lit up the world, the Cyclops built a fire

    and milked his handsome ewes, all in due order,

85   putting the sucklings to the mothers. Then,

    his chores being all dispatched, he caught

    another brace[4] of men to make his breakfast,

    and whisked away his great door slab

---

4. **brace:** pair.

C LITERARY FOCUS

What qualities of an **epic hero** does Odysseus show in this passage?

_____

_____

_____

D LITERARY FOCUS

Why doesn't Odysseus kill the Cyclops at this moment? What quality of an **epic hero** is Odysseus showing?

_____

_____

_____

E LITERARY ANALYSIS

Throughout the *Odyssey*, dawn is described as having rose-colored fingers. Do you think this is a good description for dawn? Why or why not?

_____

_____

_____

What comparison is Homer making here? What does this say about the Cyclops?

_____

_____

_____

_____

B **VOCABULARY**

Selection Vocabulary

Profusion is a noun meaning "large supply, or abundance." It comes from the adjective *profuse*. What do you think *profuse* means? Use a dictionary to check your answer.

_____

_____

_____

_____

C **READING FOCUS**

Paraphrase, or retell in your own words, what Odysseus does to the staff he finds.

_____

_____

_____

_____

_____

to let his sheep go through—but he, behind,

90   reset the stone as one would cap a quiver.[5] **A**

There was a din of whistling as the Cyclops

rounded his flock to higher ground, then stillness.

And now I pondered how to hurt him worst,

if but Athena granted what I prayed for.

95   Here are the means I thought would serve my turn:

a club, or staff, lay there along the fold—

an olive tree, felled green and left to season

for Cyclops' hand. And it was like a mast

a lugger[6] of twenty oars, broad in the beam—

100   a deep-sea-going craft—might carry:

so long, so big around, it seemed. Now I

chopped out a six-foot section of this pole

and set it down before my men, who scraped it;

and when they had it smooth, I hewed again

105   to make a stake with pointed end. I held this

in the fire's heart and turned it, toughening it,

then hid it, well back in the cavern, under

one of the dung piles in profusion there. **B C**

Now came the time to toss for it: who ventured

110   along with me? Whose hand could bear to thrust

and grind that spike in Cyclops' eye, when mild

sleep had mastered him? As luck would have it,

the men I would have chosen won the toss—

four strong men, and I made five as captain.

115   At evening came the shepherd with his flock,

his woolly flock. The rams as well, this time,

entered the cave: by some sheepherding whim—

or a god's bidding—none were left outside.

He hefted his great boulder into place

120   and sat him down to milk the bleating ewes

in proper order, put the lambs to suck,

---

5. **quiver:** case for arrows.
6. **lugger:** type of sailboat.

and swiftly ran through all his evening chores.
Then he caught two more men and feasted on them.
My moment was at hand, and I went forward
125   holding an ivy bowl of my dark drink,
looking up, saying:

'Cyclops, try some wine.
Here's liquor to wash down your scraps of men.
Taste it, and see the kind of drink we carried
130   under our planks. I meant it for an offering
if you would help us home. But you are mad,
unbearable, a bloody monster! After this,
will any other traveler come to see you?'

He seized and drained the bowl, and it went down
135   so fiery and smooth he called for more:
'Give me another, thank you kindly. Tell me,
how are you called? I'll make a gift will please you.
Even Cyclopes know the wine grapes grow
out of grassland and loam in heaven's rain,
140   but here's a bit of nectar and ambrosia!'

Three bowls I brought him, and he poured them down.
I saw the fuddle and flush come over him,
then I sang out in cordial tones:

'Cyclops,
145   you ask my honorable name? Remember
the gift you promised me, and I shall tell you.
My name is Nohbdy: mother, father, and friends,
everyone calls me Nohbdy.'
And he said:

150   'Nohbdy's my meat, then, after I eat his friends.
Others come first. There's a noble gift, now.'
Even as he spoke, he reeled and tumbled backward,
his great head lolling to one side; and sleep
took him like any creature. Drunk, hiccuping,
155   he dribbled streams of liquor and bits of men. **D**

D READING FOCUS

Summarize the events that have taken place on this page.

_____

_____

_____

_____

_____

_____

from the Odyssey   **301**

A LITERARY FOCUS

Do you think that the ability to persuade and lead others is an important quality for an **epic hero**? Why or why not?

_____

_____

_____

_____

_____

_____

Now, by the gods, I drove my big hand spike

deep in the embers, charring it again,

and cheered my men along with battle talk

to keep their courage up: no quitting now. **A**

160   The pike of olive, green though it had been,

reddened and glowed as if about to catch.

I drew it from the coals and my four fellows

gave me a hand, lugging it near the Cyclops

as more than natural force nerved them; straight

165   forward they sprinted, lifted it, and rammed it

deep in his crater eye, and I leaned on it

turning it as a shipwright turns a drill

in planking, having men below to swing

the two-handled strap that spins it in the groove.

170   So with our brand we bored that great eye socket

while blood ran out around the red-hot bar.

Eyelid and lash were seared; the pierced ball
hissed broiling, and the roots popped. **B**

In a smithy[7]

175   one sees a white-hot axhead or an adze[8]

plunged and wrung in a cold tub, screeching steam—

the way they make soft iron hale and hard—

just so that eyeball hissed around the spike.

The Cyclops bellowed and the rock roared round him,

180   and we fell back in fear. Clawing his face

he tugged the bloody spike out of his eye,

threw it away, and his wild hands went groping;

then he set up a howl for Cyclopes

who lived in caves on windy peaks nearby.

185   Some heard him; and they came by divers[9] ways

to clump around outside and call:

'What ails you,

Polyphemus? Why do you cry so sore

in the starry night? You will not let us sleep.

190   Sure no man's driving off your flock? No man

has tricked you, ruined you?'

Out of the cave

the mammoth Polyphemus roared in answer:

'Nohbdy, Nohbdy's tricked me. Nohbdy's ruined me!'

195   To this rough shout they made a sage[10] reply:

'Ah well, if nobody has played you foul

there in your lonely bed, we are no use in pain

given by great Zeus. Let it be your father,

Poseidon Lord, to whom you pray.'

200   So saying

they trailed away. And I was filled with laughter

to see how like a charm the name deceived them. **C**

---

7. **smithy:** blacksmith's shop, where iron tools are made.
8. **adze:** axlike tool with a long, curved blade.
9. **divers** (DY vuhrz): diverse; various.
10. **sage:** wise.

B QUICK CHECK

How have Odysseus and his men injured the Cyclops? Why might this be preferable to killing him?

_____

_____

_____

_____

C LITERARY FOCUS

Odysseus' fake name has prevented the other Cyclopes from coming to Polyphemus' aid. Do you think this kind of trickery is characteristic of an **epic hero**? Why or why not?

_____

_____

_____

_____

A QUICK CHECK

Why can't Odysseus and his men leave the cave yet?

_____

_____

_____

_____

B VOCABULARY

Word Study

Homer is using a literary device called *anthropomorphizing* (AN THRUH PUH MAWR FYZ IHNG)—giving human qualities to nonhuman things. What is he anthropomorphizing here? What human qualities is he giving to this thing?

_____

_____

_____

_____

_____

Now Cyclops, wheezing as the pain came on him,

fumbled to wrench away the great doorstone

205 and squatted in the breach with arms thrown wide

for any silly beast or man who bolted—

hoping somehow I might be such a fool.

But I kept thinking how to win the game:

death sat there huge; how could we slip away? **A**

210 I drew on all my wits, and ran through tactics,

reasoning as a man will for dear life,

until a trick came—and it pleased me well.

The Cyclops' rams were handsome, fat, with heavy

fleeces, a dark violet.

215 Three abreast

I tied them silently together, twining

cords of willow from the ogre's bed;

then slung a man under each middle one

to ride there safely, shielded left and right.

220 So three sheep could convey each man. I took

the woolliest ram, the choicest of the flock,

and hung myself under his kinky belly,

pulled up tight, with fingers twisted deep

in sheepskin ringlets for an iron grip.

225 So, breathing hard, we waited until morning.

When Dawn spread out her fingertips of rose **B**

the rams began to stir, moving for pasture,

and peals of bleating echoed round the pens

where dams with udders full called for a milking.

230 Blinded, and sick with pain from his head wound,

the master stroked each ram, then let it pass,

but my men riding on the pectoral fleece[11]

the giant's blind hands blundering never found.

Last of them all my ram, the leader, came,

235 weighted by wool and me with my meditations.

The Cyclops patted him, and then he said:

---

11. **pectoral fleece:** wool on an animal's chest.

304 *from the* **Odyssey**

'Sweet cousin ram, why lag behind the rest

in the night cave? You never linger so,

but graze before them all, and go afar

240   to crop sweet grass, and take your stately way

leading along the streams, until at evening

you run to be the first one in the fold.

Why, now, so far behind? Can you be grieving

over your Master's eye? That carrion rogue[12]

245   and his accurst companions burnt it out

when he had conquered all my wits with wine.

Nohbdy will not get out alive, I swear.

Oh, had you brain and voice to tell

where he may be now, dodging all my fury!

250   Bashed by this hand and bashed on this rock wall

his brains would strew the floor, and I should have

rest from the outrage Nohbdy worked upon me.' **C**

He sent us into the open, then. Close by,

I dropped and rolled clear of the ram's belly,

255   going this way and that to untie the men.

With many glances back, we rounded up

his fat, stiff-legged sheep to take aboard,

and drove them down to where the good ship lay.

We saw, as we came near, our fellows' faces

260   shining; then we saw them turn to grief

tallying those who had not fled from death.

I hushed them, jerking head and eyebrows up,

and in a low voice told them: 'Load this herd;

move fast, and put the ship's head toward the breakers.'

265   They all pitched in at loading, then embarked

and struck their oars into the sea. Far out,

as far offshore as shouted words would carry,

I sent a few back to the adversary: **D**

'O Cyclops! Would you feast on my companions?

270   Puny, am I, in a Caveman's hands?

---

12. carrion rogue: rotten scoundrel. Carrion is decaying flesh.

C **READING FOCUS**

Briefly **paraphrase** the Cyclops' speech to his ram.

_____

_____

_____

_____

_____

_____

_____

_____

_____

_____

_____

D **LANGUAGE COACH**

The adjective *adverse* means "harmful, or unfavorable." An *adversary* is an "enemy, or opponent." Use a dictionary to find one more word from this word family. Use your new word in a sentence.

_____

_____

_____

_____

_____

A **LITERARY ANALYSIS**

Odysseus' love of boasting is one of his traits. Do you think he is wise to taunt the Cyclops? Why or why not?

_____

_____

_____

_____

_____

B **QUICK CHECK**

Do you think that Odysseus should listen to his men? Why or why not?

_____

_____

_____

_____

_____

How do you like the beating that we gave you,

you damned cannibal? Eater of guests

under your roof! Zeus and the gods have paid you!' A

The blind thing in his doubled fury broke

275   a hilltop in his hands and heaved it after us.

Ahead of our black prow it struck and sank

whelmed in a spuming geyser, a giant wave

that washed the ship stern foremost back to shore.

I got the longest boathook out and stood

280   fending us off, with furious nods to all

to put their backs into a racing stroke—

row, row or perish. So the long oars bent

kicking the foam sternward, making head

until we drew away, and twice as far.

285   Now when I cupped my hands I heard the crew

in low voices protesting:

'Godsake, Captain!

Why bait the beast again? Let him alone!'

'That tidal wave he made on the first throw

290   all but beached us.'

'All but stove us in!'

'Give him our bearing with your trumpeting,

he'll get the range and lob[13] a boulder.'

'Aye

295   He'll smash our timbers and our heads together!' B

I would not heed them in my glorying spirit

but let my anger flare and yelled:

'Cyclops,

if ever mortal man inquire

300   how you were put to shame and blinded, tell him

Odysseus, raider of cities, took your eye:

Laertes' son, whose home's on Ithaca!'

---

13. lob: toss.

At this he gave a mighty sob and rumbled:

'Now comes the weird[14] upon me, spoken of old.

305 A wizard, grand and wondrous, lived here—Telemus,[15]

a son of Eurymus;[16] great length of days

he had in wizardry among the Cyclopes,

and these things he foretold for time to come:

my great eye lost, and at Odysseus' hands. **C**

310 Always I had in mind some giant, armed

in giant force, would come against me here.

But this, but you—small, pitiful, and twiggy—

you put me down with wine, you blinded me. **D**

Come back, Odysseus, and I'll treat you well,

315 praying the god of earthquake to befriend you—

his son I am, for he by his avowal

fathered me, and, if he will, he may

heal me of this black wound—he and no other

of all the happy gods or mortal men.'

320 Few words I shouted in reply to him:

'If I could take your life I would and take

your time away, and hurl you down to hell!

The god of earthquake could not heal you there!'

At this he stretched his hands out in his darkness

325 toward the sky of stars, and prayed Poseidon:

'O hear me, lord, blue girdler of the islands,

if I am thine indeed, and thou art father:

grant that Odysseus, raider of cities, never

see his home: Laertes' son, I mean,

330 who kept his hall on Ithaca. Should destiny

intend that he shall see his roof again

among his family in his fatherland,

far be that day, and dark the years between.

---

14. **weird:** fate.
15. **Telemus** (TEHL uh muhs).
16. **Eurymus** (YOO ree muhs).

C **VOCABULARY**

Academic Vocabulary

Do you think that the meeting between Cyclops and Odysseus was *destiny* (meant to happen)? Why or why not?

_____

_____

_____

_____

D **LITERARY FOCUS**

Epic heroes and their opponents often have character flaws which can cause their downfall. What character flaw has led to the Cyclops' downfall?

_____

_____

_____

_____

Do you think the Cyclops'
curse is likely to come true as
the *Odyssey* continues? Why
or why not?

_____

_____

_____

_____

_____

_____

© AKG Images, London/Badisches Landesmuseum

Let him lose all companions, and return

335   under strange sail to bitter days at home.' . . ." **A**

Here we will imagine that Homer stops reciting for the night.
The blind poet might take a glass of wine before turning in. The
listeners would go off to various corners of the local nobleman's
house. They might discuss highlights of the poet's tale among
themselves and look forward to the next evening's installment.

Applying Your Skills

from the Odyssey

VOCABULARY DEVELOPMENT

DIRECTIONS: Circle the letter of the correct definition for the boldfaced word.

1. Throughout the competition, she found him to be a worthy **adversary**.

    a. opponent

    b. teammate

2. I was surprised by the **profusion** of flowery cushions scattered all over her otherwise sleek and modern house.

    a. ugliness

    b. large supply

LITERARY FOCUS: EPIC HEROES AND CONFLICT

DIRECTIONS: In the chart below, use checkmarks to indicate whether Odysseus has certain qualities of an **epic hero.** For each quality that you check off, describe the part of the story that shows he has this quality.

Qualities	✔	Proof from Story
strength		
knowledge		
cunning		
courage		
daring		

SKILLS FOCUS

Literary Skills
Understand epic heroes and conflict.

Reading Skills
Summarize a text.

READING FOCUS: READING AN EPIC

DIRECTIONS: On a separate sheet of paper, write a paragraph **summarizing** the selection you just read.

from Shipwreck at the Bottom of the World

by Jennifer Armstrong

Tending Sir Ernest's Legacy

from NOVA Online

INFORMATIONAL TEXT FOCUS: SYNTHESIZING SOURCES—MAKING CONNECTIONS

One way to increase your understanding as you read is to **synthesize**—bring together—what you have learned from different sources on one topic. To synthesize information, **connect** what you read with your own experiences and **compare** your current reading with what you have read in the past.

Use the Skill   As you read the following selections, paraphrase (restate in your own words) the ideas in each source, and think about how the information in each source relates to the other.

SELECTION VOCABULARY

provisions (PRUH VIHZH UHNZ) *n.:* supply or stock, especially of food.
   The crew knew they were in trouble when they ran out of provisions.

plummeted (PLUHM IH TIHD) *v.:* plunged or dropped.
   The temperatures plummeted during their trip in Antarctica.

abandon (UH BAN DUHN) *v.:* leave behind.
   The crew had to abandon the ship once it became encased in ice.

priority (PRY AWR UH TEE) *n.:* something deemed of utmost importance.
   Shackleton's top priority was the rescue of his crew.

WORD STUDY

DIRECTIONS: These words were created from the vocabulary words above. Based on the definitions of the original words, what do you think each new word means? Check a dictionary. Were the new definitions similar to the old definitions?

1. provisional *adj.* _____
2. abandonment *adj.* _____

Informational Text Skills
Synthesize information from different sources on a single topic by making connections.

from SHIPWRECK AT THE BOTTOM OF THE WORLD

The Open Boat Journey: The First Ten days
by Jennifer Armstrong

BACKGROUND

In 1915, Ernest Shackleton and his crew were stranded in the Antarctic after their ship, *Endurance*, was caught in ice masses. The crew made it to Elephant Island in April 1916 in lifeboats. There was nothing on the island, and Shackleton knew they had to get help from the whaling station on South Georgia Island. After the lifeboat *James Caird* was refitted for the journey to South Georgia Island, the relief party set off. The first selection tells part of their story and the second selection is an interview with Shackleton's granddaughter.

On the morning of Monday, April 24, all hands were roused at six o'clock to help lash up and stow the *Caird*. As Wild[1] oversaw the preparation of the boat, Shackleton and Worsley climbed up a small hill they used as a lookout and surveyed the ocean. The ice was within five or six miles of the shore, drifting northeast. Large, grounded icebergs made wide gaps in the ice as they streamed past them. The rescue party would escape through one of those leads.

Below, the *Caird* was dragged down to the surf and loaded
10 with the bags of ballast,[2] boxes of stores, a hand pump, a cook pot, six reindeer-skin sleeping bags, and the rest of the provisions. **A** At noon the men heaved the laden boat out on the backwash of a breaking wave, and the remainder of the stores was ferried out on the *Stancomb Wills*. Shackleton and Worsley rejoined the group.

A VOCABULARY

Selection Vocabulary
Based on the examples in this sentence, what do you think is the definition of *provisions*?

_____

_____

_____

_____

---

1. **Wild:** Frank Wild, second-in-command of the Endurance.
2. **ballast** (BAL UHST): something heavy carried in a ship's hold to steady it.

"The Open Boat Journey: The First Ten Days" from *Shipwreck at the Bottom of the World: The Extraordinary True Story of Shackleton and the Endurance* by Jennifer Armstrong. Copyright © 1998 by Jennifer M. Armstrong. Reproduced by permission of **Crown Publishers, a division of Random House, Inc., www.randomhouse.com.**

A LITERARY ANALYSIS

What kind of a trip do you expect the men to take?

_____

_____

_____

_____

_____

_____

_____

B VOCABULARY

Word Study

Porpoise is a noun that refers to a kind of animal that lives in the ocean. Here, *porpoised* is a verb that means "to move forward with a rising and falling motion in the manner of a porpoise." Why do you think the writer included this detail about the penguins?

_____

_____

_____

_____

There were handshakes all around. The six members of the relief party boarded the boat, and they shoved off. **A**

Behind on the beach, the remaining twenty-two men cheered and waved. "Good luck, Boss!" they shouted. Shackleton looked back once and raised his hand in farewell. Gentoo pen-
20 guins porpoised along beside the boat as they raised the sail and plunged forward into the rolling waves. **B** The Boss stood with one arm around the mast looking forward, directing Worsley at the helm around the ice.

They made good speed for two hours and then reached the loose belt of ice they had seen from the lookout. They turned east along it, searching for the leads that would let them through. Huge, lopsided remnant bergs bobbed and heaved in the waves, and small chunks of broken floe[3] knocked and scraped along the sides of the *Caird*. The whole jumble of loose pack hissed and
30 rustled as it rose to the swell. After an hour's run, they found an opening and turned north to sail through it. Just before dark they were on the other side, and when they looked over their shoulders they saw Elephant Island as a small shadow far astern.

Shackleton and Worsley had agreed that the safest plan was to get as far north as possible before heading east. For one thing, they would be glad to get away from the most frigid weather as soon as they could. Furthermore, they would be sailing day and

---

3. **floe** (FLOH): sheet of floating ice.

night, and they needed to get beyond the limit of floating ice: if they rammed a chunk in the dark, their journey would be a short one. By 10:00 P.M. the water seemed relatively clear of ice, and their spirits rose: so far, so good. In the darkness, they steered by keeping an eye on the small blue pennant that streamed from the mast in the wind.

The living arrangements on board were uncomfortable and cramped. The men were divided into two watches: Shackleton, Crean, and McNeish steered, bailed, and pumped for four hours, while Worsley, Vincent, and McCarthy slept—or tried to. Then the watches traded places—watch and watch, every four hours. The sleeping bags were forward, under the improvised decking on the bow. To reach them, the men had to crawl on hands and knees over the stone ballast, then wriggle forward on their stomachs over the crates of stores. Then, with barely enough room to turn around, they wormed themselves into the sleeping bags and attempted to sleep as the boat bucked up and down through the heavy swell. At the end of each four-hour watch, the men would change places, wriggling past each other in the cramped space. **C**

It was a tossup which was worse—being pounded up and down in the bow of the boat in a sorry excuse for sleep, or huddling in the cockpit as icy seas swept across the thwarts[4] and gunwales.[5] There were no oilskins, and the men were dressed in wool, which got wet and stayed wet for the duration of the voyage. With temperatures below freezing, and no room to move around to get their blood stirred up, they were always cold. Miserably cold. Waves broke over the bows, where bucketfuls of water streamed through the flimsy decking. The bottom of the boat was constantly awash, and the two men on watch who weren't steering were always bailing or pumping. The reindeer-skin sleeping bags were soaking wet all the time, and beginning to rot. Loose reindeer hair found its way into the men's nostrils and mouths as they breathed, into their water and their food as they ate.

---

4. **thwarts:** rowers' seats extending across a boat.
5. **gunwhales** (GUN EHLZ): upper edges of the sides of a boat.

What conditions do these explorers face? Why must they have four-hour watches for the boat?

_____

_____

_____

_____

_____

_____

A **READING FOCUS**

Connect this passage with your own experiences of cooking and eating. Do you think it was easy to make good food in these conditions? Why or why not?

_____

_____

B **LANGUAGE COACH**

The verb *wreck* means "to damage badly." *Wreckage* is a **derivation** of, or word originated from, *wreck*. What do you think *wreckage* means?

_____

_____

_____

_____

Crean had taken over as cook for the journey. In the pitching and rolling of the boat, preparing meals was a tricky business. Crean and Worsley would sit on opposite sides of the boat with their feet out, bracing the Primus camp stove. Crean would light the stove and begin stirring up chunks of sledging ration[6] in water as Worsley held the pot. With each dip and plunge of the boat, Worsley swooped the pot up in the air lest their precious hoosh[7] go slopping into the bilges.[8] When the

80 hoosh was cooked, Crean doled it out into six bowls, and the men ate it scalding hot, hunched under the decking. Whoever finished first went out to relieve the man at the tiller[9] so that he could eat his hoosh before it cooled. In addition, Shackleton allowed hot milk and sugar at regular intervals: the only way to keep going was by fueling themselves constantly. **A**

By the third day of sailing, the weather turned rotten. A gale blew up with snow squalls and heavy seas, and waves broke incessantly over the boat. The *James Caird* clawed its way up the face of one hissing wave and then plunged down the other side

90 as spray lashed into the men's faces. The gale continued into the fourth day, finally blowing them north of the sixtieth parallel. Floating past them went two pieces of wreckage from a lost ship. **B** The men watched it disappear, and hunched their shoulders and struggled to keep their little boat on course. As Shackleton put it, "So small was our boat and so great were the seas that often our sail flapped idly in the calm between the crests of two waves. Then we would climb the next slope, and catch the full fury of the gale where the wool-like whiteness of the breaking water surged around us."

100 For Worsley, navigating had ceased to be a science and had turned into a kind of sorcery. To get a sight of the sun meant Worsley had to kneel on the thwart, where Vincent and

---

6. **sledging ration:** crew member's daily food allotment while on an Antarctic expedition.
7. **hoosh:** thick stew made from pemmican (mixture of dried meat, fat, and cereal), a thickener such as ground biscuits, and water.
8. **bilges** (BIHLJ IHZ): bottom of a ship's hull.
9. **tiller:** bar or handle at the stern of a boat used for steering.

McCarthy would hug him around the waist to keep him from pitching out of the boat as it bucked and leaped over the waves. Then, while Shackleton stood by with the chronometer,[10] Worsley would wait until the boat reached the top of the wave and the horizon came into sight, then shout "Now!" as he shot the sun. His books were fast turning into useless pulp. His sun sights were the crudest of guesses, and to look up positions in the tables he had to peel apart the wet pages one by one. Making his calculations with a pencil became laughably impossible. The boat pitched and rolled so badly that he could barely read his own scribbles. The weather was so foul that in the whole journey he managed to take a sight of the sun only four times.

Since leaving Elephant Island, the six men had been accompanied by an albatross, who soared and dipped through the air. The bird could have reached South Georgia in a matter of hours, if it chose, while the men in the *James Caird* were crawling like a beetle over the surface of the ocean. Each time Worsley calculated the number of miles they had put behind them, the bird seemed to mock their slow progress.

On their seventh day at sea, the wind again turned into a gale roaring up from the Pole; the temperature plummeted. **C** The men began to fear that the sails would freeze up and cake with ice, becoming heavier and heavier until the boat toppled upside down. With the gale howling around their ears, they took down the sails and rolled them up, stuffing them into the cramped space below. Then they rigged a sea anchor, a canvas cone dragged through the water to keep the boat turned into the storm.

Throughout the night, waves crashed over the *James Caird* and quickly turned to ice. At first the crew was relieved, since it meant the flimsy decking was sealed against further leaks. But when they awoke on the eighth day, they felt the clumsy, heavy motion of the boat beneath them and knew they were in trouble: fifteen inches of ice encased the boat above the

---

10. **chronometer** (KRUH NAHM UH TUHR): clock or watch that keeps exact time and is used to determine longitude at sea.

Selection Vocabulary
Plummeted means "plunged or dropped." Why does a plummeting temperature make Shackleton's journey more difficult and dangerous?

_____

_____

_____

_____

A VOCABULARY

Word Study

Resiliency is "ability to spring back." Do you think that resiliency is an important quality in a person? Why or why not?

_____

_____

_____

_____

B READING FOCUS

The situation seems to have taken a turn for the worse, according to these last two paragraphs. What similar situations have you read about or seen in film or on TV? Write about one situation on the lines below and then **connect** it to the current situation. How are they similar? How are they different?

_____

_____

_____

_____

_____

_____

_____

_____

_____

_____

waterline, and she was rolling badly. "We saw and felt that the *James Caird* had lost her resiliency," Shackleton said later. **A** "She was not rising to the oncoming seas. The weight of the ice was having its effect, and she was becoming more like a log than a boat."

The ice had to come off. Taking turns, the men crawled on hands and knees over the iced deck, hacking away with an ax. "First you chopped a handhold, then a kneehold, and then chopped off ice hastily but carefully, with an occasional sea washing over you," Worsley explained. Each man could stand only five minutes or so of this cold and perilous job at a time. Then it was the next man's turn.

And the gale continued through the next day, too. As Shackleton crawled out to relieve Worsley at the tiller, a large wave slammed the skipper right in the face. Shackleton took the tiller ropes and commented, "Pretty juicy," and both men managed a weak laugh.

As the storm continued, a large buildup of ice on the sea anchor's rope had kept the line swinging and sawing against the stern. Before noon on the ninth day, the sea anchor broke away, and the boat lurched heavily as seas hit her broadside. Before the gale ended that afternoon, the men had had to crawl onto the deck three times to get rid of the boat's shell of ice. The men all agreed that it was the worst job any of them had ever been forced to do.

By the time the gale ended, everything below was thoroughly soaked. The sleeping bags were so slimy and revolting that Shackleton had the two worst of them thrown overboard. Even before the storm, however, the men had been suffering from the constant wet. "After the third day our feet and legs had swelled," Worsley wrote later, "and began to be superficially frostbitten from the constant soaking in seawater, with the temperature at times nearly down to zero; and the lack of exercise. During the last gale they assumed a dead-white color and lost surface feeling." **B**

Exposure was beginning to wear the men down. In spite of two hot meals a day, they were hungry for fresh meat. Cape pigeons often darted and flitted around the boat, but the men couldn't bring themselves to kill the friendly birds, and ancient superstition forbade them from killing the albatross that still followed majestically above. But the men were in pain. They were cold, frostbitten, and covered with salt-water blisters. Their legs were rubbed raw from the chafing of their wet pants. Conditions below were almost unbearable: the stinking, rotting sleeping bags

180 made the air putrid, and the molting hairs choked the men as they tried to gasp for breath. Their bodies were bruised and aching from their pounding up and down in the bows, and they were exhausted from lack of sleep. McNeish, who was more than fifty, was beginning to break down. Vincent, who should have stood the conditions well, was also close to collapsing. Shackleton, Worsley, Crean, and McCarthy took up the slack. When someone looked particularly bad, the Boss ordered a round of hot milk for all hands. The one man he really wanted to get the hot drink into never realized that the break was for his

190 benefit and so wasn't embarrassed, and all of the men were better off for having the warmth and nourishment. **C**

The night after the gale ended, Shackleton was at the tiller, crouched in a half-standing, half-sitting position against the thwart with his back hunched against the cold. He glanced back toward the south and saw a line of white along the horizon. "It's clearing, boys!" he shouted. But when he looked back again, he yelled, "For God's sake, hold on! It's got us!" Instead of a clearing sky, the white line to the south was the foaming crest of an enormous storm wave bearing down on them. Worsley was

200 just crawling out of his sleeping bag when the wave struck, and for a few moments the entire boat seemed to be submerged. **D**

Worsley, Crean, Vincent, McCarthy, and McNeish frantically pumped and bailed with anything they could find—the cook pot, dippers, their hands—anything that would get the water out of the boat. For an hour they labored to keep the water from capsizing the Caird. They could hardly believe they had not

C LITERARY ANALYSIS

In what way do Shackleton's actions here show his leadership abilities?

_____

_____

_____

_____

_____

D QUICK CHECK

This paragraph has many descriptive details. Re-read the paragraph and underline any words or phrases that help you picture the scene. What was Shackleton's mistake?

_____

_____

_____

_____

A LITERARY ANALYSIS

Judging by what Shackleton wrote, how would you describe his character? How would you guess this rescue mission ended?

_____

_____

_____

_____

_____

_____

foundered,[11] and they prayed they would not see another wave like that one again.

On the tenth day, the sun showed its face long enough
210 for Worsley to get a fix. He calculated that they had made 444 miles from Elephant Island, more than half the distance. The men rejoiced as the weather cleared and they had the first good weather of the passage. They brought wet sleeping bags and clothes up on deck and hung them from the masts, halyards, and rigging.[12] The sleeping bags and clothing didn't dry, but they were reduced from soaking wet to merely damp. All their spirits were lifted. They were more than halfway to South Georgia Island.

"We were a tiny speck in the vast vista of the sea,"
220 Shackleton wrote later. "For a moment the consciousness of the forces arrayed against us would be overwhelming. Then hope and confidence would rise again as our boat rose to a wave and tossed aside the crest in a sparkling shower like the play of prismatic colors at the foot of a waterfall." **A**

They had less than half the distance left to go.

---

11. **foundered:** sank.
12. **halyards** (HAL YUHRDZ), **and rigging:** ropes used on a ship to raise or lower something, such as a flag or sail, or to support the masts, yards, and sails.

TENDING SIR ERNEST'S LEGACY: AN INTERVIEW WITH ALEXANDRA SHACKLETON

from NOVA Online

Sir Ernest could do far worse than have as his only granddaughter the Honorable Alexandra Shackleton. Life-president of the James Caird Society, which was founded to honor Shackleton and provide information about his expeditions, Ms. Shackleton looks after her grandfather's legacy about as well as the great man himself looked after his men. **B**

© Helen Atkinson

10 Based in London, she has been instrumental in furthering Shackleton historical research, has contributed forewords to books on Antarctic exploration, and consulted for the Channel Four/First Sight Films television drama *Shackleton*, starring Kenneth Branagh. She has even had the honor to christen three ships: the Royal Navy's Ice Patrol ship, *HMS Endurance*; the trawler *Lord Shackleton*; and, most recently, the British Antarctic Survey ship, *RRS Ernest Shackleton*.

NOVA: What was really pushing your grandfather to do this expedition to cross Antarctica?

20 **Shackleton:** Well, the Pole had been attained, so he had to abandon that dream. **C** I think he considered it the last great Antarctic adventure—to cross the Antarctic from the Weddell Sea to the Ross Sea, a distance of about 1,800 miles. Of course, in those days it was felt that it should be done by somebody British. All of the nationalities felt that. The Germans felt that. The Americans felt that. The French felt that. And he considered

B VOCABULARY

Academic Vocabulary
Based on this description of Alexandra Shackleton, do you think her grandfather will be *portrayed*, or described, in the same way as the previous selection? Explain.

_____

_____

_____

_____

C VOCABULARY

Selection Vocabulary
To *abandon* is to "leave behind." What do you think it felt like for Shackleton to abandon his dream?

_____

_____

_____

_____

_____

What background information about Shackleton is provided in this paragraph?

_____

_____

_____

_____

_____

Compare what you have learned about Shackleton in this paragraph with the description of him in the previous selection. Do you think the descriptions are similar? Why or why not?

_____

_____

_____

_____

he was pretty well fitted to do it, having built up a reputation as a successful leader of the Nimrod Expedition [a 1907 attempt to reach the South Pole, of which he got within 100 miles before having to turn back]. A

NOVA: It was a pretty ambitious plan, given the stage of Antarctic exploration at that time. Was the monumental challenge part of the attraction?

Shackleton: It was ambitious, but I think he thought it was possible. He was a very practical person, and he would have never attempted anything that he thought could not be done. The main reason was that, above all, he had the lives of his men to consider.

NOVA: How do you think your grandfather felt at the moment when the *Endurance* was finally stuck in the ice, and he realized he would never attain his goal of crossing Antarctica?

Shackleton: Well, when the ship got locked in the ice, it wasn't a sudden event, of course. The realization gradually dawned on them that the ship was not going to get out, that she was stuck— I think one of the crew members said "like an almond in toffee." Eventually, it became clear that she was being crushed by the ice and had no chance of rising above it. And my grandfather said to the captain, Frank Worsley, "the ship can't live in this, skipper." Then he started making plans for what could be done when the ship finally had to be abandoned. He was a great planner who was always working out what to do in every conceivable eventuality. B

For several weeks the ship had been letting out terrible creaking and groaning noises like a human in agony, and then eventually my grandfather called out, "she's going boys," and they saw her disappear. He wrote in his diary, "I cannot write about it." He found it extremely distressing. Of course, it was the abandonment of his dream.

Yet he said to his men, quite calmly, "ship gone, stores gone, now we will go home." And he wrote in his diary, "a man must set himself to a new mark directly the old one goes." And what became his new mark was bringing every one of his 27 men home alive, from a part of the world where nobody knew they were. He knew there was no chance whatsoever of rescue. There were no communications. They might as well have been in space. **C**

NOVA: That was probably one of the toughest tests of his character, because he must have been bitterly disappointed.

Shackleton: Bitterly. Also, a ship is more to a sailor than just a floating home. It is a symbol. It's distressing for any captain, any leader of an expedition, to lose his ship.

NOVA: And yet he held himself together.

Shackleton: Indeed, and the men apparently felt reassured. After losing the ship, they felt rather adrift in every sense of the word, and yet he helped them to feel reassured. **D** There was something to set themselves to do.

NOVA: How did you think he felt when he realized that his plan to travel over the ice was just not going to work?

Shackleton: When that method didn't work, I think he simply switched to the next method. He was extremely pragmatic,[1] and he always had many alternatives in his mind. Ernest Shackleton did not go in for soul-searching and self-recrimination.[2] He would have called it a complete waste of valuable time. **E**

NOVA: Now, on the journey to South Georgia aboard the *Caird*, how did your grandfather help the men cope with the horrendous conditions?

Shackleton: Well, he was well aware of the importance of a hot drink. Every man was fed every four hours, but if he noticed any member of the expedition failing slightly, he would order hot milk then and there, not just for him, but for everybody, so this man would not, as he put it, have doubts about himself. When he noticed one man suffering particularly from cold, he would rummage in the damp supplies and dig him out a pair of gloves.

NOVA: How do you think your grandfather felt when South Georgia appeared on the horizon?

---

1. **pragmatic** (PRAG MAH TIHK): practical
2. **self-recrimination:** blaming oneself

C QUICK CHECK

What new information does Alexandra Shackleton tell you about her grandfather and his leadership style?

_____

_____

_____

_____

_____

D VOCABULARY

Word Study

If you don't already know its meaning, use a dictionary to look up the word *adrift*. What synonym (word with a similar meaning) could you use to replace *adrift* in this sentence?

_____

_____

_____

E LITERARY ANALYSIS

Does Shackleton's attitude surprise you, or do you think that kind of thinking is to be expected in a leader? Explain.

_____

_____

_____

Shackleton: When they saw South Georgia for the first time, and he realized that Worsley had accomplished his miracle of navigation, he felt huge relief, but sadly that was tempered[3] instantly by the fact they could not land. There was a lee shore,[4] and they were very nearly driven onto the reefs and sunk. It took two days of agonies of thirst before they could actually land. While they were struggling to land, Worsley said he felt this almost detached resentment that no one would ever know what they had accomplished. They would just be sunk as if they had been sunk at the beginning of the journey. **A**

NOVA: Even today that journey is seen as nothing short of miraculous.

Shackleton: Yes. They had accomplished what many regard as the greatest small boat journey in the world, 800 miles across the stormiest seas in the world in a little boat not even 23 feet long—all the while encountering extremely harsh weather and suffering gales, privations[5] of thirst, hunger, and everything. It was a colossal achievement, and when they saw the black peaks of South Georgia, they felt huge relief and happiness.

NOVA: Was the Endurance expedition the greatest achievement of his life?

Shackleton: I think so, because against almost impossible odds he brought his 27 men home safely. The boat journey to South Georgia was an epic in itself, and climbing across the uncharted, unmapped island of South Georgia with no equipment was remarkable. To this day, no one has ever beaten his record of 30 miles in 36 hours. **B**

NOVA: What did your grandfather think were the most important qualities for a polar explorer to possess?

Shackleton: Well, he actually listed them. In order of priority, he said first optimism, second patience, third imagination (with which he coupled idealism), and fourth, courage. He thought every man had courage. **C** Now, those are very practical qualities,

---

3. **tempered** (TEHM PURD) counter-balanced; offset by
4. **lee shore:** term used to describe a shoreline that is hard to reach by sea because of wind conditions.
5. **privations** (PRY VAY SHUHNS): lack of necessities

130　and yet Ernest Shackleton was a very romantic man who wrote poetry. This was an era in which fine words abounded, and I might have thought he would have chosen qualities such as self-sacrifice or going for glory. After all, the search for the pole was likened to the search for the Holy Grail.[6] But his practical qualities did not war against his romantic aspects. They made a harmonious whole, which I think was one of his strengths.

NOVA: What qualities do you think he possessed that made him such a compelling leader and instill such loyalty in his crew?

Shackleton: I think that the fact that his men were so important.

140　Leadership was a two-way thing for him. It wasn't a case of men following him just because he was the leader; he was devoted to them. It was a reciprocal, very close relationship. That's why any discord and disobedience he took personally. He was the ultimate leader because his men were his priority at all times. **D** It took four attempts to rescue his men from Elephant Island and he visibly aged, particularly after the third one did not succeed. But when he got to Elephant Island, counted the heads frantically, and found all safe all well, well, the years rolled away.

NOVA: Do you think he was happiest when he was in the

150　Antarctic?

Shackleton: Grandfather was, I think, happiest in the Antarctic, yes. He wrote once to my grandmother, "I'm not much good at anything else but being an explorer." He loved her and he loved his home, but he chafed in the confines of this country. For a man who loved wide open spaces, Antarctica does get a grip of one. If one has never seen it, it's like nowhere else. He wrote once to a little sister, "you cannot imagine what it is like to tread where no man has trod before." **E**

　　　　　　　—Interview conducted by Kelly Tyler, NOVA producer,
　　　　　　　　　　"Shackleton's Voyage of Endurance"

---

6. **Holy Grail:** The Holy Grail was the cup or dish said to be used by Christ in the Last Supper. The quest for the Holy Grail formed the basis of many Arthurian legends.

D VOCABULARY

Selection Vocabulary
How do Shackleton's actions prove that his men are his *priority*?

_____

_____

_____

E READING FOCUS

How do the two accounts of Shackleton **compare**? Are they mostly similar or mostly different? Explain.

_____

_____

_____

Skills Practice

from Shipwreck at the Bottom of the World *and* Tending Sir Ernest's Legacy

USE A VENN DIAGRAM

DIRECTIONS: Compare and contrast (find similarities and differences between)
"Shipwreck at the Bottom of the World" and "Tending Sir Ernest's Legacy."
What kind of information did you find in both selections? Write the differences
in the outer sections of the ovals. Write the similarities in the section where the
two ovals overlap.

Shipwreck at the Bottom of the World   Tending Sir Ernest's Legacy

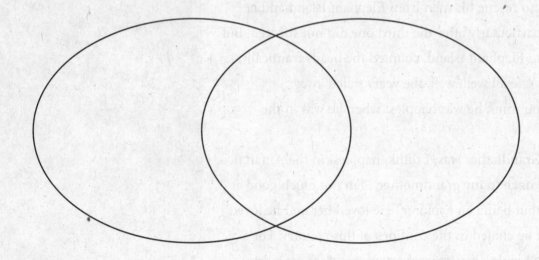

Applying Your Skills

from Shipwreck at the Bottom of the World and Tending Sir Ernest's Legacy

VOCABULARY DEVELOPMENT

DIRECTIONS: Complete each sentence by filling in the correct vocabulary word from the Word Box.

Word Box

provisions
plummeted
abandon
priority

1. Finishing my homework will be my first _____ tonight.

2. During our camping trip, a bear ate our _____, so we had to head back home early.

3. The ship _____ into the ocean after it hit an iceberg.

4. She vowed that she would never _____ any project so dear to her heart.

INFORMATIONAL TEXT FOCUS: SYNTHESIZING SOURCES—MAKING CONNECTIONS

DIRECTIONS: Review the two selections, and create a list of the important leadership qualities you think Ernest Shackleton had. Then use checkmarks to show whether you found that information in "Shipwreck at the Bottom of the World," "Tending Sir Ernest's Legacy," or both.

Leadership Qualities	"Shipwreck at the Bottom of the World"	"Tending Sir Ernest's Legacy"

SKILLS FOCUS

Informational Text Skills
Synthesize information from different sources on a single topic by making connections and comparing.

Skills Review

Collection 9

VOCABULARY REVIEW

DIRECTIONS: The sentences in the table below include boldfaced academic and selection vocabulary words from this collection. Use a checkmark to show if each word is used correctly. If a word is used incorrectly, write a sentence using the vocabulary word correctly.

	Correct	New Sentence
1. Her good friend had been an **adversary** for years.		
2. Over the years of working together, they had developed a strong **mutual** respect for one another.		
3. He was very happy to **abandon** his dream.		
4. He showed his **express** about seeing the play.		
5. He is sure that it is his **destiny** to become a famous singer.		
6. The hero is **portrayed** as a brave and ambitious man.		
7. A **profusion** of leaves lay scattered on the lawn.		
8. Safety is our first **priority**.		

Skills Review

Collection 9

LANGUAGE COACH

DIRECTIONS: The endings of some words can be changed to create a new word. Sometimes this changes the word's part of speech and its meaning. The following words are related to selection and academic vocabulary words from this collection. Based on what you know about the original vocabulary words, try to guess the definitions of the new words. Use a dictionary to check your answers. Which words have very similar meanings to the originals?

1. abandonment, *n.*: _____

2. adversarial, *adj.*: _____

3. destined, *adj.*: _____

4. expressive, *adj.*: _____

5. mutually, *adv.*: _____

6. prior, *adj.*: _____

7. profuse, *adj.*: _____

WRITING ACTIVITY

DIRECTIONS: Each of the selections in this collection deals with heroes and the character traits that make a person a hero. What traits do you think a hero should have? Write a short essay (one or two paragraphs) listing the traits and why you think these traits are important. You may want to think about Odysseus' and Shackleton's heroic traits. Are any of those traits on your list? Why or why not?

Collection
10

Reading for Life

© Masterfile Royalty Free

Literary and Academic Vocabulary for Collection 10

consequences (KAHN SUH KWEHNS EHZ) *n.:* results, outcomes.
The consequences of poorly written directions could be confusion and frustration.

function (FUHNGK SHUHN) *n.:* typical action of something.
The function of consumer documents is to inform consumers about products or services.

coherent (KOH HIHR UHNT) *adj.:* clear, connected logically; understandable.
It is usually easy to understand a coherent document.

specify (SPEHS UH FY) *v.:* state in detail.
Product information on clothing labels may specify the size, material, and laundry instructions.

consumer (KUHN SOO MER) *n.:* someone who buys or uses something.
When you buy food at the supermarket, you are a consumer.

public document (PUHB LIK DOK YUH MUHNT) *n.:* any document that is made for all to read.
Once the letter was printed in the paper, it became a public document.

Following Technical Directions

INFORMATIONAL TEXT FOCUS: FOLLOWING TECHNICAL DIRECTIONS

Instructions for using computers as well as other scientific, mechanical, and electronic products are called **technical directions**. You follow technical directions when you read instructions on how to do an experiment in a chemistry lab, program your cell phone, or install software on your computer. Technical directions may seem complicated, but if you read carefully and follow each step, you can accomplish the task.

READING FOCUS: SKIMMING AND SCANNING

These skills can help you when you first encounter technical directions:

- **Skimming** helps you get an overview of the document. Glance at the title, heads, subheads, and read the first line or two of each paragraph.

- **Scanning** helps you locate the specific information you need. Search for boldfaced or italicized words, graphics, and other details.

SELECTION VOCABULARY

scan (SKAN) *v.:* copy text or graphics from paper into a computer file.
You can scan any photograph into your computer to use on your Web site.

image (IHM IHJ) *n.:* visual illustration; graphic.
Most presentations are improved by the addition of interesting images.

options (AHP SHUNZ) *n.:* choices.
Computer menus offer you many options.

WORD STUDY

DIRECTIONS: Write "Yes" if the vocabulary word is used correctly in each sentence below. Write "No" if it is not and rewrite the sentence so that the word is used correctly.

1. I tried to **scan** the photograph so I could save it to my computer. _____

_____

2. Because of all the **options**, there were no choices. _____

_____

3. I will write an **image** that summarizes the paragraph I just read. _____

_____

SKILLS FOCUS

Informational Text Skills
Follow technical directions.

Reading Skills
Skim and scan technical directions.

FOLLOWING TECHNICAL DIRECTIONS

MANUAL

Adding Graphics to Your Web Site

(A)(B) The following technical directions show how to *scan*, edit, and save an *image* for your Web site using a made-up photo-editing program called PhotoEdit. The directions assume you have a scanner and it is set up properly to work with your computer. Reading through these instructions will make you familiar with the process of following **technical directions** so that when you choose your own picture-editing program, you'll have no trouble getting the results you want. (C)

Setting Up

1. Make sure the scanner is turned on.

2. Place your image in the scanner. The image should lie face down on the glass, aligned according to the page-size indicators on the scanner.

3. Open up the PhotoEdit program.

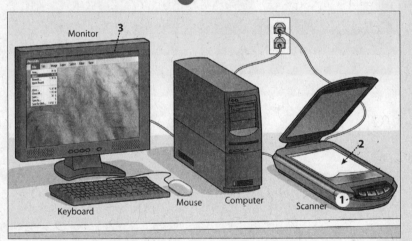

Monitor — 3

Keyboard

Mouse   Computer   Scanner — 1

2

A LANGUAGE COACH

The word *scan* has multiple meanings. Here, to *scan* is to "copy text or graphics from paper into a computer file." What is another definition of *scan*? Use a dictionary if you need help.

_____

_____

B VOCABULARY

Selection Vocabulary

An *image* is a "visual illustration, or graphic." List several types of images you might see on a Web site.

_____

_____

C READING FOCUS

Skim the title and first paragraph. What does this quick read tell you about the selection?

_____

_____

_____

_____

_____

A VOCABULARY

Selection Vocabulary

Options are "choices." Name three options listed in the File menu.

_____

_____

_____

B READING FOCUS

Scan this paragraph for boldfaced sentences. Why do you think this sentence is boldfaced?

_____

_____

_____

C QUICK CHECK

Why should you scan your image at a larger size than the original?

_____

_____

_____

Scanning

4. In PhotoEdit, under the File menu, choose Import; then select your scanner's name under the list of options. This will open up a scanning dialogue box within PhotoEdit. A preview of your picture will also appear. **Do not remove original image from the scanner.** **B**

A

5. With the cursor, select the area of the image you want scanned.

6. Set the size and resolution of the image. In general, scah your image at a larger size than the original (such as 200%) to provide more options for editing later on. For Web use, it is best to set the resolution to 72 dpi (dots per inch).

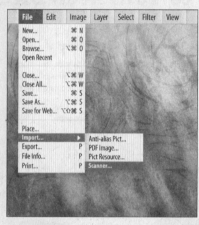

7. Click on SCAN. Your image will now open as an untitled document in PhotoEdit, ready to be edited. **C**

Vocabulary **options** (AHP shuhnz) *n.*: choices.

Editing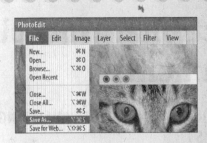

8. You may now perform any number of edits to ready your image for Web use. You can crop, adjust the color, retouch, and sharpen the image in PhotoEdit.

9. In order to resize the image, you must decide how big you want it to appear on the Web page. First, make sure you are viewing the image at 100% (actual size). Next, go to the Image menu and choose the Image Size option. A dialogue box will open. If you want your image to be large, you may set the pixel size to 800 width x 600 height. If you would like your image to be a thumbnail size, set the width to a size of around 180 pixels. If the "Constrain proportions" option is enabled in this box, the image height will be set automatically. **E**

10. Once you have entered the desired values, hit OK. You will now see the resized image.

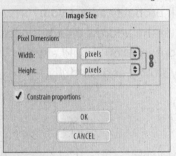

Saving

11. When you are satisfied with the way your image looks, go to the File menu and select Save As.

12. When you name your file, be sure not to exceed 31 characters, including the file extension.

13. Choose JPEG under file format (a JPEG is a compressed version of the file, suitable for Web use). When saving an image as a JPEG, you will have the option of setting the image quality and file size. For the Internet, it is best to choose a "medium" setting for these options.

14. Click OK. Your image is now ready to be uploaded onto your Web site. **F**

D — READING FOCUS

Scan the Editing section for information on how to change an image. Briefly summarize what you learned from your scan.

_____

_____

_____

_____

_____

_____

_____

_____

E — VOCABULARY

Academic Vocabulary

To *specify* is to "state in detail." What does this paragraph specify?

_____

_____

_____

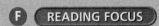

F — READING FOCUS

If you had **skimmed** this document looking for information on suitable file formats for Web site images, what section would you now want to read more closely?

_____

_____

Functional Workplace Documents

INFORMATIONAL TEXT FOCUS: ANALYZING FUNCTIONAL WORKPLACE DOCUMENTS

Workplace documents often follow a specific **structure** and **format** (the arrangement of sections). For example, Web sites usually include attention-grabbing graphics such as icons and colorful type. User guides and technical directions often include **graphics** such as **charts**, **diagrams**, and **illustrations**.

READING FOCUS: ADJUSTING READING RATE

When you read workplace documents, you will probably **adjust your reading rate**. For example, you may quickly skim the address on a business letter and slow down to pay attention to its content. You should always read contracts and other legal documents very slowly and carefully.

SELECTION VOCABULARY

diligent (DIHL UH JUHNT) *adj.*: hard-working.
  A diligent student puts a lot of time into studying.

differentiate (DIHF UH REHN SHEE AYT) *v.*: distinguish by creating a difference between.
  I couldn't differentiate between the two cars because they looked alike.

en route (AHN ROOT) *adv.*: along the way.
  You may discover many adventures en route to your destination.

WORD STUDY

DIRECTIONS: Answer the following questions about the vocabulary words.

1. If your guests got lost *en route* to your house, what happened to them?

_____

2. If you were assigned to a group to complete a classroom assignment, would it be good to be teamed up with *diligent* students?

_____

3. If you were asked to *differentiate* between three different food products, what would you have to do?

_____

SKILLS FOCUS

Informational Text Skills
Analyze functional workplace documents.

Reading Skills
Learn to adjust your reading rate.

FUNCTIONAL WORKPLACE DOCUMENTS

BUSINESS LETTER

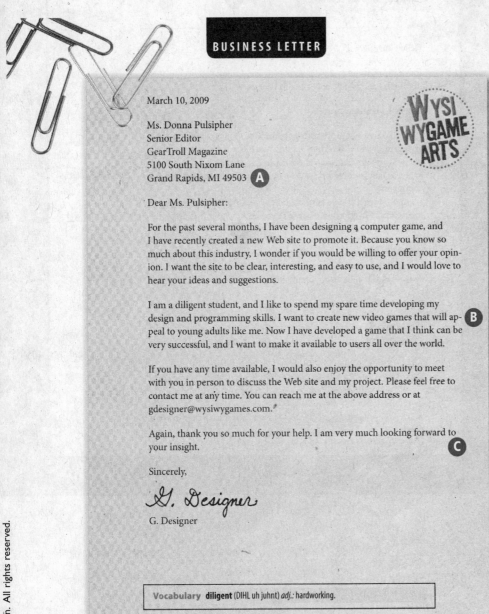

March 10, 2009

Ms. Donna Pulsipher
Senior Editor
GearTroll Magazine
5100 South Nixom Lane
Grand Rapids, MI 49503 **A**

Dear Ms. Pulsipher:

For the past several months, I have been designing a computer game, and I have recently created a new Web site to promote it. Because you know so much about this industry, I wonder if you would be willing to offer your opinion. I want the site to be clear, interesting, and easy to use, and I would love to hear your ideas and suggestions.

I am a diligent student, and I like to spend my spare time developing my design and programming skills. I want to create new video games that will appeal to young adults like me. Now I have developed a game that I think can be very successful, and I want to make it available to users all over the world. **B**

If you have any time available, I would also enjoy the opportunity to meet with you in person to discuss the Web site and my project. Please feel free to contact me at any time. You can reach me at the above address or at gdesigner@wysiwygames.com.

Again, thank you so much for your help. I am very much looking forward to your insight. **C**

Sincerely,

G. Designer

G. Designer

Vocabulary **diligent** (DIHL uh juhnt) *adj.*: hardworking.

A **READING FOCUS**

What **reading rate** did you use as you read this part of the letter? Why?

_____

_____

_____

B **LANGUAGE COACH**

Diligent has a short *i* sound in its first syllable. Write a word that begins with *di–* that has a long *i* sound.

_____

C **READING FOCUS**

What is the main idea of this letter? Did you need to adjust your **reading rate** to find the main idea? Explain.

_____

_____

_____

_____

A) READING FOCUS

How does this heading **structure** help you understand the meaning of the email message?

_____

_____

_____

_____

B) VOCABULARY

Selection Vocabulary

To *differentiate* is "to distinguish by creating a difference between." Use the word in a sentence of your own.

_____

_____

_____

_____

C) QUICK CHECK

What changes does Donna Pulsipher recommend that G. Designer make to his Web site?

_____

_____

_____

_____

_____

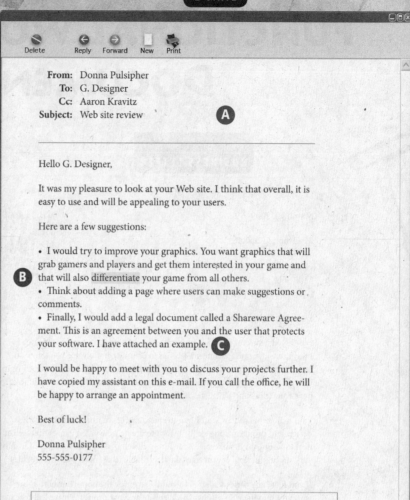

E-MAIL

Delete   Reply   Forward   New   Print

From: Donna Pulsipher
To: G. Designer
Cc: Aaron Kravitz
Subject: Web site review   **A**

Hello G. Designer,

It was my pleasure to look at your Web site. I think that overall, it is easy to use and will be appealing to your users.

Here are a few suggestions:

B
- I would try to improve your graphics. You want graphics that will grab gamers and players and get them interested in your game and that will also differentiate your game from all others.
- Think about adding a page where users can make suggestions or comments.
- Finally, I would add a legal document called a Shareware Agreement. This is an agreement between you and the user that protects your software. I have attached an example. **C**

I would be happy to meet with you to discuss your projects further. I have copied my assistant on this e-mail. If you call the office, he will be happy to arrange an appointment.

Best of luck!

Donna Pulsipher
555-555-0177

Vocabulary **differentiate** (dihf uh REHN shee ayt) *v.:* distinguish by creating a difference between.

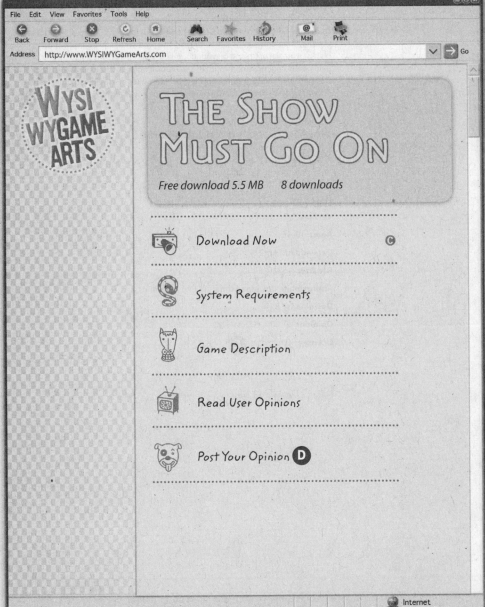

File   Edit   View   Favorites   Tools   Help

Back   Forward   Stop   Refresh   Home   Search   Favorites   History   Mail   Print

Address   http://www.WYSIWYGameArts.com   Go

WYSI WYGAME ARTS

THE SHOW MUST GO ON

Free download 5.5 MB   8 downloads

Download Now   C

System Requirements

Game Description

Read User Opinions

Post Your Opinion   D

Internet

D   READING FOCUS

How quickly did you read the text on this page? Did the **graphics** help you to read and understand the text more quickly or did they slow you down? Explain.

_____

_____

_____

_____

_____

_____

Game Description

You, Candy Rapper, are trying to get to the stadium to sing at the big benefit concert to aid the farmworkers. En route, though, you are stopped by different characters—Terry Techno and Coyote Cowboy, for example—who demand that you play them *their* songs before they let you pass. With a quick check of the playlist, you dial up a song on your boombox. If you play the right song, you gain points and move on toward the stadium. If not, you lose points and have to stay until you find the right song. Can you make it to the stadium in time? If you do, you perform to a standing ovation accompanied by a fireworks display. **B**

Would you recommend this game?

 YES   NO   Post My Opinion

Game Facts

Version 1.0

Ages: 10–16

Date added: April 6, 2009

File size: 5.5 MB

Approximate download time: 13 min. at 56 kbps

Downloads: 8

Opinions (5): 80% YES; 20% NO

Licensee: Shareware **C**

Download Now

Internet

A VOCABULARY

Selection Vocabulary

En route means "along the way." Describe three things that you saw en route to school today. What happens to Candy Rapper en route to the stadium?

B READING FOCUS

What **reading rate** would you use to decide if you would want to play this game?

C QUICK CHECK

What type of information is shown in the Game Facts section?

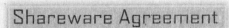

File   Edit   View   Favorites   Tools   Help

Back   Forward   Stop   Refresh   Home   Search   Favorites   History   Mail   Print

Address   http://www.WYSIWYGameArts.com   Go

WYSIWYGAME ARTS

Shareware Agreement

This is a legal agreement between you, the end user, and WYSIWYGame Arts, the proprietor. By using the WYSIWYGame Arts software [hereafter called the SOFTWARE], you indicate your acceptance of these terms.

1. **GRANT OF LICENSE**   WYSIWYGame Arts grants you the right to use the SOFTWARE on a single computer. The SOFTWARE is considered in use on a computer when it is loaded into RAM or installed in permanent memory.

2. **PROPRIETARY RIGHTS**   The SOFTWARE is owned exclusively by WYSIWYGame Arts. This license does not transfer any ownership rights of the SOFTWARE to you.

3. **RESTRICTIONS**   You may not translate, reverse program, decompile, disassemble, or otherwise reverse engineer the SOFTWARE.

4. **NO WARRANTY**   This SOFTWARE is licensed to you "as is" and without any warranty of any kind, expressed or implied, including but not limited to warranties of merchantability and fitness for a particular purpose.

5. **LIMITATIONS OF LIABILITY**   In no event shall WYSIWYGame Arts' liability related to any of the SOFTWARE exceed the license fees, if any, actually paid by you for the SOFTWARE. WYSIWYGame Arts shall not be liable for any damage whatsoever arising out of, or related to, the use or inability to use the SOFTWARE, including but not limited to direct, indirect, special, incidental, or consequential damages.   **D**   **E**

Internet

D   READING FOCUS

In a step-by-step **format**, the steps have to be followed in order. In a point-by-point format, the points can be taken in any order. Which format is followed in this contract?

_____

_____

E   VOCABULARY

Academic Vocabulary

An object's *function* is its purpose or typical action. What is the function of this contract?

_____

_____

_____

_____

Following Technical Directions *and* Functional Workplace Documents

USE A READING RATE CHART

DIRECTIONS: Re-read each document listed below and think about how quickly or slowly you read each section of the documents. Use the chart below to describe how you adjusted your reading rate while reviewing each document.

Document	How I adjusted my reading rate
Adding Graphics to Your Web Site	
Business Letter	
Email Message	
Shareware Agreement	
Web Site	

Applying Your Skills

Following Technical Directions *and* Functional Workplace Documents

Word Box

scan

image

options

diligent

differentiate

en route

VOCABULARY DEVELOPMENT

DIRECTIONS: Choose four of the words from the Word Box and write sentences of your own using the vocabulary words correctly.

1. _____

2. _____

3. _____

4. _____

INFORMATIONAL TEXT FOCUS: ANALYZING FUNCTIONAL WORKPLACE DOCUMENTS

DIRECTIONS: Copy this diagram onto a separate sheet of paper and use it to compare and contrast the information and formats in "Following Technical Directions" and "Functional Workplace Documents."

Technical Directions   **Workplace Documents**

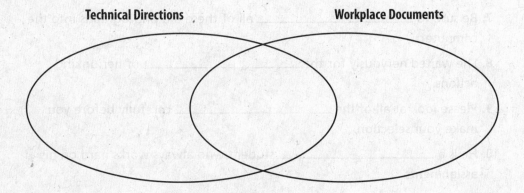

READING FOCUS: ADJUSTING READING RATE

DIRECTIONS: On a separate sheet of paper, answer the following questions about the two selections.

1. How did **skimming** help you read about adding graphics to a Web site?

2. How did **scanning** help you read about adding graphics to a Web site?

3. How did your **reading rate** change as you read the workplace documents?

Informational Text Skills
Analyze technical directions and workplace documents.

Reading Skills
Learn to adjust your reading rate.

Skills Review

Collection 10

VOCABULARY REVIEW

DIRECTIONS: The Word Box to the left includes academic and selection vocabulary words from Collection 10. Read each sentence below and write the correct vocabulary word in the blank.

Word Box

coherent

consequences

differentiate

diligent

en route

function

image

options

scan

specify

1. Sometimes it is very hard to _____ between similar products.

2. Be sure to _____ that you need four seats for you and your three friends.

3. When you visit the Web site, the first _____ you see is a large picture of an island.

4. Even though my car is very small, it serves its _____ well, and always gets me where I need to go.

5. I feel lucky that the car has never broken down _____ to an important appointment.

6. She was so excited and nervous that she had a hard time telling her story in a _____ way.

7. Be sure to _____ all of these old photographs into the computer.

8. She waited nervously for the _____ of her unkind actions.

9. Please look at all of the _____ carefully before you make your selection.

10. He is a _____ student who always works hard on his assignments.

Skills Review

Collection 10

LANGUAGE COACH

DIRECTIONS: Sometimes words that begin with *di–* have a long *i* sound, such as in *diary* and *diet*. The vocabulary words *diligent* and *differentiate*, however, have a short *i* sound.

Place the following words in the correct column of the chart below. You may use a dictionary to help you.

digress	digest	distinct
dissent	dissect	diagram
dimension	disperse	diction
dial		

Long *i* sound (EYE)	Short *i* sound (IH)

ORAL LANGUAGE ACTIVITY

DIRECTIONS: Suppose that you need to teach a group of students how to scan an image for use in a Web site. Look back at the instructions in the "Following Technical Directions" document. Based on those directions, prepare and give a short speech explaining the process to your classmates. Be sure to clearly list each step, and explain any complicated procedures in more detail.

Index of Authors and Titles